# Doc, Donnie, the Kid, and Billy Brawl

# Doc, Donnie, the Kid, and Billy Brawl

How the 1985 Mets and Yankees Fought
for New York's Baseball Soul

## CHRIS DONNELLY

University of Nebraska Press
LINCOLN

Library of Congress Cataloging-in-Publication Data
Names: Donnelly, Chris, author.
Title: Doc, Donnie, the Kid, and Billy Brawl: how the 1985
Mets and Yankees fought for New York's baseball soul / Chris
Donnelly.
Description: Lincoln: University of Nebraska Press, [2019] |
Includes bibliographical references and index.
Identifiers: LCCN 2018027836
ISBN 9781496205537 (cloth: alk. paper)
ISBN 9781496214386 (epub)
ISBN 9781496214393 (mobi)
ISBN 9781496214409 (pdf)
Subjects: LCSH: New York Mets (Baseball team)—History—
20th century. | New York Yankees (Baseball team)—History—
20th century. | Sports rivalries—New York (State)—New
York—History—20th century. | Gooden, Dwight. | Carter, Gary,
1954–2012. | Martin, Billy, 1928–1989.
Classification: LCC GV875.N45 .D64 2019 |
DDC 796.357/64097471—dc23
LC record available at https://lccn.loc.gov/2018027836

Set in Scala OT by E. Cuddy.

For Jamie, Erin Elisabeth, and Claire Ella,
who make every day the greatest day of my life.

Another book "Big" would have loved.

# CONTENTS

Acknowledgments . . ix

1. A Seismic Shift . . 1
2. "Never Played the Game" . . 15
3. Attendance Envy . . 33
4. Fun to Be a Met . . 55
5. Billy and George, a Love/Hate Story . . 85
6. The Russians Attack Atlanta . . 119
7. Hospital Management . . 153
8. "I'm Going to Kill You" . . 201
9. "One Tremendous Baseball Season" . . 235

Epilogue . . 265

Notes . . 275
Bibliography . . 287
Index . . 289

# ACKNOWLEDGMENTS

NO ONE DOES IT alone. Writing this book was an eight-year odyssey (with a few stops here and there) that could not have happened without the support and assistance of so many people. First and foremost, what kind of son would I be if I did not thank my mother, Sandy, and my father, Tim? In any and all endeavors of my life, I have received nothing but support from both of them.

To my brothers, Tim and Mike; my sisters-in-law, Taylor and Kori; my brothers-in-law, Glenn and Derek; my mother- and father-in-law, Karen and Roy; the Donnellys, Kassabs, Praschils, Leahys, Dudases, Salzanos, and Kennedys, my sincere thanks for everything you do to make mine and my family's life better.

I am ridiculously fortunate to have a great group of friends that have been supportive, ball-busting companions for decades. From Lincoln to Lakeside to PLHS to TCNJ to those I have come to know through work, thanks to all of you for the laughs, the drinks, the jokes about my hair and athletic ability (or lack thereof), and for just being around.

Special thanks to Jay Horwitz of the New York Mets, who was instrumental in putting me in touch with various members of the '85 team. Thanks also to Pat O'Connell, Martin Coco, Sally Gunter, Michael Brown, Bruce Markusen, Louis Barricelli, Brintan Madonna, Dave Campanaro, Kate McGowan, Casey Lynn, Casey Wilcox, Morgan Ballard, Gina DiDomenicis, Mike Vander Woude, Mark Zwolinski, and Sean Darcy, who helped connect me to various Yankees, Mets, Cardinals, and Blue Jays players or assisted with endorsements.

Big thanks to my editor, Rob Taylor, for shepherding me through this process and for having faith in the project.

# Doc, Donnie, the Kid, and Billy Brawl

# A Seismic Shift

THE CALLS WERE STARTING to come in. It was late in the day on Monday, December 10, 1984. The baseball winter meetings had closed up the Friday before, and the offices of most Major League Baseball teams were relatively quiet. But in the offices of the Montreal Expos and New York Mets, things were just starting to heat up. The press sensed something. They knew that Mets general manager Frank Cashen and vice president Al Harazin had flown down to West Palm Beach, Florida, that day. West Palm Beach just happened to be where Montreal Expos All-Star catcher Gary Carter lived. This was more than a coincidence thought many of the Mets' beat writers. Few details had leaked out, but they knew something big was going on. Really big. And they wanted in on the news.

They were right to be suspicious. Behind closed doors over the previous three days, the Mets and Expos had been working out a deal. Somehow, they had managed to keep it quiet for most of the weekend. The plan was to announce a blockbuster trade between the two teams the next day, Tuesday the 11th, in an early morning press conference. But that was no longer possible. The news was going to get out before they could officially announce it, and neither side wanted to lose control over the story. Instead, the two teams rushed together to hold a dual telephone press conference that Monday night. Some players were trading uniforms, and the makeup of the National League East was officially about to change for the rest of the 1980s.

A FEW WEEKS BEFORE Cashen and Harazin made the flight to southern Florida, Gary Carter felt the need to have a chat with

Montreal Expos president John McHale. It was Thanksgiving Day, but something was weighing on Carter's mind, and he needed an answer. Rumor had it the Expos wanted Carter gone.

"Is there any truth to it?" Carter asked McHale.[1]

Montreal, perennial contenders in the late '70s and early '80s, had fallen off the last few years. They won eighty-two games in 1983, then dropped to seventy-eight wins in 1984. Attendance from 1983 to '84 had dropped by nearly seven hundred thousand. The team reportedly lost $3 million. Coincidentally, Carter made nearly $2 million a year. Now, it was a price the Expos could no longer afford to pay. That made Carter a primary target as the team looked to make changes.

Born in Culver City, California, Carter played ball with his older brother and his friends growing up. Playing with older kids not only acclimated Carter to performing against those older and bigger than him, but also showed him he could compete against a higher class of athlete. Carter was dealt a severe blow when his mother died of leukemia when he was just twelve years old. But a deep religious faith pushed Carter to always give it everything he had as he felt his mother was watching him and would expect nothing less.[2]

Despite the fame he acquired playing catcher, Carter did not play that position until the last week of his senior year in high school. He had been a pitcher and shortstop, but when told he would have a better shot of making the Major Leagues as a catcher, he converted. Drafted by the Expos in 1972, he made his Major League debut in 1974. Carter's ascension was matched by that of fellow future Hall of Famers Andre Dawson and eventually Tim Raines. Montreal had a core group of talented players that made the Expos a formidable opponent.

"Where we were as a team, if you remember 1979, 1980, the Expos came into their own. We finished second to the 'We Are Family' Pittsburgh Pirates in '79. We lost out to them by two games. If there was the wildcard back then we would have been in the playoffs. We lost to the Phillies that next year. They went on to win the World Series. We lost out to them by one game and then of course the strike shortened season in '81, we won the second half, beat the Phillies and then lost to the Dodgers, and three of those teams went on to win the World Series," said Carter.[3]

As the Expos emerged as contenders, Carter, known by fans as "The Kid," became an offensive force unparalleled among National League catchers. Nineteen-eighty-four saw him produce his greatest season, setting a career high in hits (175), runs batted in (106), and batting average (.294). He had also, at the behest of Expos management, taken the extra measure of assimilating into the Montreal community. He and his wife bought a home in the city, and Carter even learned French.

Now, after a decade with the team that included their only postseason stop and seven All-Star Game appearances, Carter was compelled to ask if they no longer wanted him. "Yes," replied McHale, the rumors were in fact true. Expos owner Charles Bronfman had been complaining about Carter's performance for years. Bronfman felt Carter did not give enough, even though Carter played all of 1983 with tendinitis in his left elbow. Even though he could have been the National League MVP in 1984 had the Expos been in contention. Even though he now lived in Montreal, had learned French, and was a fan favorite. Bronfman had even gone so far as to once tell Carter, "Whenever you get up in key situations, I go to the bathroom."[4]

Somehow, the Expos' drop in the standings and their loss in attendance was Carter's fault. "We finished in fifth place. So I started hearing rumblings that the front office, including Charles Bronfman, the owner, and the rest of the board of directors were possibly interested in trading me . . . or at least that's what was filtering through the newspapers. And it got back to me and I was asked a question. 'What do you think of that?' Well that's news to me. I thought I was gonna be with the organization my entire career," said Carter.[5]

It was not just Bronfman who wanted him gone. Carter had worn out his welcome with his teammates. They talked behind his back about how he was always jumping in front of microphones, smiling for pictures, doing advertisements for any product under the sun. They derided him by calling him "Camera Carter" and "Teeth." The smiling and happy-go-lucky attitude was all an act, they thought. Carter was a phony who valued his stats and camera time more than his team. After all, if they were miserable in Montreal, how could Carter possibly be genuinely happy there?

"Well I just looked at it as they were jealous and it goes without saying. You just move on. And if that's the way they felt about me, it's their own choice of words, and it's freedom of whatever they want to say and that's fine. You know, I just took it with a grain of salt. . . . I did get a lot more maybe attention and recognition maybe because I did commercials up in Montreal. And I had a lot of opportunities," said Carter. "Hey, you try to take advantage of opportunities that exist, and when we started getting good as team, '79, '80, those years, I had the opportunity of doing some commercials for companies like 7-Up and Chrysler and Warner Lambert and stuff like that. And I made the effort of staying up there and making myself available, of getting involved in the community and the society up there. And a lot of them were so disenchanted over the transition of living in Montreal because of the changeover in money, the taxes, the language barrier."[6]

If the team no longer wants me, thought Carter, maybe it is just better to move on. "When a team doesn't want you anymore, it comes to that point in time where it's time to move on. And that's really the feeling I was getting," said Carter.[7]

Having been in the Major Leagues for ten years and with the same team for five, Carter had the right to veto any trade. But if the Expos wanted to move on, he was not going to get in the way. Instead, Carter asked McHale to at least send him somewhere competitive. A list of teams was compiled that Carter would be willing to go to. It included the Los Angeles Dodgers, Atlanta Braves, and New York Mets. Carter wanted to stay in the National League, where he knew the parks and the players.

The Dodgers would be nice. After all, Carter was from Southern California. He wouldn't mind the Braves either. Carter had a house in Florida, so playing in Atlanta would keep him relatively close to home. The Mets, while on the list, did not seem like a possibility. No way he was getting traded within the division, Carter thought (before realignment in 1994, the Braves played in the National League West, not the East). A deal was discussed that included Carter going to the Braves for Craig McMurtry, Biff Poco-roba, Rafael Ramirez, and/or Andres Thomas. The trade never happened though. Instead, the Expos informed Carter of a potential deal with New York.

The Mets had actually been after Carter for over a year. Cashen had first broached the subject of a deal involving the catcher toward the end of the '83 season when Montreal was in town. It was not much more than talk.

"I went to my friend John McHale and said, listen I am interested in Carter," recalled Cashen. "I will trade you for him, some good young ballplayers. He said, 'Frank, if they heard up here that I was thinking of trading Gary Carter I would be run out of Canada.'"[8]

But each time Cashen spoke to the Expos, the conversation grew a little more serious.

"I only had one guy in my organization who knew about it and that was Al Harazin. We must have had twenty-five meetings . . . we had five meetings face-to-face and about twenty phone calls between us," said Cashen.[9]

The winter meetings in December 1984 yielded more progress. Once they concluded, Cashen and McHale finally got down to business. The Expos would need another catcher to replace Carter, along with a pitcher. Most important for them, however, was acquiring a shortstop. They wanted Hubie Brooks, a New York fan favorite who had been one of the few bright spots during the Mets' bleaker years. Cashen agreed to part with him. Additionally, catcher Mike Fitzgerald, pitcher Floyd Youmans, and outfielder Herb Willingham were included. In return, the Mets would get Carter. Once the details were finalized, the deal was presented to Gary, who had to approve it.

Carter sat down with his wife to discuss the proposal. New York would be different—vastly different. The pressure to perform would be beyond anything they had experienced in Montreal. The benefits, however, would also exceed Montreal's. The Carters both agreed it was time to move on. "Basically, it was a decision that I was not gonna make unless I had my wife's approval and everything. And she was for it and thought it was time to make the move," said Carter.[10]

The Monday after the meetings concluded, Cashen and Harazin flew down to West Palm Beach for a face to face meeting to discuss New York with the Carters. Gary wanted to make absolutely certain this was the right thing to do before he officially said yes. If he had any lingering doubts, the meeting with Cashen and Harazin quashed them.

"All in all . . . I had to accept the trade and I said yes. Going to New York was a shock because of obviously it being the media capital of the world. I was welcoming the change because of the fact that the Expos front office were so interested in wanting to trade me, so I said you know what, it's time to move on," said Carter.[11]

"I think I have somewhere around a Christmas napkin with Gary's name on it to kind of commemorate the visit. We had a very nice time and enjoyed the company, he and his wife, and again we did some selling of the job of what we were trying to do in New York," said Harazin.[12]

And with that, on December 10, 1984, the greatest trade in Mets history was completed.

THE DEAL WAS A stunner, both for the Mets and the rest of the National League. Carter, as he was well aware, was being deemed the final piece of the puzzle for the Mets. The fact that the Mets even had a puzzle to complete was rather amazing.

Fewer franchises had struggled harder for success, at least in the 1970s and '80s, than the Mets. Having entered baseball as loveable 120-game losers in 1962, the Mets surprised the nation when they won the World Series in just their eighth season. A core group of young, solid talent helped them make the World Series again in 1973, though they suffered a seven-game defeat to the Oakland Athletics. After that, it was mostly downhill for the franchise. They remained marginally competitive until 1977, when things fell completely apart. That year, the team finished 64-98. Even worse, in June they traded away ace pitcher Tom Seaver to the Cincinnati Reds. Seaver's trade was widely decried in New York. "What really surprised us in '77 was the demise of Seaver, in June, going to Cincinnati," said Bud Harrelson, the team's shortstop for much the

1970s and eventually the third-base coach on the '85 team. "It was starting to get a lot different than it was in the past with a lot of guys being there together winning in '69 and losing in '73. When Seaver left, it was tough. He was my roommate, so it was real tough mentally on me. It gave everyone a sense of hey, anything can happen. Which it did the next year for me. I end up getting traded to Philadelphia in spring training."[13]

Soon, other mainstays from the good years were gone. By 1980 the Mets were an embarrassing franchise to both players and fans.

"During the mid to late 1970s, the stench of stagflation and the Vietnam/Watergate hangover was in no way alleviated at Shea Stadium," said Mike Riordan, history department supervisor at Pompton Lakes High School in New Jersey and a devoted Mets fan. Riordan's mother used to take him to games whose sole highlight would be seeing John Stearns, a .260 career hitter who represented the best the Mets had to offer, get a hit or two. "Luckily, for the older members of Generation X, alcohol was becoming an appropriate partner for Met-related suffering."[14]

They were some of the few who were actually showing up to Shea, as the Mets were constantly overshadowed by New York's other team, the Yankees. While the team in the Bronx had future Hall of Famers like Reggie Jackson and Rich "Goose" Gossage, the Mets had players like Jerry Morales and John Pacella. The results were predictable. The 1980 Yankees scored 772 runs and won 103 games. The 1980 Mets scored 554 runs and won 67 games. The Yankees won the American League East. The Mets just barely avoided finishing last in the National League East for the fourth consecutive year.

"In those early years when I first joined the Mets, the fall of 1980, the Mets were pretty bad," said Mookie Wilson. "They had great guys, don't get me wrong, but the team was not the team that was capable of winning any ball games. The pitching was probably the strong suit. They didn't have a lot of speed. Didn't have much power. As I remember they were pretty strong up the middle, but everything else was pretty much a toss-up. John Stearns was catching at the time and was probably one of the better players on the team at that point. Everywhere else we were pretty weak. I was somewhat disappointed. I had expected more out of Major League Baseball. Reading and watching Major League Baseball, I had expected more, and I really began to wonder if I had made a mistake."[15]

A media campaign designed by Della Femina, Travisano and Partners, which tried to entice fans to Shea by claiming "The Magic Is Back!" was widely ridiculed. What magic? Early in the 1980 season the St. Louis Cardinals' team bus drove by Shea Stadium. When the players caught a glimpse of the slogan plastered on the stadium's exterior, they broke out laughing.[16]

The team was so lackluster that management actually began promoting opposing players to draw fans to the park. "I get a little tired when I look up at our own scoreboard and see constant plugs for a visiting team and a visiting pitcher," said then-manager Joe Torre in 1981, when the Mets were plugging the impending Shea Stadium debut of Dodgers rookie phenom pitcher Fernando Valenzuela.[17]

"It was bad," said Wally Backman, a second baseman who was called up to the team in 1980. "The team was terrible. It was a lot of older players."[18]

After enjoying a mini hot streak in midseason, the team lost twenty-four of twenty-seven games. Fortunately for most fans, they had not bothered to show up to witness the performance.

"The first time I came up there, I remember a big crowd was about fourteen thousand people," said Terry Leach, a pitcher who started his career with the club in 1981. "We were not very good, and heck I didn't know any better. That was my first time being up in the big leagues."[19]

Nineteen-eighty-one was not much better than 1980 for the team, as they were already thirteen and a half games out of first by May 19. Starting pitcher Pat Zachary tied with relief pitcher Neil Allen for the team lead with seven wins, amazingly low even for a strike-shortened season. Outside of Hubie Brooks, no starting position player hit over .271. Pitcher Pete Falcone hit as many home runs (1) in 22 at bats as starting second baseman Doug Flynn and starting shortstop Frank Taveras hit in 608 combined at bats.

"When I got back, it was not a good team," said Rusty Staub, who had played with the Mets from 1972 to 1975 and then rejoined the team in 1981. "They had a lot of people that had been around there for a while. Some had talent. Some overestimated their talent."[20]

Staub saw an immediate difference between the competitive Mets teams he had been on in the '70s and the clubhouse he was now entering. "That was probably the most enjoyable period, that last month of the season [1973] where we all came together and we won all these big games. You know we couldn't lose anything. As a memory that is about as good as it gets, to be able to come together as a unit and to do that. The second time [around], the team wasn't like that."

The team's horrid performance led to the firing of Torre, replaced for the 1982 season by George Bamberger. Expectations were not high. One player recalled Bamberger holding a meeting in spring training in which he said if the team played .500 ball he "would be happy."[21] Still, the change seemed to work at first, as the team was 34-30 and just three games out of first on June 20. But it all fell apart. At one point in August, the Mets lost fifteen games in a row. It was the second-longest streak in team history, bested only by a seventeen-game streak in their initial season. For their fifteenth loss, they went down 4–0 to the Astros before 9,500 fans at Shea. Nolan Ryan, a former Met, held the Mets hitless until the eighth inning. Oddly, the idea of being no-hit took the team's mind off losing another game. "At least for seven innings, we weren't thinking of the score," said the Mets' Bob Bailor at the time. "We were thinking of whether or not we were going to get a hit. It managed to take our minds away from the losing for a while."[22]

They finished August with a 5-24 record, the second worst single-month performance in team history. After June 20, they lost forty-nine of their next sixty-five games and eventually finished the year 65-97. No one batted over .300, and only one pitcher managed to win more than nine games.

"When I first got there we weren't very good," said Walt Terrell, a pitcher who made his Major League debut with the club in 1982. "I guess, I think there was kind of a transition going on. And I don't mean this to sound disrespectful to the guys that were there, but it was kind of that older to younger transition was going on. . . . We had some guys that had played a long time. Older players towards the end of their career with that infusion of younger guys that were coming up. We weren't very good. Hell, when I first got up to the big leagues we were forty-two games out of first place."[23]

For Tom Gorman, a pitcher who joined the team in 1982, it was only slightly better. "We were really lousy. We were terrible. I remember when I showed up, and it would have maybe been the first of September, we were twenty-eight games out of first," said Gorman.[24]

Nineteen-eighty-three was not much better. A poor start caused Bamberger to step down as manager forty-six games into the season. His replacement, Frank Howard, took over a team in last place. They remained there for the rest of the season, finishing 68-94. Terrell ended up with as many home runs in forty-four at bats that year as did the Mets' shortstop, second baseman, and two starting catchers combined. During the last game of the season, just 6,393 fans showed up at Shea.

Though the play on the field was awful, in reality the team's future had begun to turn in 1980 when Cashen was hired as general manager. Cashen, rarely seen without his trademark bow tie, worked for Jerry Hoffberger's National Brewing Company in the 1960s. When the company purchased the Orioles in 1965, Cashen moved into the team's front office and helped develop the franchise into perennial winners throughout the late '60s and early '70s. He moved out of baseball temporarily in the mid-1970s, going back to the National Brewing Company and serving as senior vice president of marketing and sales.[25] Eventually Cashen returned to baseball, going to work in the commissioner's office. That is where he was when he was informed that the Mets, under new ownership, were looking for a general manager. Hoffberger, who thought the world of Cashen, and for good reason, had been informing the Mets' new management that they would be wise to give Cashen a call.

"Nelson Doubleday called me and asked me to come and talk with him . . . he wanted me to become general manager," said Cashen. "To tell you the truth, the team was so goddamn bad at that point in time, they had been last or next to last for five straight years. They had only drawn like 788,000 the previous year. They were so bad. I looked into the farm system and that had been just allowed to dwindle into nothing. It was such a big goddamn job, at least I thought it was . . . well that is why I really took it, because I thought it was such a big challenge."[26]

"I had worked for Frank Cashen [in Baltimore], who hired me out of the Minor Leagues, and so when Frank went to New York he brought Lou Gorman and Joe McIllvane and I along," said Harazin. "I had . . . never thought that I would work in New York because I could have gone to New York out of law school and never had any interest in going to New York . . . and the east in particular and instead went to Cincinnati to practice law. But the opportunity to work for Frank again, combined with, at that time, if it wasn't the worst club in baseball it was certainly close . . . to try and build something was what appealed to me."[27]

Behind the scenes, Cashen began amassing a wealth of talent that gradually brought the Mets back into prominence.

"I went in and started to rebuild it," said Cashen. "Nelson Doubleday was a fantastic owner. He was like Hoffberger had been in Baltimore. You ran the team, and he didn't question anything you did. All he asked was he didn't want to read things in the paper. Whatever was going on, I would let him know. We had a great one-on-one relationship. I went ahead and, as far as I know, rebuilt the ball club, rebuilt the farm system, and turned it into one of the better franchises in baseball."[28]

The first major move was acquiring outfielder George Foster from the Reds. Foster, one of the game's major power threats in the late '70s, was not only acquired to improve the team; he was also Cashen's way of showing the rest of the National League East that the Mets meant business.

"I was looking for somebody to help, you know, we had to start getting some players," said Cashen. "I showed an interest in Cincinnati and Foster 'cause I had seen him and I knew him to be a good offensive player."[29]

While they gave away little in return, Foster did not come cheap. The team, wanting to lock him in long term, immediately inked him to a five-year deal worth $2 million a year. It was the second largest contract in baseball history at the time, second only to the Yankees' Dave Winfield, whom the Mets had attempted to sign but whose offer did not come close to that of the Yankees.[30]

"We were certainly looking for a punch, and here was a guy who had some tremendous years in Cincinnati on really good ball clubs of course. We had Dave Kingman, so we had sluggers, but here was a guy, you know, a real proven RBI guy. At the time it seemed like a no brainer to be interested in him," said Harazin.[31]

The Foster trade and subsequent signing, even if it did not mean an immediate turn around, displayed that the Mets were no longer going to be a laughingstock. Along the way, Cashen also traded for young prospects like Ron Darling and Sid Fernandez. These players complimented other young prospects the Mets had drafted, like Roger McDowell, Darryl Strawberry and Dwight Gooden. In June 1983 Cashen made one of the biggest steals in baseball history when he traded relief pitcher Neil Allen to the St. Louis Cardinals for first baseman Keith Hernandez.

"That fell into my lap," said Cashen. He was sitting at his desk one day when Joe McDonald, a former Mets general manager who now held the same title in St. Louis, gave him a call. The Cardinals were interested in Allen, who had been one of the Mets' better relief pitchers. No dice, Cashen told him. If you talk about Allen, McDonald said, then we will talk about Hernandez. "Let's talk," replied Cashen. The two worked out the terms of a deal over the next day.[32]

"The change in the club started, I am talking about having a championship club, when they made the trade for Keith Hernandez," said Staub. "That was a momentous break for the Mets. He was a very aggressive, good, experienced player, with a very young team, with a lot of young pitchers coming up. He was as good at the bunt plays as anybody ever. And fielder? Come on. He was the catalyst of what started to happen with the Mets again."[33]

In 1984 Cashen coupled all his newfound talent with a new manager: Davey Johnson. The team was not given much of a chance. When the season began, their odds of winning the pennant were 75 to 1.[34] But the newly formed Mets surprised everyone. Behind one of the league's dominate pitching staffs, they emerged as contenders for the National League East crown. At the All-Star break, they were in first place, the first time in their existence they led the division going into the second half of the season. After years of putrid offense, the Mets finally had reliable, consistent players at the plate, like Keith Hernandez, Mookie Wilson, and Hubie Brooks. "The Mets are for real," commented Dodgers manager Tommy Lasorda at the midseason break.[35]

But they were unable to keep up the pace. During a twelve-game stretch from late July to early August, the team went from four and a half games in front of the Chicago Cubs for first place to four and a half games behind them. The culmination of the collapse took place at Wrigley Field, where the Mets were swept in a crucial four-game series. During the final game, the team blew a late-inning 3-run lead. When Terrell and Johnson were ejected after Terrell hit Bob Dernier in the head, Cubs fans began belting Mets players with beer. It was a carryover of anger that had stemmed from beanball incidents the day before. As a result, several Mets nearly charged the stands, with first base coach Bill Robinson having to be restrained by Wrigley Field security.[36] Eventually, the Mets were escorted from the stadium to the airport by the police.[37]

While the Mets never recovered from their sweep at Wrigley, there was no shame in their second-place finish in 1984.

"Of all the positive things I've seen happen to this team this season, the most important was that the guys were disappointed," said Wilson, who had put up with several last-place finishes in his time in New York. "They're not content with second place."[38]

Despite their disappointment, the end result of 1984 was great. "Finishing second and winning ninety games would have been reason for a ticker-tape parade in some previous Mets seasons, when the one thing the players used to hope for was staying out of last place and the main thing the managers would hope for is not getting fired," noted the *Newark Star-Ledger*'s Dan Castellano.[39]

The team, however, was still missing something. That was where Gary Carter came in. Carter was the most exciting and important trade in Mets history. It not only brought added star power to the

Mets, it also earned them the back pages of the New York newspapers and stole the momentum away from New York's other team only a week after they had pulled off a blockbuster trade of their own. That other team, the Yankees, had been the city's team for nearly decade. But that was changing, fast. The Carter deal was the unofficial beginning of New York becoming a Mets town.

# 2

# "Never Played the Game"

THREE YEARS. THAT WAS how long it had been since a member of the Yankees referred to himself in the third person. That streak came to an end on December 5, 1984. The Yankees, shut out of the playoffs for three straight seasons, had acquired baseball's flashiest and perhaps most eccentric player by acquiring Rickey Henderson from the Oakland A's in a mega seven-player deal. It was the biggest trade of the off-season, for at least the next week anyway. Henderson was the game's greatest lead-off hitter and the fastest man to ever don a pair of cleats. It was not a stretch to say he was the most talented player the Yankees had traded for since Babe Ruth.

RICKEY, AS HE SOMETIMES called himself, grew up in Oakland, California, and might have become a football player had his mother not feared him getting injured on the gridiron. Drafted by the A's in 1976, he made it to the club in 1979. Outside of 33 stolen bases, his first season was nothing remarkable. The following year, however, people in baseball began to take notice of Rickey after he stole 100 bases and hit .303. It was only the third time in the twentieth century a player stole 100 or more bases. In 1981 he hit .319 and stole 56 bases in a strike-shortened season, a performance that earned him enough votes to finish second in the American League Most Valuable Player voting. Under the tutelage of manager Billy Martin, the A's surprised many when they reached the playoffs that year, though they were eliminated in the American League Championship Series by the Yankees. By 1984 Henderson was one of the premiere players in baseball. He shattered the single-season stolen-base record in 1982 when he swiped 130 bags. The next year, he stole 108, marking the third time in four seasons he reached the 100 plateau. He led the league in swipes every season from 1980 to 1984. Only six years into his career, Henderson was already halfway toward breaking the all-time stolen base record held by Lou Brock.

While speed was his most renowned talent, Henderson was also an excellent hitter who could be counted on to bat .300 or better. But Henderson's most valuable asset at the plate was his batting eye. He was patient, rarely swung at the first pitch, and wore pitchers down. His eye was coupled with an unusual batting stance: he crouched his body toward the back end of the plate, drastically shrinking the size of the strike zone. Pitchers could either throw something down the heart of the plate and take their chances, or walk him, which with Rickey's speed was the equivalent of giving up a double. As a result, Henderson led the league in walks in 1982 and '83. His on base percentage hovered around .400.

But Henderson was set to become a free agent after the '85 season, and he had already rejected a seven-year offer the A's put to him before the '84 season. It seemed obvious Oakland would not be able to retain him. They began talking trade with the Yankees during the winter meetings. The Yankees were amendable to a deal so long as they could discuss a contract with Henderson beforehand. When the negotiations stalled, Yankees owner George Steinbrenner contemplated backing out of the deal. "Get him," Martin, then an advisor to the Yankees, told Steinbrenner. "He could be the most exciting Yankee since Mickey Mantle."[1]

The Yankees eventually worked out a contract and the deal was done. Richie Bry, Henderson's agent, made a statement after the trade was announced that was rather telling in terms of his client.

"This is an excellent opportunity for Rickey to be with the Yankees, to have more fame and fortune than he's had before," said Bry.[2]

While perhaps unintended, the statement indicated Henderson wanted the deal not because it could lead to a championship, but for what it could bring him personally.

Many teammates, however, spoke highly of Henderson, and he made clear he wanted to win a ring in New York. But there was another element to him outside his talent. Henderson had a personality to match his skills.

"Rickey was Rickey," said teammate Rich Bordi. "It sounds weird, but people in the baseball world would know what I mean when I say that. Rickey was in his own world."[3]

A fitness fanatic who rarely drank and did not smoke (two qualities that would make anyone on a 1980s baseball team an outcast), Henderson did not hesitate to make grievances known through the papers. If Rickey was unhappy, people were going to hear about it. Moreover, stories had emerged from Oakland that Henderson had not played in games simply because he did not feel like it.

"He asked out last season when the A's were still in contention, claiming he had a cold. On many occasions, he refused to steal," reported the *Trenton Times'* Bus Saidt.[4]

He also had a flair for the dramatic that surpassed anyone else's who had been in a Yankees uniform. When Henderson hit a home run, he would tug at the collar of his uniform before taking his sweet time rounding the bases. It was beyond ironic: the fastest man in baseball took perhaps the longest amount of time to circle the bases on a homer.

"I will never forget how he wore leather outfits in the summer. No matter how hot it was," recalled teammate Rex Hudler.[5]

Rickey also brought the famous "Snatch" catch along with him, which was a method of catching fly balls where Henderson essentially snatched them out of the air with his glove. Usually he would give his upper thigh a good pat or two with his glove before he did this. Yet, while Henderson could be a headache for managers and owners, to his teammates he was as good as they came.

"He was the first guy to give a kid in camp or rookie [something]. He'd give you spikes, give you a glove," said Dale Berra.[6]

The Yankees were aware of Henderson's personality. Everyone was. But they saw the skills as far exceeding any problems that might arise off the field.

"Rickey Henderson is the most exciting player in baseball," said Martin after the trade. "There's no player I'd rather have if I was starting a team."[7]

The deal was meant to solidify the outfield and provide more RBI opportunities for the Yankees' middle of the order, which was perhaps the strongest in baseball. Rickey's speed would be an element the Yankees had not had in years (he stole more bases in 1984 than the entire Yankees team combined). The trade was an important statement by the Yankees that they did not wish to repeat their performance of 1984, when a bad first half effectively killed the season before the All-Star break. Of course, 1984 was supposed to be an improvement over what happened in 1983. Nineteen-eighty-three was supposed to be an improvement over what happened in 1982. And 1982 was supposed to be an improvement over what happened in 1981.

FROM 1976 TO 1984, the same period in which the Mets were falling apart only to gradually rebuild, fewer teams had greater success than the New York Yankees. During that nine-season span, they made the postseason five times, reached the World Series four times, and won the championship twice. Removing the strike-shortened 1981 season, the Yankees averaged ninety-three wins a season during this time. No other team performed better during that period.

Statistics and win-loss records, however, only tell part of the story of the Yankees of that era. And in many ways they are an insignificant part. Because regardless of how many games they were or were not winning, the Yankees were a team of internal chaos. While the players liked each other, mostly, and maintained a spirit of camaraderie, each had their own issues to deal with. One faction of the club had to deal with lack of playing time. Another had to deal with the attitude of whoever the manager was. And in one way or another, directly or indirectly, each had to deal with the daily soap opera the owner was creating. The Bronx Zoo–era Yankees teams of the late '70s have become famous for turmoil, but the Yankees of the early and mid-1980s surpassed those teams in terms of drama. The only difference was the Bronx Zoo teams won championships, and the 1980s teams did not. The drama would only increase as the Mets became a force to be reckoned with. Regardless of what one player might be bitching about on any given day, the disorder and tension surrounding the Yankees always came back to one man.

TO UNDERSTAND THE DIFFERENCE between the Yankees and Mets during the course of the 1980s is to understand the difference in ownership. Nelson Doubleday called in Frank Cashen because he wanted his team to get better. He knew that meant leaving Cashen alone, for the most part, to make the trades and obtain the talent he felt would best give the Mets a chance to contend. The New York Yankees' owner, George Steinbrenner, did no such thing in every way possible.

George Michael Steinbrenner III was born on July 4, 1930, the son of a demanding Cleveland ship-building magnate. Steinbrenner's personality would be greatly shaped by his father, a man who required his son to answer "Yes, sir, no sir" and who accepted nothing other than success. It appears Steinbrenner was never truly able to please his father, or at least he never thought he did. It was the kind of relationship Freud could write a textbook about.

"The fact that George was so dismissive of and often even abusive toward his employees can probably be directly attributed to his failure ever to win his father's approval," wrote Bill Madden in his biography of Steinbrenner's life.[8]

A decent high-school athlete, Steinbrenner highly desired to be involved in sports. In the mid-1950s he landed a job as an assistant coach of the Northwestern University football team. He was fired after a year. Afterward, he took a position with his family's company, Kinsman Marine Transit Company. While he may not have pleased his father, Steinbrenner proved an efficient worker who made shrewd deals that helped expand the company, which was eventually bought by American Ship Building Company. At the same time, he also became involved in professional sports. He bought the Cleveland Pipers of the National Basketball League. Though George tried feverishly to get the Pipers into the National Basketball Association, the attempt ultimately failed, and the team went bankrupt.

It was during this time that the devious side of Steinbrenner first began to emerge. He attempted to oust the Pipers' popular coach,

John McClendon, because he did not think he was argumentative enough with referees or his own players. His attempt failed. Steinbrenner fired his first general manager after word of a big player signing accidentally leaked before he wanted it announced. When trying to raise $250,000 to pay the entry fee into the NBA, Steinbrenner manufactured a pile of telegrams he claimed represented a portion of the down payment. The move backfired severely.

"It threw basketball in Cleveland back six or seven years because no one would touch Cleveland after that, and it wasn't until George left Cleveland that Cleveland was able to get a franchise," said McClendon.[9]

Serendipitously, a deal in 1971 to buy the Cleveland Indians fell through at the last minute. Afterward, Steinbrenner focused his energy on buying the New York Yankees. The team had fallen into disarray during the late 1960s. They had failed to adequately replace many of their aging superstars in large part due to their hesitancy to embrace black and Latino ballplayers. So as Mickey Mantle and Whitey Ford edged into retirement, the Yankees edged toward the bottom of the standings. Attendance at Yankee Stadium began to decline and the team's owners, CBS, were desperate to sell. Along with minority partner Michael Burke and ten other investors, Steinbrenner bought the team in January 1973 for $8.7 million. A press conference was held in New York to announce the deal. In one of the greatest misstatements in the history of the spoken word, Steinbrenner told the assembled media that, "We plan absentee ownership as far as running the Yankees is concerned. We're not going to pretend we're something we aren't. I'll stick to building ships."

Steinbrenner's meddling in team affairs began almost immediately. On his first opening day as owner, he made a list of players whose hair he felt was too long. Since he did not know their names yet, he identified them by uniform number and demanded they get a haircut.[10] By the end of the '73 season, which saw the team finish in fourth place, manager Ralph Houk had had enough. He had been with the team since 1966 and had previously led the Yankees to two world championships in the early '60s. But the new owner became too much for the man known as "The Major."

Houk resigned and was replaced with Bill Virdon. Under Virdon, the Yankees made a surprising run for first place in 1974, finishing in second. But the team faltered in 1975, and Virdon was replaced in midseason by Billy Martin.

Martin helped rebuild the team into perennial contenders as he led the Yankees to the World Series in his first full season as manager. Though they were swept by the Reds, they returned in 1977 bolstered by the signing of All-Star outfielder Reggie Jackson. They reached the World Series again, this time beating the Dodgers in six games. In 1978, however, the team was beset by injuries and inconsistent play early on. By July, they had fallen fourteen games behind the first place Red Sox. Martin, Steinbrenner, and Jackson were in a never-ending feud with one another over issues of playing time, hustle, and who was really in charge of the team. After making some derogatory comments about both Steinbrenner and Jackson to a reporter, Martin tearfully resigned before he was fired.

Bob Lemon replaced Martin, the fourth manager under Steinbrenner in just five years. Under Lemon, the Yankees staged one of the greatest comebacks in history, ultimately winning the World Series a second time in a row. Yet two consecutive titles were not enough for Steinbrenner. In '79, the team was hurt by a string of injuries, and some felt Lemon was simply not the same manager after his son was killed in a car accident during the off-season. Sixty-five games into the season, Lemon was let go and replaced with Martin. Martin managed a badly injured and, because of the death of team captain Thurman Munson, devastated club to a 55-40 record. But shortly after the season ended, Martin punched a fifty-two-year-old marshmallow salesman in the face during an altercation outside a hotel bar in Bloomington, Minnesota. Steinbrenner fired Martin shortly thereafter.

The Yankees slogged through a difficult period during the early 1980s. They won the American League East in 1980 but were overwhelmed and swept by the Kansas City Royals in the American League Championship Series. Their manager Dick Howser, who had replaced Billy II as the Yankees' sixth manager under Steinbrenner, won acclaim for his performance, which included winning 103 regular-season games. But the team's failure to get to the World Series, especially after being swept like that, left a bad taste with Steinbrenner. During the Championship Series, third-base coach Mike Ferraro had sent Willie Randolph home during a critical moment in Game Two. Randolph was out by a mile, and after the season, Steinbrenner moved to have Ferraro replaced with Don Zimmer. Hearing that a coach of his would be replaced without his input, Howser, responding to a question from the press, said it would have been nice had he been informed of such a move since, after all, he was the manager. Steinbrenner did not take kindly to Howser's remarks and immediately moved to fire him under the charade that Howser was leaving because of a real-estate deal.[11]

Howser was replaced with Gene Michael, who had one of the stranger tenures as Yankees manager. The 1981 Yankees were in first place when, in midseason, the players went on strike. When the strike ended forty-nine days later and play resumed, Major League Baseball decided that the season would be split into two parts. Teams that were in first place the day the strike began would automatically make the postseason. The teams that posted the best record in their division in the second half would also make the playoffs, or if the same team was in first place for both halves, the team with the second-best record would make it. Since the Yankees were in first place in the American League East when the strike hit, they were guaranteed a spot in the playoffs. But when they returned, Steinbrenner was not happy with the play on the field. He began to make life a living hell for Michael. He constantly phoned Michael so he could second-guess his decisions, and he did his best to pit him against Reggie Jackson when Jackson went into a slump. Finally, Michael snapped.

"I'm tired of getting the phone calls after games and being told it's my fault that we lost," he told the press in late August. "I thought I knew what I was getting into when I accepted this job, but I didn't expect it to be this direct and this constant."[12]

The comments naturally drew the ire of Steinbrenner. But instead of firing him immediately, he let Michael twist in the wind by cutting off all communication between his manager and front-office staff. After a week, Michael was put out of his misery. Even though his team was headed to the postseason, Michael was fired with twenty-five games remaining. He was replaced by Lemon.

The Yankees advanced to the World Series only to blow a two-games-to-zero lead to the Dodgers, ultimately losing in six games. Lemon stayed on in 1982, the first Yankees manager to last two consecutive seasons since, well, Bob Lemon in 1978 and '79. Not only that, but Lemon was promised he would manage the entire '82 season. That promise lasted all of fourteen games. The Yankees struggled out of the gate, and almost immediately Steinbrenner began telling reporters he had made a mistake bringing Lemon back. What's more, Steinbrenner had always been leery of Lemon's seemingly superhuman ability to drink. Rightly or wrongly, he hinted that it was impacting the team. Moreover, Lemon, who had now twice rescued the Yankees during times of peril, had grown fed up with Steinbrenner's constant meetings and phone calls. The guy had managed the Yankees twice, and they had made the World Series both times. What more did Steinbrenner want? So out was Lemon. In was, of course, Michael, now the ninth manager in Steinbrenner's nine years as owner. Michael lasted eighty-six games, going 44-42 with a squad full of aging veterans and poor acquisitions. Clyde King, the third manager of the '82 season, finished the year off at the helm, as the Yankees landed in fifth place.

In 1983 Martin returned for a third time. He managed to last the entire season, but that was it. During the course of the year, Martin engaged in strange behavior, including being caught on TV passing love notes to his girlfriend during a game. The Boss could not tolerate his actions, and so, for a third time, he was let go. Nineteen-eighty-four saw Yogi Berra, a much-beloved former Yankees catcher and outfielder, sign on as the twelfth manager under Steinbrenner.

IT WAS NOT JUST the constant managerial changes that drove players, fans, and the media crazy. Steinbrenner was intimately involved in every aspect of trades and free-agent signings. He also continuously vowed to step back from his incessant meddling, only to reemerge before anyone even knew he had made the vow to begin with. Moreover, Steinbrenner constantly questioned the ability and character of his players in print. It was a tactic he often felt would encourage those he questioned to do better. George never realized his football mentality simply did not translate to baseball. Often, all it did was piss them off and make them want to leave New York.

Steinbrenner's act was mostly ignored as long as the Yankees were winning. But that began to change drastically following the team's loss in the '81 World Series. In fact, the descent could probably be pinpointed as having come before the World Series. In the division series against the Milwaukee Brewers, the Yankees won the first two games of the best-of-five series, only to lose the next two. An irate Steinbrenner stormed into the Yankees' clubhouse, berating the team's performance.

"Fuck you, you fat son of a bitch," shouted Yankees catcher Rick Cerone. "You never played the game. You don't know what you are talking about."[13]

The Yankees won Game Five to advance. During the World Series, Steinbrenner claimed to have gotten into a fight with two Dodger fans while trying to protect the Yankees' honor. The fans in question never surfaced, and many suspected George just made it up. The team's eventual collapse to the Dodgers especially infuriated Steinbrenner, who took the almost unheard-of step of issuing a public apology to fans of the team: "I want to sincerely apologize to the people of New York and to the fans of the New York Yankees everywhere for the performance of the Yankee team in the World Series. I also want to assure you that we will be at work immediately to prepare for 1982."[14]

Steinbrenner was true to his word, immediately restructuring the Yankees for 1982. Unfortunately for fans, the majority of moves he made soured quickly. First and foremost, Steinbrenner decided against bringing back outfielder Reggie Jackson. A future Hall of Famer who had overcome extreme scrutiny in his initial years with the club, Jackson was a lethal threat with the bat. But instead of re-signing with the Yankees, Jackson went to the West Coast, inking a deal with the California Angels.

"He has one decent year left, at best," Steinbrenner told friends before Jackson left.[15]

The Yankees never even made him an offer, and rather tellingly, after Jackson signed with the Angels, Steinbrenner issued a statement where he essentially put the blame on his manager for Reggie having left. "One of the negotiating points made by Gary Walker [Jackson's agent] was Reggie's desire to play the outfield every day, which the Yankees could not commit to at this time, since that is the responsibility of manager Bob Lemon."[16]

In his first game back at Yankee Stadium after signing with the Angels, Jackson homered into the upper deck off former teammate Ron Guidry. In response, Yankees fans began chanting, "Steinbrenner sucks." Jackson ended up leading the American League in home runs in 1982, as the Angels won the Western Division. The "one decent year" decree did not pan out either. Jackson's career lasted until 1987. After leaving New York, he was a three-time All-Star, averaging 23 home runs a year.

Heading into '82, Steinbrenner decided the Yankees were going to focus more on their running game and less on the power they had come to be known for. He acquired Ken Griffey and Dave Collins to add speed to the lineup. During spring training, he had Olympic sprinter Harrison Dillard in camp to conduct special running drills with the players. The result was a paltry sixty-nine stolen bases, with Griffey and Collins combining for just twenty-three of them.

Doyle Alexander, acquired just before the beginning of the season to bolster the starting rotation, went 1-7. Worse, he proved a headache in the clubhouse, once punching a wall and injuring his pitching hand. After one particularly horrid start in Detroit, Steinbrenner announced that he was "having Doyle Alexander flown back to New York to undergo a physical. I'm afraid some of our players might get hurt playing behind him."[17] Alexander was exiled from the Yankees in 1983, but it would not be the last they heard of him.

As the season began slipping away, Steinbrenner made erratic decisions. He traded for John Mayberry, a once legitimate power threat now in the twilight of his career with Toronto. The Blue Jays did not want him anymore, and lucky for them, a scout for the Yankees just happened to be in the stands to see Mayberry hit 2 home runs in a game against the Red Sox. They were the only two Mayberry had hit so far that year. Steinbrenner, based on the scout's report, pulled the trigger on a deal for Mayberry, who in turn batted just .209 for the Yankees with 8 home runs.

When the team's performance failed to pick up, Steinbrenner began using petty tactics disguised as elixirs to punish his players. His favorite method was the mandatory team workout on scheduled off days. To Steinbrenner, you could never work hard enough, practice hard enough, try hard enough. There were no off days to him. A day off really meant a day to hone your skills in the batting cage or to take a few ground balls. To the players though, his workouts were complete bullshit. They felt a day off would do far greater good than an hour of batting practice. "We are being punished, that's all," said pitcher Goose Gossage after an early morning workout late in the '82 season. "A slap on the wrist for losing too many games. The workout doesn't accomplish anything, even he [Steinbrenner] must realize that. But we're getting used to this shit."[18]

Steinbrenner spared no one when his team was failing to meet his expectations. In addition to players and his own personnel, he went after umpires with just as much vigor. In late August '82, umpire Dallas Parks made calls on consecutive nights that went against the Yankees. In turn, Steinbrenner issued a press release suggesting that Parks had a beef with the team that went back years and that the state of umpiring should be discussed at the winter meetings. In response, American League president Lee MacPhail said that one of the things they would look at during the winter meetings was "placing on that agenda the matter of intemperate, petulant and problem-causing public statements by baseball personnel and the question of how the league feels such should be dealt with."[19]

The end result of all the trades, managerial changes, workouts, and tirades was a disappointing 79-83 record in 1982.

The following year, the team played better, finishing 91-71. But they were never able to catch up to the division-winning Orioles. Steinbrenner continued his erratic behavior and disastrous moves. He inked Pirates outfielder Steve Kemp to a lucrative five-year deal only to see Kemp miss over fifty games due to injury and hit just .241 with 12 home runs. During the season, Steinbrenner was fined and suspended a week for public comments he made critical of umpiring calls against the Yankees.

Nineteen-eighty-four saw veterans like Graig Nettles and Gossage leave for San Diego. Their departures were due in no small part to their yearning to break free of their owner and the chaos that surrounded the club. Before signing with the Padres, Gossage, who had once famously referred to Steinbrenner as "the fat man," had declared that he would not "return and play for George Steinbrenner." That in turn led to Yankees general manager Murray Cook paying Gossage a backhanded compliment.

"I believe that he'll perform better over the long run in the National League," said Cook. "As he loses his stuff, he'll do better in the bigger ball parks there. He's a fly ball pitcher and the bigger the parks, the better for him."[20]

Nettles, upset over the team acquiring another third baseman just after he had signed a new two-year contract with the club, made his unhappiness evident during spring training.

"I can't believe they would give me that kind of money and then tell me I'm a platoon player," said Nettles. "It doesn't make any sense to me. But I guess most things they do around here don't make much sense."[21]

Comments like that were guaranteed to get you run of out of town. Manager Yogi Berra made it known that he felt Nettles would be a negative influence on the club, but Steinbrenner doubled down on it, making it abundantly clear that trading Nettles was not his decision.

"Yogi and the coaches told me that it would be best for the team if Nettles was traded. I gave them three chances to change their minds and three times they said he had to go. That was good enough for me," said Steinbrenner.[22]

It was a typical comment. If Nettles flourished in San Diego, Steinbrenner could easily blame Yogi and crew for making the move. If Nettles faltered, Steinbrenner would take all the credit for listening to his coaches and making a shrewd move that was unpopular at the time.

In the end, though San Diego had yet to make the playoffs in their existence, the calmer shores of southern California were much more welcoming for Gossage and Nettles than the chaos of the Bronx. They helped lead the Padres to the World Series in '84.

There was some hope for Yogi going into the '84 season. Perhaps a highly respected Hall of Famer like Berra would not have to endure the same kind of crap previous managers had under Steinbrenner, who by now had become known simply as "The Boss." But Berra soon enjoyed the same headaches departed Yankees managers had. The team got off to a sluggish start, going 8-13 in April. Couple that with the Detroit Tigers historic 35-6 record to open the season, and the Yankees were out of it before the middle of May. The team's offense struggled mightily. Outside of first baseman Don Mattingly, the starting infield combined for only 5 home runs and 82 RBIS. Despite a surprising first half by forty-five-year-old Phil Niekro, the pitching staff faltered as well. Ron Guidry, hampered by injuries, failed to follow up on his twenty-win season in 1983. Instead, he suffered the first losing season of his career. Guidry was not the only one felled by injuries. In fact, the Yankees ended up using thirteen different starting pitchers during the course of the season, and only two (Guidry and Niekro) won more than ten games. The starting rotation was also short one lefty when Dave Righetti, in a controversial move, was shifted to the bullpen to become the team's closer after Gossage departed.

Around the All-Star break, Steinbrenner sat Berra and his entire coaching staff down for a meeting. Instead of it being about how to improve the team, it turned into a Steinbrenner gripe session. He belittled Yogi and his staff for the team's performance, placing the blame squarely on them. Steinbrenner specifically kept referring to the team as "your team." The ranting went on for some time. Those in the meeting could see that Yogi was starting to boil. The public persona of Berra was one of almost a class clown. Yogi was the aloof goof who came up with those funny Yogism's like, "No one goes there anymore, it's too crowded." Berra certainly was a nice person, well loved and respected. He rarely blew up or sought confrontation. But even someone like Yogi had his limit, and Berra had now taken enough shit from Steinbrenner.

"I don't want to hear any more of this," Berra shouted at The Boss. "This is your fucking team, not my team. You put this fucking team together. You hire all these fucking players that nobody else wants and pay them more money than they should get."

With that, Berra threw a pack of cigarettes across the table Steinbrenner was seated at. It bounced off the table and hit Steinbrenner in the face. Yogi then stormed out.[23] Steinbrenner, perhaps shocked at how combative Berra had been, did not take any action against his manager. Not then anyway.

By the All-Star break, with their record at 36-46, there was essentially nothing left to play for. The Yankees decided to call up some Minor League talent and give them a chance to show what they had. Players like Mike Pagliarulo, Bobby Meacham, Joe Cowley, and Dennis Rasmussen were all given an opportunity to perform at the Major League level. The result was a 51-29 second-half record, the best in baseball.

Steinbrenner remained largely unseen during the second half of the season. And coincidentally or not, the team picked up its play. Still, the late resurgence was not nearly good enough for The Boss. On the last day of the season, he held a pow wow with reporters in which he brought up various topics that no one had asked about, including how Berra had fought to bring in the young talent but still had not managed to get to the postseason. He proved less than reassuring when, asked about the status of Berra's job, he said he would make a decision by Thanksgiving.[24] The Boss went on, chastising the way decisions were made by committee within the organization, though he failed to fault himself for that kind of process being in place to begin with. It was Steinbrenner's way of saying everyone was at fault but him. It did not end there.

"You can say the Mets were hot, but you can't say that on the road," said The Boss when discussing the Yankees drop in attendance for both home and away games. "Is it because my team is less exciting?"[25]

The answer, which no one dared say, was yes. The Yankees

were less exciting. Steinbrenner's shtick—manageable and even quaint when the Yankees were winning divisions and world championships—had grown increasingly stale since the last Word Series appearance in 1981. It was not just that the Yankees were not as good as those other clubs but that their drama had also worn thin. The soap opera that was the Bronx Zoo–era Yankees only added to the entertainment value of the club. Fans could tune in on any given day to see what Billy Martin had said about Reggie, or The Boss had said or done to Billy, or vice versa. Then they could watch the Yankees win.

Now, they were not watching the Yankees win, and they laid blame at Steinbrenner's door. The lack of a pennant winner made the daily soap opera--like story lines aggravating, not interesting. Fans wanted some calm so that the ship could be righted. They were not getting it, and so they started to drift away. They were not the only ones. Players, coaches, and managers all started to become leery of being in the Bronx. Even one of the best story lines of the year provided unneeded tension.

Throughout 1984, Winfield and Mattingly battled it out for the American League batting title. The race came down to the season's final game against Detroit. Mattingly ended up with four hits against the Tigers that day, besting Winfield for the batting crown, .343 to .340.

It should have been a great story that drew fans to the park well after the Yankees had been out of contention. Instead, it created tension within the clubhouse as the media drew more attention on the race—in Mattingly's favor some thought—and fans began to take sides. By and large, they sided with Mattingly, and some certainly thought the fact that Mattingly was white and Winfield black had something to do with that. Moreover, the fact that people did not want Winfield to win the title despite his having put up four stellar seasons in New York stung the outfielder.

"Every time Donnie steps up to bat cheers fill the stadium, standing O's in fact," Winfield later wrote in his autobiography. "Every time I step up to bat there are boos."[26]

After the season's final game, Winfield quickly showered and left the clubhouse before the media could talk to him. He was afraid he would say something negative, and he did not want to take away from Mattingly's accomplishment. While there were no hard feelings between the two players, the tension was an example of what went on in the Bronx. Even the minute successes were covered in gray clouds.

While the Yankees offered daily aggravation, the Mets offered genuine excitement. Both teams had their share of personalities, whether they be reclusive superstars, down-to-earth country boys, or hard partying scumbags. But the Mets' internal issues, whether good or bad, were generally kept just that way: internal. What little drama they did have made them more endearing.

Exacerbating the situation was that Steinbrenner had an intense dislike for his crosstown rivals. In 1980 the Mets engaged in a highly visible marketing campaign to draw fans to Shea. One of the ads disparaged the Yankees as the "Bronx Zoo." Even worse, Jerry Della Femina, who crafted the ads, was quoted knocking the Yankees in the paper, saying the Mets' Lee Mazzilli, not Reggie Jackson, was the real star of New York. The Boss fired back hard.

"My advice to the Mets folks," said Steinbrenner, "and their Madison Avenue ad agency approach to the fans of New York is to forget sniping at the Yankees and the American League—the one league that never left New Yorkers high and dry—and start concentrating on players who can hit the ball, catch the ball and throw the ball better than other guys."[27]

The next year, Cashen made what he thought was an off-the-record comment in which he questioned the safety of the neighborhood around Yankee Stadium. The comment made the back page of the *Daily News* and The Boss was livid. He demanded an apology from Cashen. It never came.

"I started covering the Yankees in '76 and I remember Steinbrenner made such a big deal of spring training games against the Mets," recalled Moss Klein, who covered the Yankees for the *Newark Star-Ledger*. "The managers used to joke that these were the biggest games of the year—counting the regular season—because Steinbrenner was obsessed. These are the days back when the games were telecast in New York on Channel 9 or Channel 11, and Steinbrenner was always convinced that if the Mets beat the Yankees in spring training games, that was going to mean more ticket sales for the Mets and fewer ticket sales for the Yankees."[28]

The Mets cared about, well, the Mets. Steinbrenner cared about the Yankees, the Red Sox, the Mets, the Brooklyn Dodgers [apparently] . . . anyone he deemed a threat to his team's success. His paranoia over what the Mets were doing and how it might affect ticket sales for the Yankees drove many of his strange actions and manic behavior. This behavior only got worse as the Mets got better. And ironically, it only drove more people, be they players or fans, away from the Yankees and into the hands of the Mets.

As both teams headed into spring training in 1985, the Yankees, successful for so many years, were on their way down. The Mets, disgraceful for so many years, were on their way up. Nineteen-eighty-five is where they intersected, and it would be one of the greatest baseball seasons in New York's history.

# 3

# Attendance Envy

AS THE YANKEES HEADED into the 1985 season, all their drama served as a backdrop to what would happen on the field. That drama was starting to wear thin for fans. It was a base that had been used to and demanded results. Three years without being in the play-offs was simply too much. What made it worse were all the side stories that emanated from the clubhouse on a daily basis. While the Mets headed into spring training relatively drama free, the Yankees came to spring training engulfed in drama. The specter of Yogi being fired hung in the air like the sword of Damocles. From the first day of spring training the watch was on to see when, not if, Yogi might get the boot.

The atmosphere could not have been more different for the Amazin's. Youth, exuberance, and excitement permeated every element of the Mets' clubhouse in St. Petersburg. A good portion of the '84 team was returning, bringing with it all the excitement and expectations that had grown out of the team's surprising run for the National League East title. Those who were new, like Gary Carter and Howard Johnson, were gladly welcomed. Davey Johnson was confident in his club, and most importantly, his players were confident in him.

There come times in baseball when the right group of talent is brought together under just the right person to oversee that talent. For the Mets, Davey Johnson was that right person. He was young. He was confident. He understood the need to blow off steam. And he drank beer. He was perfect!

Johnson was born in the middle of World War II. His father was a decorated military man who spent part of the war in a German prison camp. As a kid, Johnson was a military brat, hopping around from base to base. After settling in Texas, Davey found he excelled at baseball and was drafted into the big leagues in 1962.

A second baseman for most of his career, Johnson was a part of the Orioles team that challenged the Mets in the 1969 World Series. In fact, Johnson made the last out of the Series in Game Five. He put together some solid years in Baltimore and then a few more in Atlanta, including setting the single-season home run mark for second baseman, before retiring. But Johnson's play on the field was not what set him apart. Rather, he was one of the most intelligent minds in the game. He had a degree in mathematics. He worked in a brokerage firm. Knew how to make smart investments. Owned businesses. He did it all.

In an age before analytics took over the game, Johnson was one of the first people in baseball to turn to computers for answers. Computers fascinated him, even at a time when they were the size of board rooms and no one else in the game cared or even thought about how to use them.

Johnson began taking courses on how to best utilize this new technology. The results were interesting. Well, at least they were to Johnson.

"Actually, what I did was to recreate the 1968 season to determine the best batting order," said Johnson during his playing days, referring to his Orioles team. "I don't know whether to tell [Orioles manager Earl] Weaver, but the sixth-worst lineup was the one we used most of the time last season."[1]

Johnson's analysis went to waste, but his baseball acumen was well known. Shortly after retiring in 1978, the Mets hired him to manage in the Minor Leagues. He led their Double-A team to a championship. Then, he did the same thing with their Triple-A team. When the Mets finished the 1983 season twenty-two games out of first place under Bamberger and Howard, it was time to try something new.

"When I went looking for a new manager for the Mets I felt we needed a change of pace," said Cashen. "We had had three fraternal managers—Joe Torre for all his macho image was kind of a paternal kind of father-type to the guys, and so was George Bamberger and so was Frank Howard. . . . I just felt we needed somebody different, preferably someone younger, who could communicate a little better with the ballplayers."[2]

Shortly after the '83 season ended, Cashen sat down with Johnson in an Atlanta airport. Cashen did not want the press catching on to what was happening. Who the hell would be looking for them in Atlanta, he figured. Cashen made clear what he wanted: a young manager who would be patient with his even younger players, help nurture them along, and keep an open line of communication. I'm your man, Johnson told him. After haggling over a contract, the two reached a deal. On October 13, 1983, Johnson was announced as the eleventh manager in team history.

The Cashen-Johnson relationship was not without its problems. Cashen would make moves without input from Johnson, driving the manager crazy to no end. After the 1983 season, Cashen decided to protect younger players on his forty-man roster over Tom Seaver in the free-agent compensation draft. No one would pluck the aging star and his contract away, rationalized Cashen. He was wrong. The White Sox grabbed him. Seaver won fifteen games the next season. Johnson was livid that he had not been consulted on the decision.

Johnson, however, gave as good as he got. Cashen wanted his new manager to keep his players in check: in other words, stop them from doing anything remotely fun off the field. Johnson was not interested in doing that. He had been a player. He knew the pressures that came with it—the strain of constantly being on the road and dealing with injuries. And he loved a good drink. So who was he to tell these adult men what they could or could not do? So long as their off-field antics did not impact their on-field play, he would take a pass on being a disciplinarian.

In his first spring training, Rusty Staub asked Johnson what his policy was on hotel bars. The previous year, they had been off limits to players. "It's open to everyone," replied Johnson, including himself and his coaches. The players started hanging out with one another, rather than spreading out throughout whatever city they were visiting. It helped create greater bonding experiences and bring them closer together.

"He wasn't a bullshitter," said Sid Fernandez. "He told you to your face. He just let you play. I think guys liked that because he really was a players' manager. We had three rules: come on time; don't embarrass the team; and be professional."[3]

Johnson was by no means, however, a hands-off manager. Having seen firsthand the kind of talent the Mets had in their farm system, he was cognizant of which players were going to perform well in the big leagues. Moreover, he had an underlying faith in veterans to perform in big moments.

"Whenever he talked to us, the players in the room were grown men, and he expected the game to be played professionally," said Roger McDowell. "He expected guys to show up every day and be accountable for that day, whether it was good, bad or indifferent."[4]

"What he did is allow players to go out and play the game," said Mookie Wilson. "He didn't overmanage. He would allow players a lot of leeway in a lot of areas until it was shown that you could not do your job. Then he would have something to say."[5]

Johnson had insisted that Dwight Gooden was ready for the big time, even if he was just nineteen. Johnson was right. He had insisted on keeping Staub on the team, even though Rusty was at the end of his career and merely a pinch hitter at that point. Johnson was right. He had insisted in bringing in Dr. Saul Miller, a psychologist from Los Angeles, to help keep players focused on their roles in the 1985 season. Johnson was right, even if the players sometimes lost focus after hours.

After shocking the baseball world with their performance in '84, there was no way Nelson Doubleday could even dream of tossing his manager. Davey Johnson was here to stay.

NO ONE WAS SAYING the same thing about Yogi Berra. Having baseball's best record in the second half of the '84 season did nothing to protect Yogi's job status. From the day Berra walked into camp in Fort Lauderdale, the countdown to when he would be fired began. Ironically, in an attempt to make the situation better, George Steinbrenner only made things worse. During a press conference on February 20, The Boss informed the press corps that

"Yogi will be the manager the entire [1985] season, win or lose . . . a bad start will not affect Yogi's status."[6]

In Mafia circles, a comment like that would be referred to as the "Kiss of Death." The press corps knew as much. They had heard it before. In 1982 Steinbrenner had guaranteed Bob Lemon would manage the team the entire season. Lemon lasted fourteen games. To the media, it was another empty promise by a man who would surely flip out the second the Yankees lost two games in a row.

For Berra, the added pressure was an unwelcomed distraction for what was an already fractured clubhouse. Internal strife had reverberated through the Yankees in '84. As Moss Klein of the *Star-Ledger* noted in March of '85, "When the Yankees dropped out of contention in the AL East by last June, team officials agreed there were seven high-salaried, unhappy players who didn't figure in future plans and whose departure would be in the best interests of all concerned."[7]

That meant nearly a third of the team was unhappy, at least publicly, being on the Yankees in '84. Six of those players, Toby Harrah, Roy Smalley, Rick Cerone, Oscar Gamble, Steve Kemp, and Tim Foli were dealt away or released during the off season. The remaining disgruntled player was Omar Moreno, who, with a salary of $600,000 a year was not going to be easy to ship off. But even if most of the unhappy players had been banished, you don't have one third of your team wishing they played for someone else by accident. That kind of mentality has to be driven by something . . . or someone, and it carries over from season to season if that someone or something does not change.

Nineteen-eighty-five was no exception. For one reason or another—though the reason was usually George Steinbrenner—a large share of the Yankees' clubhouse was unhappy. More than one player had a trade request into the front office. Omar Moreno was on the list of course. But for some time Ken Griffey had been unhappy that the Yankees hesitated from playing him against left-handed pitching. Only a few days into spring training, he complained that he would have to "fight for a job" in the outfield, even though Griffey was the only Yankee with a career batting average above .300.[8] Dave Winfield and Steinbrenner had feuded with each other essentially since the day Winfield became a Yankee. Don Mattingly, fresh off a batting title, thought Steinbrenner had short-changed him during recent contract negotiations. It began when the Yankees renewed Mattingly's contract for $325,000 a year, slightly below what Gooden of the Mets was making. Gooden had been the benchmark the Yankees were willing to make Mattingly's deal around. The problem was that Darryl Strawberry had just signed a five-year contract worth over $1 million a year and Mattingly was not happy that the Yankees had compared his deal to Gooden's and not Strawberry's. Based on arbitration at the time and the contract between the owners and the union, Mattingly had little say in the matter, which just made him even angrier.

"I learned a lot the last few days, I grew up," Mattingly told the press. "This is business, that's all. It won't affect the way I play but I won't forget it. This year, the Yankees had the hammer. Next year [when Mattingly would be eligible for salary arbitration], I'll have the hammer."[9]

Mattingly also directly jabbed Steinbrenner because The Boss eventually turned the negotiations over to the team's vice president for baseball operations, Woody Woodward.

"We were at this for a year and went face-to-face with Steinbren-ner, and it gets down to the last three days, and he turns it over to somebody else. I felt like I was cheated a little bit there. I lost some respect," Mattingly said.[10]

Never one to be outdone, Steinbrenner immediately fought back with a popular tactic. He painted his batting champion first baseman as an overpaid complainer who could not relate to working stiffs.

"I'm overlooking what Don Mattingly said this time," said Stein-brenner, who clearly wasn't overlooking the comments by how in depth he then commented on them. "I remember he said that the money wasn't the most important thing but it always comes down to money. The farmers in Indiana [Mattingly's home state] are los-ing their farms, steelworkers are out of work . . . you tell them it isn't a matter of money."

Steinbrenner then said Mattingly made the comments due to

stress over the contract, a knee injury, and the fact this his wife was due to deliver their first child any day.

"Sometimes, young people say things under emotional strain that they don't mean."

The next day, Mattingly pulled back a bit, saying he did not want to get into a public feud with the owner. The two seemingly made up, but it would not be the last time they fought publicly over contracts.

Dave Righetti was also displeased. Righetti had begun his contract as a starter for the team but had since been converted to their closer. His agent asked that relief-oriented incentives be placed into his deal to make it more fair. The same had been done for other relief pitchers. The Yankees refused.

"It's not about the money, it's the principle," said Righetti. "I just wanted someone to recognize that I had a helluva year last year."[11]

In response to both his and Righetti's situation, Mattingly referred to themselves as "the farm boys" because they had come up through the system and were not being given the same money as the free agents Steinbrenner gobbled up with huge contracts. Taken all together, while the players by and large liked each other, the Yankees' clubhouse was an unpleasant place to be in the beginning of March. And keep in mind that just a week before he sparred with his players, Steinbrenner had declared he wanted peace.

"I don't want 'em popping off at the owner, the front office, or the manager," said Steinbrenner about his players. "And by the same token, they're not going to get it from me. This is a year when we need to have everybody working together."[12]

IN ST. PETERSBURG, THINGS were different. Few, if any, players exhibited displeasure with their personal situation. The biggest controversy occurred when George Foster and Ray Knight both showed up late for camp. Privately, Johnson reamed Foster out telling him that just because he made millions a year did not mean he did not have to "earn his time."[13] But publicly, Foster's teammates made light of the situation by taping a picture of a fifty-foot limousine to his locker (Foster traveled to and from the ballpark in a limo).

"That's the limo the whole team is going to drive to the World

Series in," replied Foster lightheartedly.[14] The affair quickly blew over. It was a sharp contrast between New York's two teams. One handled their family business in private. The other aired it out in the press, usually deliberately to try to gain the upper hand.

In the meantime, outfielder Darryl Strawberry was signed to a lucrative long-term contract, one that did not have him complaining in the papers. In fact, the outfielder was nothing but smiles.

"I'm pretty much taken care of the rest of my life," said Strawberry after the deal was officially announced on his twenty-third birthday. "It's the best birthday I've ever had."[15]

The Mets' camp emanated with joy and excitement.

"It reminds me of when I was with the Orioles," Davey Johnson said, referring to his playing days with Baltimore when the team was constantly making the postseason. "The guys are anxious for the season to start already."

The change in demeanor and attitude from previous springs was evident to all.

"It's more serious, more professional," said Hernandez. "It's a winner's camp. You can tell the difference."[16]

All this newfound attention for a previously inconsequential team forced the Mets to bring in consultants to assist the players with the press.

"In recent years, the Mets were second citizens to the Yankees in New York, not only in terms of competitiveness on the field but also in terms of media attention," noted the *Bergen Record*'s Jack O'Connell. "But last season, the Mets moved closer to first place in the National League East standings, moving them closer to Broadway in terms of exposure."[17]

So the team hired Andrea Kirby, a news reporter with Channel 5, to help players, particularly the younger ones, deal with the media. Players took part in seminars where they conducted and then reviewed simulated interviews with newspaper, radio, and television reporters. While the front office was pleased with the sessions, Johnson was worried that too much exposure would hurt some of his players, particularly Gooden. Still, the sessions were rather mundane, stressing such things as eye contact and remembering names. In the end, many of the players simply laughed it off.

"I think I get along well with the press anyway. Maybe it helped some. I do dress better," said pitcher Doug Sisk, who was wearing a T-shirt, jeans, and flip flops when he made the comment.[18]

Still, there was one distraction the team was going to have to face, even if it was not yet public.

THERE WAS NO QUESTION about it, Keith Hernandez was the leader of the Mets' clubhouse. It was not sanctioned. There was no ceremony or "C" on his uniform—that would come later. He was not the oldest guy on the team, nor had he played the most games. But he was the leader.

"Keith is a natural leader, maybe more to me than anybody else," said Wally Backman that spring. "I play right next to him in the infield and he's always talking to me and telling me where to play certain hitters. He helps me all the time. He goes out of his way to help."[19]

By nature of his first-base position, Keith took charge on the field. He told players where to place themselves. He told pitchers what to throw. He positioned himself against his manager's wishes when he felt he knew better about the situation. He also called out those he felt were dogging it or not putting the team first. Hernandez had a knack for using the media as a means to an end when it came to himself or to motivate a lackadaisical teammate. Most players were grateful for his leadership. Some, not so much.

Hernandez was just a different kind of ballplayer. He loved history, touring battlefields, and painting pictures of Confederate generals like "Stonewall" Jackson and Robert E. Lee. Though his surname was of Mexican origin, his speech was more northern Californian. Before games, he sat in the clubhouse, devouring crossword puzzles while smoking a cigarette. He was intense, but not the overbearing jock type of intense. There was no bigger critic of Keith Hernandez than Keith Hernandez.[20]

John Hernandez, Keith's father, had once been a prospect in the Cardinals' farm system. It did not pan out. His eyesight worsened after being hit in the head by a pitch. But his talents passed down to his son. The younger Hernandez was a good player himself, good enough to earn a forty-second-round pick by the Cardinals in 1971. It was not exactly the top of the list, but it would do.

Hernandez emerged as a good hitter in the late '70s, before exploding in 1979. He led the National League in batting average and won the MVP. The following year he led the league in runs scored and on-base percentage. In 1982 the Cardinals won the World Series thanks to a solid season from Hernandez. But Keith and Cardinals manager Whitey Herzog were just never on the same page. Herzog despised the pregame rituals of crossword puzzles and smoking. Why wasn't this guy out on the field providing leadership for his team? Even worse, Hernandez had a tendency to jog down the first base line on balls in play that he thought were obvious outs.

"I hustle like hell when I need to," said Hernandez during his playing days. "When I'm clearly out at first on a grounder, no, I don't sprint across the bag to break the tape. If Pete Rose wants to do this, fine, but my legs and ankles are sore enough, and I have miles to go before I sleep at the end of the season."[21]

Maybe that line of reasoning made sense, but it sure did not sit right with Herzog. Moreover, there were questions about Hernandez's extracurricular activities and whether they were impacting his game. All told, it was enough for Herzog and the Cardinals to finally say they had enough.

On June 15, 1983, they shipped Hernandez to New York for Neil Allen and Rick Ownbey. Hernandez was horrified by the news. The Mets?! This was a last-place team that had been a joke of an organization for his entire playing career. Hell, the Cardinals used to laugh at the Mets and how poor the entire organization was. The "Siberia of baseball" they called it.[22] And he was not too excited about New York City either. The New York City of that era was a hellhole. People were mugged in broad daylight on the street. Times Square was just a mix of peepshows, prostitutes, and pimps.

No thank you, thought Hernandez, so upset by the deal he sat and cried in the shower. He would just as soon retire than play for the Mets. In fact, he asked his agent if he could do so. Could he afford to live on a retired ballplayer's pension? The answer was no.

Now what? He had no choice but to fly to Montreal and join up with his new team on the road. But when he got back to New York, Staub took him around the city. He showed him the best places to eat, to get a drink and since Hernandez was separated from his wife, the best places to find beautiful women. Then Cashen took him aside and walked him through the Mets' farm system. He described all the players on their way up who were going to transform the organization. Hernandez was sold. After the '83 season, he signed an extension with the club. Something special was going to happen here, and Keith wanted to be a part of it.

It did not take long for New Yorkers to fall in love with their new mustachioed player. They could see from the start they had a different kind of ballplayer here. Even in the 1980s, first base was considered a dumping ground for aging stars who could still hit but could not play anywhere else in the field. So long as they could catch the ball and make the occasional move to their left or right, they could play the position. Hernandez changed that in a way few players had revolutionized an individual position. He changed how first baseman could hold runners on, yet still manage to take away base hits in the hole between first and second. He showed that instinct could deaden the impact of sacrifice bunts, turning them into gimme outs at second—not first—and even the occasional double play. Moreover, Hernandez was constantly visiting the mound, either to provide advice, give a unique perspective that only he, as first baseman, could see about the game, or merely just to stay in motion.

Hernandez was a talent, without question. But his greatest asset could not be measured in statistics or Gold Gloves. For Hernandez had a unique ability to see what was before him on the field, sense possible outcomes, and react accordingly.

"Hernandez has built his career upon . . . an innate feel for the rhythms a game produces," wrote the *New York Times'* Craig Wolff.[23] He knew when someone would bunt, knew when a catcher was trying to trick him into thinking a different pitch was coming, knew

knew knew everything about the game. And when the game was over, you could often find Hernandez in the clubhouse or at the bar, drinking a beer and rehashing the game just played. Keith Hernandez loved baseball. He ate, drank, breathed it.

"He is the most intense player I've ever played with, to the point that sometimes he's a total mess," said Staub, who became Hernandez's closest friend on the team.[24]

Hernandez was the leader of the clubhouse heading into the season. Of that there was little question. But 1985 would bring its own set of challenges for him, which he would have to do his best to keep off the field.

IN THE TWENTY-FIRST CENTURY, drug use by Major League athletes was not a page-one scandal. Players who tested positive for marijuana use were even defended by fans, while others who suffered from addiction were praised if and when they underwent rehabilitation.

In the 1980s, however, that was not the case. While cocaine had become the drug of the celebrity scene, and crack cocaine was just about to begin decimating the inner cities, most everyday Americans still reacted with shock and indignation when an entertainer or athlete was revealed to have done drugs. In perhaps no sport was this truer than baseball, for in the early 1980s, several of the game's players—including some of the biggest stars—were using cocaine. Keith Hernandez was one of them.

The epicenter for players looking to score the drug was, randomly enough, Pittsburgh. Several Pirates players were using. A Phillies clubhouse caterer named Curtis Strong was supplying the drug to several Major Leaguers. Hernandez was one of them. Attempting to deal with a separation from his wife, he began using in 1980, and continued into '81 and '82, all while he was a member of the Cardinals.

By 1983 players were starting to get busted. Their dealers were getting picked up too. Eventually, prosecutors nailed Strong. While most dealers copped pleas, Strong insisted on going to trial. That meant players who used were going to be called as witnesses against

Strong. They were going to be publicly outed as cocaine users and were going to have to name other players they did drugs with.

It was no secret among teams that Hernandez had used, or at least that he had been suspected of using. It was one of the reasons the Cardinals had traded him. But the public did not know. In fact, no one, outside of those he bought from and did drugs with, actually knew for sure. But early in '85, Hernandez informed his parents and his brother of the extent of his usage. He also told them he was being called in front of the grand jury, where he would have to testify to what he did, and who he had done it with.

The grand jury came down with an indictment of Strong that spring. A trial was set for the fall, meaning Hernandez would most likely have to miss at least one, maybe two games during a crucial period, to go testify. That also meant he was going to be publicly outed. There was an uncertainty over how fans would react. This was the era of "Just Say No," the antidrug catchphrase made popular by first lady Nancy Reagan. While it was not as simple as that, the sentiment caught on. However the fans reacted, what was certain was the drug issue would hang over Hernandez for the rest of the season.

ON MARCH I TICKETS for '85 regular-season games went on sale at Shea Stadium. A team record twenty-eight thousand of them were sold, sixteen thousand for opening day alone. The twenty-eight thousand shattered the old record, which had been five thousand.[25] On March 9 the Mets played their first intersquad game in front of a packed house of one thousand fans. It was eight times larger than the normal turnout and by far the biggest crowd for a practice game anyone associated with the team had ever seen.

"I've seen Shea Stadium crowds smaller than this," said Mookie Wilson, who no doubt had in the early '80s.[26]

A week later, the Mets announced that opening day at home against the Cardinals was sold out. It was the first time in team history that opening day sold out during spring training. Shortly thereafter, New York City announced an agreement with the team to provide $36 million in renovations to Shea Stadium and a ten-year extension on their lease. Mayor Ed Koch called for the deal so "that the magic of the Mets will continue to be with us for a long time."[27]

Even though Knight was injured with bone chips, it seemed like every day in spring training brought good news and excitement for the Mets. On March 13 the team traveled to Sarasota for a match with the White Sox. But it was no ordinary match up. Gooden would be facing off against Seaver. Media swarmed the stadium, unable to resist the stories about the Mets' past and future facing off in the same game.

"Five television crews were there," reported the *Bergen Record.* "Among them was a unit from the CBS news program *60 Minutes,* which is planning a feature on Gooden."[28]

The match up did not disappoint, as both men went five innings and did not give up a run. The Mets eventually lost, putting them at 0-3 for the spring. But no one cared that they were winless. This was all too exciting for anyone to care.

MEANWHILE, TWO HUNDRED MILES southeast, each day brought some sort of new drama to the Yankees. The fact the team the team started off 0-5 did not help. Still, Steinbrenner at first tried to present an air of calm.

"It's early yet, and that's what spring training is for," he told the press, before issuing the almost obligatory shot across the bow. "I'm not concerned, but if we look like this after ten or twelve games, then I'll be concerned."[29]

But Steinbrenner clearly was concerned, because he followed those comments up by issuing a veiled threat toward Berra.

"We looked like this last year and Yogi kept saying 'Don't worry, we'll be okay.' Well, we weren't okay. We'd better be ready this time."[30]

It had been only three weeks since The Boss said Berra was safe for the season. The next day, the Yankees blew a 7–4, eighth-inning lead to the Rangers, losing 10–7. Still claiming to be waiting it out for another week's worth of games, The Boss spent fifteen minutes by himself in his rooftop box after the game was over. Then the guy who wasn't concerned knocked pitcher Dale Murray for giving up a 2-run home run in the ninth inning and took a shot at pitching coach Mark Connor.

"We're finding out about some guys. We found out about Dale Murray today. We're finding out who can pitch and who can't. Our pitching coach can't seem to get our pitchers to finish out," he told the press. Then he codified his remarks on Murray. "You can't be critical of pitchers on just one outing. This was the second outing for Murray."[31]

This shot at Murray came only a week and a half after the *New York Times* ran a story saying The Boss would not be taking public shots at his players.

The team rebounded to win three in a row, but it wasn't without consequences. Henderson suffered an ankle injury sliding late into third base. The next day, Winfield fouled a ball off his foot and had to walk with the aid of crutches. Worse, after falling to the ground in pain, he injured his elbow. The elbow then became infected, an injury that placed Winfield in the hospital through the rest of March. Just like that, the Yankees lost two-thirds of their starting outfield. Mattingly, Griffey, Willie Randolph, and Pagliarulo also sustained injuries that caused them to miss time.

The injuries all just happened to take place right before the Yankees and Mets faced off on March 19 in their first spring-training game. The Yankees, with most of their marquee players ailing, put together a lineup of backups and Minor Leaguers. They lost, 8–2. Oddly, it was the Mets who added more fuel to the fire, not Steinbrenner.

"It seems they never have their big guys in there so as not to lend credence to the game," said Davey Johnson.

"I'm just getting to know this so-called rivalry thing," said Carter. "I sense it more and more. The Yankees dominated for years and won championships. The Mets are here now. That's good for New York."[32]

"Nobody wants to admit it," added Mets outfielder Danny Heep, "but this game mattered to us and I'm sure it mattered to the Yankees."[33]

The Yankees, most notably Berra, were lucky they could fall back on not having their A-team that day. Few, if any, games were more important to The Boss than the preseason games the Yankees played against the Mets. Losing could result in dire consequences.

"Don't play bad against them in spring training, cause if you played bad, you are going to get traded that day cause that's just the way it is," said Mike Pagliarulo about spring games against the Mets.[34]

"I remember spring training in '83 we played them [the Mets] and guys were like, 'Wow,'" said Bobby Meacham, the Yankees' shortstop. "I said, 'Why is everybody so worried about this team?' and they said, 'Oh gosh, George takes it hard if we lose.'"[35]

In 1981 Mike Griffin, once a top prospect in the Yankees organization who had faltered when called to the Majors, made the mistake of getting hit hard by the Mets in a spring-training game that not only was Steinbrenner in attendance for, but was also broadcast live in New York. As a result, Steinbrenner banished him to the Minor Leagues, never again to see the Bronx in a Yankees uniform.[36]

"God, how we used to laugh at the Yankees," recalled Gooden in his autobiography. "Our attitude was, Fuck the Yankees. Even in spring training we wanted to beat them and we rooted for them to lose one hundred games a year."[37]

The Boss did not directly address the team's 8–2 beat down. Instead, he got defensive and went after Davey Johnson and the Mets organization after Johnson said the Mets were winning over some Yankees fans.

"Maybe he's right," said Steinbrenner. "Maybe the Mets took a *few* fans. But over the last 10 years, we've taken *thousands* of fans from them. And when the season starts, the fans won't be fooled. The proof is in the pudding. We're in the toughest division in baseball, an exciting division. The Mets are in the National League East, a weak division."[38]

A week later, the two teams faced off again. A strong performance by outfielder Billy Sample helped the Yankees prevail 6–5. Righetti, who had walked a fine line in the ninth inning before getting the save, knew what blowing the game might have meant.

"Losing to the Mets is supposed to be a sin around here," he told reporters afterward.[39]

Instead of the game itself though, the focus afterward, at least for Steinbrenner, was on Johnson's comments from a week earlier.

"I love Davey, but when he doesn't play [George] Foster and [Keith] Hernandez, he's just hedging his bets in case he loses, because we didn't have [Dave] Winfield, [Don] Mattingly, and [Rickey] Henderson in the lineup," said The Boss.[40]

It was telling. Steinbrenner would not have gone after his crosstown rivals if he didn't feel they were a legitimate threat to the Yankees' dominance of the back-page headlines. If Steinbrenner loved winning, he loved back-page headlines almost as much, if not more. The idea of losing those back pages to the Mets, a reality that was emerging daily, certainly incensed him. He would have none of it.

The following day, Mattingly returned after a knee injury had sidelined him briefly. But even that bit of good news was not without controversy. After Mattingly played in two different games in one day and experienced some soreness in the surgically repaired knee, Steinbrenner publicly chastised Berra and his staff.

"I'm a little upset by the way Mattingly was handled by the trainer and the staff and the front office," he said. "I'm a little concerned, let's put it that way. You've got to hold him back easy coming off a knee injury. They made a mistake letting him play two games in one day. That was crazy."[41]

A few days later, the Yankees were getting beat badly at home. Steinbrenner left the game early, apparently unable to stomach the sight of his team any longer. When leaving the stadium, a group of children looking for autographs recognized him and asked him why he was leaving so early.

"I'm going to get my money back after watching this one," he told him. "And that's what you should be doing."[42]

As spring wound down, the two teams began assembling their final rosters. Luckily for the Mets, they were drowning in an abundance of pitching talent. Highly rated prospects like Sid Fernandez and Calvin Schiraldi were shipped back to Triple-A. Fernandez had been the predicted number-four starter, but struggled that spring. Schiraldi had pitched exceptionally well, but there simply was not enough room on the roster. The Mets began the year with Gooden, Ron Darling, Ed Lynch, and Bruce Beneryi in the starting rotation. The schedule allowed them to go without a fifth starter until late April.

The bullpen was anchored by veteran left-hander Jesse Orosco, while rookie sinker baller Roger McDowell would complement him from the right side. Doug Sisk, Tom Gorman, and Bill Latham rounded out the rest of the bullpen. The lineup was the strongest the team had ever assembled, with Carter catching, Hernandez at first, Backman at second, Rafael Santana at short, Howard Johnson at third for the injured Knight, Foster in left field, Wilson in center field and Strawberry in right field. That starting eight boasted two MVP awards, four world championships, and seventeen All-Star appearances. The writers began making their preseason predictions, and most expected the Mets to be contenders again. They were not so bold as to say they would take first. That honor, by and large, went to the defending National League East champions, the Cubs. But many saw the Mets finishing a close second.

The writers were not thinking the same for the Yankees. Their lineup was possibly the strongest in the Majors, featuring two future Hall of Famers in Henderson and Winfield, and two borderline Hall of Famers in Mattingly and Don Baylor. The rest of the group was solid as well, with Pagliarulo, Meacham, Randolph, Butch Wynegar, and Griffey rounding out the lineup. The problem, as most saw it, was the pitching. Ron Guidry was coming off the worst season of his career, and some people thought he was finished. Phil Niekro was back after leading the team with sixteen wins in 1984, but he had struggled in the second half of the season and entered '85 at the ancient age, for baseball anyway, of forty-six. Moreover, Niekro was sixteen wins short of three hundred career victories, and as the season wore on, his pursuit of that milestone was sure to become a distraction. After Guidry and Niekro, there were several question marks. Ed Whitson was their biggest off-season pitching acquisition, but he was coming off only a marginally good season for the National League West champion Padres. There were already questions about how small-town, country boy Whitson would handle the pressure of New York. Joe Cowley had talent, but he had serious issues finding the strike zone. Plus, he was a nutcase. Cowley had a habit of getting under his teammates' skin with his eccentric behavior to a point where some would just directly tell him to shut up and speak only when spoken to. Such talk went nowhere. They might as well have been explaining quantum physics to a puppy.

The number-five starter was unknown after John Montefusco went down with an injury. Rich Bordi, Tim Foli, and Murray, yes the same Dale Murray that Steinbrenner had singled out during the spring, would pitch in middle relief. Righetti returned as the team's closer, but whether or not he should be put back in the rotation was a debate that would pop up throughout the year. Despite trading for the greatest lead-off hitter in baseball history, the Yankees faced serious obstacles.

"The average annual salary on the Yankees last season was $458,544, highest in the major leagues," noted Klein. "And unless a lot of developments go the Yankees' way, the season is shaping up as another expensively futile stretch in the AL East, a division which allows little room for error." Klein predicted they would finish fourth. "As far as all the talk about a Subway Series: Unless there's a special subway going from Wrigley Field to Tiger Stadium, forget it."[43]

As opening day approached, injuries continued to cripple the team. Rickey Henderson would start the season on the disabled list. His sprained ankle had continued to swell after sustaining the injury, and he would not be ready until at least the second week of the season. Winfield, while active, was still hobbled by the injured elbow. Three days before the season began, Randolph was diagnosed with a stress fracture in his foot. Guidry would miss his opening day start due to a stiff neck. Steinbrenner, worried about a now sagging offense, made inquiries about trading for Cardinals shortstop Ozzie Smith and Seattle Mariners designated hitter Ken Phelps. Nothing materialized, leaving Steinbrenner to brood over the state of his team.

"I don't like what I'm seeing," said The Boss less than a week before opening day. "I'm not going to use the injuries as excuses. The season is dangerously close and we're not finishing strong. We're looking the way we did at the end of spring training last year, and I don't want a repeat of last season."[44]

Not only that, but the success of the Mets brought even more pressure to bear on his manager and players.

"Don't forget, his [Steinbrenner's] impatience won't be fueled only by the AL East rivals," noted the *Star-Ledger*. "These days, he's feverishly studying the record and attendance figures of the Mets."

The team left Florida and flew up to Boston to start the season with three games against their archrival Red Sox at Fenway Park. It would end up being one of the worst season-opening series in team history.

THE METS COULD NOT have left Florida in better shape. With the exception of Knight, they had stayed relatively healthy throughout the spring. They were confident and cocky and believed they had the upper hand this year.

"First of all, I think it's going to be a two-team race between the Cubs and us," said Backman, before making clear who he thought would emerge on top. "Some of their players had their greatest seasons last year. I don't think they can do it again. I just don't think the Cubs can beat us."[45]

That kind of confidence would become a staple of Backman's. The scrappy second baseman, born and raised in a small Oregon town whose only two stores were a grocery and a gas station, would embody the Mets can-do spirit that year. Backman did not hit for power, but he got dirty, took the extra base, leapt into bases head first, and sprawled over the field to make a play. Even though he only had a few full seasons under his belt, he would emerge as one of many players who spoke for the team. And when Backman spoke, it was often blunt and cocky. New Yorkers would eat it up.

The serenity of the clubhouse was marred only by a minor spat in which Davey Johnson questioned the communication abilities of the front office. The incident was quickly resolved. Whereas the Yankees' public disputes only seemed to further heighten the tension of the clubhouse, or at least the public perception of tension, the Mets doing so seemed to close any schisms that might exist. The Yankees stated the problem, generally let it linger, and then failed to fix it, or by trying to fix it, only made it worse. The Mets stated the problem, solved it, and that was that.

How loose were the Mets? Loose enough to pull off one of the greatest pranks in sports history just before leaving for New York to start the season. On April 1 the latest edition of *Sports Illustrated* appeared on newsstands. In it was a story titled "The Curious Case of Sidd Finch," authored by George Plimpton, the well-known writer and sports enthusiast. Plimpton detailed the story of Sidd Finch, a Mets pitching prospect who went to Harvard, played the French horn, was raised by Buddhist monks, and pitched with one bare foot and the other foot in a boot. Most incredibly, Finch was recorded as throwing a 168-mile-an-hour fastball (something that is physically impossible for a human to do).

According to the story, Finch was the talk of Mets camp, a phenom they were keeping in secret to then spring on the rest of the league. Players could not believe their eyes. Ronn Reynolds, the team's backup catcher, was told he would be Finch's special catcher. The story included photos of Reynolds, clearly in pain, after catching a few pitches from Finch. Other players, like Len Dykstra and John Christensen, were seen gazing under a tarp—the Mets would not allow outsiders to view their prized prospect—and gawking in amazement. Mel Stottlemyre and Jay Horowitz, the team public-relations director, were quoted, and there were pictures of Finch doing quirky things, like riding a camel in front of the pyramids of Egypt.

The whole thing, however, was a fabrication—an elaborate April fool's joke concocted by Plimpton and an editor at the magazine. In fact, the first letters of each of the words included in the subtitle of the story spelled out, "Happy April Fool's Day—ah fib." Finch was really Joe Berton, an art teacher from Illinois who was friends with a *Sports Illustrated* photographer and who just happened to fit the description of Finch as written by Plimpton. Several Mets players and key members of the organization were in on the joke.

Many others, however, took the initial story seriously. Managers complained about how they could possibly keep their players safe batting against someone throwing so fast. Fans were giddy with excitement, wanting to know when Finch would appear in a game so they could buy tickets. News organizations wanted to do follow-up interviews with the mysterious Finch. When the story was revealed as a hoax, many were angry.

The Mets, however, did not care. The whole thing was emblematic of the kind of team they were developing into: carefree, fun-loving pranksters who could laugh at the joke because they were both winning and winning over fans. And if people did not get the joke, well, that was their problem. They could go root for the joyless, corporate Yankees.

While both teams were flying up the East Coast to start the season, metaphorically they seemed to be heading in opposite directions. One team nearly injury and controversy free and looking forward to capturing the heart of the city. Another team injury riddled, bloated with controversy, and run by an owner desperately clinging to the city's back pages.

Despite the differences, curiously enough the *Star-Ledger* ran a piece the weekend before opening day discussing a possible subway series. It may have seemed off the mark at the time, but when October came rolling around, it would come ever so close to reality.

**4**

# Fun to Be a Met

MONDAY, APRIL 8, 1985, was a bright, sun-filled day in New England. That sunshine, however, betrayed a cold, early spring afternoon in Boston. Filing into Fenway Park were 34,282 fans ready to see their beloved Red Sox. The Sox had fallen on hard times since a resurgence in the 1970s. Their offense was outstanding, featuring guys like Wade Boggs, Jim Rice, Dwight Evans, and Bill Buckner. Like the Yankees, their problem was a lack of pitching. Few expected the Sox to contend in '85, but on opening day, hope springs eternal. There were few better ways to make a statement to the rest of the league than by beating up on the Yankees.

In the cramped visitor's clubhouse of seventy-three-year-old Fenway Park, Phil Niekro suited up for his opening-day start. At forty-six, Niekro was not nearly as old as the place he was about to pitch in, but some teammates may have joked he just might well have been. Already grey haired, Niekro took plenty of ribbing over his age. It was all in good fun though, because there were few better teammates in baseball than Niekro.

"He was one the funniest human beings probably to ever put on a uniform," said Rich Bordi, a relief pitcher on the Yankees in 1985. "We were in Boston and he stuck a rubber mouse in Stick's [third-base coach Gene Michael] shoe. Stick had a phobia about that kind of stuff. And he had a ritual of when he took his shoes, he would tap his shoe to make sure nothing was in it. So Stick tapped his shoe before he put it on, and this rubber mouse comes out and he goes flying over his chair, lying on his back."[1]

Phil grew up in the small town of Lansing, Ohio, just a few miles west of Wheeling, West Virginia. His father played ball for a coal-mining team, a common practice in an area where coal mining was the basic source of employment and income. By the time organized Little League came around to that section of Ohio, Niekro was too old to play. Instead he learned the game from his father and from pickup games he played with his friends. When high school came around, Phil made the varsity team as a freshman.

After high school, Niekro saw an ad in the Wheeling paper for baseball tryouts.

"Milwaukee scouts were gonna have a tryout camp," said Niekro, referring to the Braves. "Anybody could walk on, so I went there with about 150 other guys from the area."[2]

By the time he got back from the tryout, a Braves scout had already reached out to his father saying they were interested. The Braves offered him a contract, which, surrounded by his entire family in the Niekro's kitchen, he accepted. There was a $500 signing bonus.

"He [his father] said let's take it, 'cause I don't know if my dad made that much money in a month," said Niekro.[3]

The following spring, Phil boarded a train for Waycross, Georgia, and his professional baseball career was under way.

Niekro spent twenty seasons with the Braves, becoming one of the most popular players in team history and amassing statistics that placed him among the all-time franchise leaders in just about every single pitching category. Only Warren Spahn threw more innings, only Spahn and Kid Nichols won more games, and only John Smoltz struck out more batters for the Braves than Niekro. Phil was also first in games pitched, fifth in complete games, and third in shutouts. Of course, he also lost more games for the Braves than any other pitcher, but that was more a combination of Niekro's having pitched late in so many games and playing for several mediocre teams over the years.

In all that time with the Braves, Niekro made the postseason only twice, and never once did his team advance to the World Series. Somewhat unexpectedly, Atlanta decided not to retain Niekro after the '83 season.

"Ted Turner called me into his office," said Niekro. "John Mullen was there, who was the general manager of the Braves at the time. He [said] we are gonna go with the youth movement, and we are gonna release you from the Braves. They are both sitting there saying we know you can still win. We know you can win in the big leagues, but we are gonna go with youth."[4]

With that, for the first time in his career, Niekro had to seek the employment of another franchise.

Two years removed from a season in which he went 17-4, he was still clearly capable of pitching, and there was no shortage of suitors for his services. The Cardinals, A's, and Pirates all inquired about him. Each offer was tempting in its own way. But in early January of '84, his agent called him and said that Steinbrenner was interested in him.

"No way," thought Niekro, as he explained in a book he wrote detailing the '85 season. "There's just no way I'm gonna become just another puppet on Steinbrenner's purse strings. No way, not after all the shit I've heard about the Yankees, all the newspaper stories, and the firing of managers, the firing of bat boys, the firing of ball girls, ushers, janitors, and the firing of this and the firing of that."[5]

In the end, Steinbrenner's offer was just too good to refuse. Phil signed a two-year deal with the Yankees. Niekro immediately excelled in New York, going 11-4 with a 1.84 ERA in the first half of the '84 season. He faltered in the second half though, going 5-4 and seeing his ERA rise to 3.09. Still, Niekro ended up leading the team in wins. He entered the '85 season sixteen wins short of three hundred career victories, something only sixteen pitchers had done to that time and an accomplishment that would all but guarantee him a spot in the Hall of Fame. Still, Niekro's chase for three hundred was not what he was about. He would either get it or he wouldn't. Niekro wanted a World Series ring. That was what he was all about. He had few, if any, seasons left after this one. He knew his time to reach the World Series was short. The 1985 Yankees could be his last chance.

Niekro's success could be attributed to one pitch: the knuckleball. Generally held with the knuckles or the tips of two fingers (usually, but not always, the index and middle fingers) pressed against the ball, when thrown toward home plate, the result is a lack of rotation of the ball. As it moves toward home plate, generally revolving only a few times, physics takes over. The air ends up doing crazy things to the ball. It can move left, right, down, or all three. Unlike most pitches, no one can determine with certainty where a knuckleball will end up. Pitchers who throw it well can eat up innings because there is little wear and tear on the arm, as most knuckleballs are thrown below eighty miles per hour. A well-thrown knuckler is difficult to hit. At the same time, because the ball changes direction unpredictably, knuckleball pitchers rack up tons of walks, and any knuckler that spins too much becomes nothing more than a batting practice fastball.

Few pitchers threw it, because it was difficult to master. But no one in baseball history had thrown it with more success than Niekro, who had learned the pitch from his father.

"One day he threw me a knuckleball. I just opened my eyes and asked him what it was and he showed me how to hold it. And after that it was just about playing knuckleball in the backyard," said Niekro.[6]

Eventually, he earned the nickname "Knucksie." The book Niekro was writing would end up being called *Knuckleballs*.

So out went forty-six-year-old knuckleball throwing Niekro to get the Yankees' 1985 season off on the right foot. Oddly enough, of his 284 career wins to that point, not one had happened on opening day. And none ever would.

"The first guy up was Wade Boggs," recalled Niekro. "I had no balls and two strikes on him, and I threw him a knuckleball. Must have been a foot outside, and he threw his bat at it and hit a fly ball to left. I said there's my first out. . . . I turn around and saw Ken Griffey's number playing it off the big wall out there. And I said oh boy, this is gonna be tough."[7]

The game was a disaster. Staked to a 2–0 lead after the top of the second, Niekro gave up 5 runs in the next three innings. He later referred to his performance as "horseshit."[8] A 3-run home run by Rice in the bottom of the sixth opened the Sox' lead to 9–2, the eventual final score. As if the loss was not bad enough, the Yankees went through the indignity of seeing several of their players knocked to the ground by Red Sox starting pitcher Dennis "Oil Can" Boyd. It was hardly the kind of performance that could have pleased their owner.

TUESDAY, APRIL 9, WAS a bitterly cold, dreary day in New York City. The weather—the temperature reaching only the low forties—was more suited for an NFL playoff game. But the cold could not stop 46,781 fans, the Mets' first ever sellout opening day crowd, from assembling at Shea Stadium.

The Mets home park was ugly, dull, and minus any frills. Shea was a remnant of the cookie-cutter age when stadiums were designed for multiuse purposes. They were all circular in shape, with steep upper decks whose seats seemed miles from the action. The outfield dimensions were almost always the same. However far it was down the right field line, that is how far it was down the left-field line. However far it was to right-center, that is how far it was to left-center. Perhaps the only thing that separated it from the cookie cutters in Philadelphia, Pittsburgh, St. Louis, or Houston was that Shea had natural grass, not AstroTurf, and the stands ended just after the right- and left-field foul poles. In most other multipurpose stadiums, the stands were continuous around the entire ballpark.

Shea also had a few other distinguishing characteristics. Whenever the home team hit a home run, a large red apple with the Mets' insignia would pop up from behind the center-field wall. The stands were an interesting mix of orange, green, and bluish seats. Out behind the right-center-field wall was one of the largest digital scoreboards in baseball. The overwhelming number of presumed chop shops in the area, as opposed to bars, made tailgating before a game almost a necessity. To top it off, Shea stood not too far from LaGuardia Airport, so it was not uncommon for players and fans to be serenaded by the sounds of landing or departing 747s during the course of a game.

Still, for Mets fans, Shea was home. And it had not seen excitement like this in a long time. Team announcer Tim McCarver described a World Series–like feel to the park before the first pitch was even thrown. Vice President George H. W. Bush, a former college ballplayer himself, was on hand to throw out the first pitch, something that surely most have riled Steinbrenner. Mayor Ed Koch was on hand as well, though he was known for sneaking out of games as early as possible.

Fans had their "K" posters at the ready and for good reason. Taking the mound for the Mets on this day was the reigning National League Rookie of the Year, Dwight Gooden. As with so much else during that spring, the opening-day starters for the Mets and Yankees could not have been more different. Niekro was a forty-six-year-old white guy from rural Ohio who'd been in the Majors for twenty-one seasons and whose success was based on throwing the slowest pitch in baseball with a short, easy pitching motion. Gooden was a twenty-year-old black guy from urban Tampa who had just thirty-one starts to his credit and who succeeded by throwing a blazing fastball with a full flowing motion. Gooden had not even been born when Niekro made his Major League debut.

Hailing from Tampa, Florida, Gooden's father had played semipro ball. Nothing too serious, but enough to instill a lifelong love of the game. He passed it on to his son at an early age. Living in Tampa, the weather was warm enough to play ball year round. And young Gooden was just a few miles away from the Detroit Tigers training facility in Lakeland.

"There, we got to watch the great Al Kaline hit," wrote Gooden in his autobiography. "He crushed a home run the very first time I saw a Tigers game, and ever since then, I was an Al Kaline fan. I was only six, but I made up my mind that I wanted to be a Major Leaguer."[9]

Under the tutelage of his father, Gooden quickly moved through the ranks in Little League, playing with kids two years older than him. His team went to the Little League World Series in 1979 but lost. Even at an early age, he could throw the ball a lot harder than most kids. But pitching was not his interest. He loved hitting. He loved the idea of being involved in every inning of a game in the field and at the plate, not on the mound.

Gooden, however, was too good not to pitch. As he tells it, one day on the mound he had a hitter down two strikes. Someone in the crowd yelled, "Go get him Dwight. Operate on him, Doc."[10]

The nickname stuck. Scouts started showing up to see "Doc" Gooden blow the ball past his high-school opponents.

Though he had signed a letter of intent with the University of Miami, the Mets drafted Gooden fifth overall in the 1982 draft. It was hard to believe later that four players went ahead of Gooden. When the Mets attempted to sign him, his father held out for more money. Doc was horrified. He would have agreed to just about anything to pitch in the big leagues. But his dad was right in the end. The Mets knew what they had and agreed to give Gooden more money. Suddenly, the eighteen-year-old was on his way to some town in northeastern Tennessee he had never heard of. His professional career was about to begin.

How hard did Gooden throw? In his first start in professional baseball, with the Mets' Minor League Kingsport, Tennessee, affiliate, Gooden broke the thumb of his battery mate in the second inning. The two mixed up signs: catcher Marlin McPhail thinking a curve was coming, Gooden thinking McPhail had called for a fastball. When the crossed up McPhail felt the fastball hit the thumb of his unprotected hand, he "knew it was broken right away."[11]

At six feet two and 190 pounds, Gooden was not a physically overpowering presence. Nor did he tend to stare hitters down or brush them off the plate. Instead, he simply overpowered them with a fastball that exploded out of his hand and a curve ball that dropped out of sight. Gooden utilized a high leg kick to generate power and hide the ball from hitters. The big, smooth motion was somewhat deliberate, lulling hitters into a false sense of security before the ball came charging at them at speeds near one hundred miles an hour.

"His ability to tune it up a notch with a man on third base and one out or less was amazing," said Mel Stottlemyre. "It was something you usually don't see in a nineteen-year-old pitcher. But he had the uncanny ability to reach in his back pocket when he got in trouble and tune it up a little bit."[12]

Gooden's arm was not the only thing that impressed people

though. Even as a nineteen-year-old rookie he had an extraordinary baseball intellect, knowing exactly what to do with hitters in any given situation.

"We had him throwing the ball on the side, and at 17 he had outstanding command," said Davey Johnson. "One day I asked him how he gripped his fastball and he told me, across the seams when he wanted to fire it, with the seams when he wanted movement. For a kid that age to know that is a rarity."[13]

In the Minors, Gooden was a highly touted prospect who seemed destined for great things. But Frank Cashen did not want to rush him to the big leagues, despite Davey Johnson's pleas. In fact, Johnson had wanted to use Gooden at Triple-A Tidewater in 1983, when the organization thought it was too soon for the eighteen-year-old to be pitching at that level. Johnson, then the Tidewater manager, knew what he had and knew that he wanted him on his team. Cashen hesitated. He had been burned before. In 1981 he had allowed twenty-two-year-old top pitching prospect Tim Leary to make his debut on a cold April day at Wrigley Field in Chicago. Leary lasted two innings before developing a muscle strain in his throwing elbow. He missed the rest of the year and did not pitch again until 1983. Cashen was not someone to be fooled twice. But Johnson insisted that Gooden pitch one game for him in the playoffs. Cashen relented. When Tidewater advanced, he asked for one more Gooden start. Cashen relented.[14] Then, in spring training of '84, Johnson asked for Gooden to come up north with the team. Cashen again relented.

There would be no Tim Leary repeat. Doc took baseball by storm. Gooden went 17-9 and established a rookie record by striking out 276, which also led the National League. He ran away with the National League Rookie of the Year award and finished second in Cy Young voting. In that year's All-Star Game, Gooden struck out Lance Parrish, Chet Lemon, and Alvin Davis in his first inning of work.

Gooden's first year led some to compare him with Hall of Famer Bob Feller. Not bad for a twenty-year-old. He inked an endorsement deal for Diet Pepsi that netted him $150,000.[15] Not bad for someone who could not legally drink alcohol yet. On Forty-Second Street near Ninth Avenue in the city, there was a ninety-five-foot mural of Gooden—on the mound at Shea Stadium just a millisecond away from delivering what was surely a devastating fastball—plastered on the side of a building. Not bad for a kid who still exhibited a boyish shyness whenever he talked to the press.

Now, here was Gooden starting the most exciting opening day at Shea in over a decade. At twenty years, four months, and twenty-four days, he was the youngest opening-day starting pitcher in modern baseball history. No one knew or foresaw the troubles that were to come in the years ahead. The drugs, the lying, the injuries, the suspensions, none of that existed on this chilly April day. All there was was the most exciting pitcher baseball had seen in decades, taking the mound in front of thousands of cheering fans, with nothing but all the world could possibly offer standing in front of him.

PERHAPS NO ONE WAS more excited about the first game of the year than Gary Carter. Driven from Canada by an owner who failed to appreciate him, Carter was surrounded by an organization and fans who could not wait to see him in a Mets uniform.

"The Mets are just as good as last year, and now they have Gary Carter," said fan John Weiss before the game.

"We expect a big year out of our Metsies," said fan Mike Higgins. "Some people think the Cubs will repeat, but we have Carter. The guy hit 25 home runs [actually 27], hit .295 [actually .294], and had 106 runs batted in. All we gave up is a guy named Hubie."[16]

As Carter approached the plate for his first at bat with his team—with debris strewn across the field from the cold wind blowing through the park—fans stood and cheered for their new catcher.

It was a great moment, emblematic of the new hope emanating out of Shea. Then that hope was almost instantly shattered. In the first inning, with the Mets already leading 1–0 on a Keith Hernandez RBI single, Cardinals starting pitcher Joaquin Andujar drilled Carter in the left elbow with a fastball. It would have hurt on any day, but it was especially painful given the bitter coldness of the early April afternoon. Carter flung his bat toward the Mets' dugout, then walked briskly toward first, appearing as if he was trying to shake off the pain by staying in constant motion. But once he got to first, Gary was barely able to endure the numbness shooting through him, and he doubled over, clutching his arm. Obviously in pain, he shook off the team trainer. Carter remained in the game and got an ovation just for that alone. The season was mere minutes old, but it was clear fans were in love with this team.

The Mets eventually jumped out to a 5–2 lead after five innings. Gooden, blowing into his hand before nearly every pitch, was clearly uncomfortable in the early spring cold. Though he allowed eight base runners over six innings, Doc left the game in the seventh with a lead. But the Cardinals battled back to make it a 5–4 game, and they had the bases loaded with two outs in the top of the ninth. On the mound for New York stood Doug Sisk.

BY ALL ACCOUNTS, SISK was and is a funny, likeable guy. That sense of humor was on fierce display when it came to perhaps Sisk's most important contribution to the Mets. He was a founding member of the Scum Bunch. The infamous group, which formed during spring training in '85, was mostly made up of relief pitchers. After all, you have a lot of time out there just sitting and staring. Decades later, baseball would change. Relief pitchers could enter a game at any time. But in 1985 relievers were still largely relegated to the later innings. It was rare for more than two or three pitchers to enter a game, unless it went into extra innings or if no one could get anyone out.

So, what do you do when you have hours to kill and you are a Major League ballplayer? You play cards—for Roger McDowell and Jesse Orosco the game was often spades—you play pranks, you break balls, and, when the game is over, win or lose, you drink. And you drink a lot. The drinking leads to more pranks and more breaking balls. On the plane. On the bus. In the topless bar. Wherever their travels took them, the Scum Bunch partied and attacked their less-willing teammates.

It was Darwinism in action. The weak were chewed up and spit out. The more irritated you were by their antics, or the more meek your response, the more likely you were to be a victim. They were merciless.

"One thing I remember, and this was a normal occurrence, [was when] we'd go on the road, and [if] we were on the bus between the ballpark and the airport, or once we landed and gotten on the bus to go to the hotel, everything was fair game," said Joe Sambito, a relief pitcher who spent his only time with the Mets in 1985. "I mean, insults started flying like you wouldn't believe. *Everything* was fair game. Nothing was sacred from your mother to your sister to your wife to your grandma."[17]

When flights taxied in at three in the morning, they were still up drinking. When the bus pulled into the hotel just before sunrise, they, seemingly by instinct, found the nearest strip joint and kept partying.

Sisk, along with Orosco, McDowell, and Tom Gorman, was one of the ring leaders of the group. The Scum Bunch went on to attain a mythic status among Mets fans and players over the years. Whereas most teams would try to bury a history of drinking and ogling strippers, over the decades the organization seemingly embraced the stories. No documentary about the 1986 championship team is complete without mention of their afterhours activities.

Most of the Scum Bunch were held in high esteem by fans. Sisk, however, was not. And by most accounts, it had a lot to do with July 28, 1984. That day, Sisk entered the eighth inning of a 3–3 game against the Cubs at Shea. The Mets, hot off a seven-game winning streak, were four and a half games ahead of Chicago for first place. They had taken the first game of a four-game series and were now trying to keep the score tied so they could take the second with late-game heroics. But Sisk walked the first batter, gave up two consecutive singles, and then committed an error on a bunt. He was pulled after the error, but the Cubs went on to score 8 runs in the inning. The Cubs won that game, as well as the two final games of the series. A week later, the Mets were swept in Chicago, and their improbable 1984 season was all but over.

No one on the team bore the brunt of the fans anger over dropping the division to the Cubs more than Sisk.

"The fact that the Mets still led the N.L. East by 3 1/2 games that day is forgotten by the fans," wrote the *Star-Ledger*'s Dan Castellano.

"The fact that a lot of other players went on to blow bigger games than Sisk did is also forgotten. The fact that, to that point, Sisk was having as good a year as any reliever in the league with 14 saves and an ERA of 0.92 also seems to mean nothing."[18]

That same day against Chicago was also the day Sisk began to have soreness in his throwing shoulder. A week later, he went on the disabled list, but in the limited appearances he did make for the remainder of 1984, he was booed by the home crowd, to a point where he preferred pitching on the road.

"I love the fans. Love the ballpark. But they want to see their club win. I had people follow me home. I would go into a bar and have altercations. I had my wife stop coming to games at home. Fans would call the hotel room. They would send vile messages in the mail. Davey really stood up for me," recalled Sisk.[19]

The start of 1985 seemed to offer no reprieve. While nearly every player was cheered loudly during introductions before the start of opening day, Sisk was booed. Now, here he stood, with everything on the line in the most anticipated Mets game in years.

With the based loaded, Sisk did not want to leave something over the plate for Jack Clark, the dangerous Cardinals first baseman. Clark had already taken Gooden deep earlier in the game and could turn on a fastball like few other hitters in baseball. So Sisk pitched him carefully. Too carefully. He walked Clark, forcing in the tying run. What looked like a great start to the '85 season had now seemingly dissipated with one walk. Orosco replaced Sisk, who left the mound to a chorus of boos. Unfortunately for Doug, this would be the first of many times Mets fans would boo him off the field in 1985.

Orosco got out of the inning without further damage. But the Mets failed to score in the bottom of the ninth, sending the game into extra innings. The score remained tied into the bottom of the tenth, with Neil Allen now pitching for St. Louis. Allen had once been a popular relief pitcher coming out of the bullpen for the Mets. That ended when he was swapped for Hernandez. While Allen would not last through the '85 season in St. Louis, and time would reveal how lopsided the deal was, at the time the Cardinals thought they had made out well. They had rid themselves of someone that Herzog had perceived as a clubhouse cancer and in return, Allen had pitched solidly for them as both a starter and reliever. Now, starting the bottom of the tenth inning of opening day, Allen struck out the man he had been traded for.

That brought Carter to the plate with one out. The Kid had caught the entire game with an elbow that still throbbed from his first-inning beaning. His debut so far had not gone as hoped for. He had been hit twice by pitches, grounded out with two runners on, allowed a run on a passed ball, and even allowed Andujar to steal a base. If there was a moment from Carter to step up, this was it.

The sun had long since disappeared behind an overcast sky when Allen wound up and delivered an 0-1 curveball low and away. Carter, though appearing momentarily fooled, adjusted to the sudden drop, reached out, and quickly drilled the ball toward left field. It was not clear if it had enough to get out of the park. Perhaps on a warmer day there would have been no doubt. Cardinals left fielder Lonnie Smith drifted back tentatively, mindful of the quickly approaching left-field fence. Finally, he reached the wall, right where the clear Plexiglas was that allowed relief pitchers to watch the game. Smith leapt and for a split second, it looked like he might come away with the ball. But he misjudged how far he was from the wall, leaping too close and crashing into it before he could hit full stride. The ball slammed into the Cardinals' bullpen, landing just before the pitching rubber of the first warm-up mound. As the Shea faithful let out a roar of mass elation, Carter rounded first base and triumphantly raised his right arm. It was the first opening day walk-off hit for the Mets in ten years and the most exciting moment the team had seen in some time.

"There was a lot of magnetism in the stands," said Carter after the game. "In one day here, I've already had a curtain call. This script couldn't have been written any better than it turned out, could it?"[20]

The excitement did not end with Carter's heroics. After a day off, the two teams met again. This time, comedian and actor Rodney Dangerfield threw out the first pitch. He did not exactly have the gravitas of a vice president, but it seemed oddly fitting for a team that, in twenty-three years of existence, had seldom gotten any respect.

The game turned into a pitcher's duel, with Ron Darling and John Tudor each giving up only a run. The bullpens eventually took over for both teams as the game went into extra innings. In the bottom of the eleventh, singles by Hernandez and Carter along with an intentional walk to Foster set up the bases loaded with no outs for Danny Heep. A pinch hitter extraordinaire, Heep drew a walk from Allen, giving the Mets a 2–1 win.

It was the first time in team history they had played two consecutive extra-inning games to open the season. Carter had again played a heroic role, while Allen had again played the goat. It was just the first series of the year, but everything was falling in place for the Mets.

The Gary Carter Show continued the next night when the Reds came to Shea. In the fourth inning of a scoreless game, Carter took Cincinnati ace Mario Soto deep into the left-field bleachers for a solo home run. It was the only run of the game, as Bruce Berenyi and Sisk combined for a three-hit shutout.

"Gary Carter's act is getting a little old," wrote the *Star-Ledger*'s Rich Chere, tongue-in-cheek. "For that matter, the Mets are becoming just too predictable."[21]

In his first three games as a Met, Carter hit 2 game-winning home runs and delivered a key single in extra innings to help win a game. It had not taken long for fans to adore their new catcher. Unlike Montreal, his teammates embraced him too.

"[Carter's] enthusiasm and raw energy seemed to make things happen from right out of nowhere and infected the entire team with a spirit," said Strawberry. "It was *fun* to be on the Mets now."[22]

The next day featured yet another pitcher's duel, this time between the Mets' Ed Lynch and the Reds' Tom Browning. Both pitchers each gave up 1 run over seven innings before yielding to the bullpen. McDowell held the Reds scoreless for two innings before Strawberry led off the bottom of the ninth against John Franco.

Strawberry was nursing a sore right wrist after diving for a ball in the second game against the Cardinals. The fact that he was in the lineup at all was a great sign—not regarding his health, but regarding his maturity. For, even though he was only twenty-three years old and had been in the league just two years, Strawberry was already showing signs of the onerous, standoffish teammate reputation he later cemented. At the same time, he was also showing signs of becoming one of the game's elite all-around players.

DARRYL STRAWBERRY: THE NAME just jumped out at you. It had marquee written all over it. And behind that name was one of the greatest talents people had seen in a long time. He was branded as the "Black Ted Williams." Tall and lanky with a swing so graceful it seemed like something out of a painting they keep behind velvet ropes in an art museum. The talent was all there. It was just a matter of attitude.

Strawberry grew up in the Crenshaw neighborhood of south-central Los Angeles. It was not affluent, but it was not the ghetto that many would automatically assume it to be based on geography. It was a neighborhood of working-class people trying to make ends meet. That included Strawberry's parents. Unfortunately, his father's idea of making ends meet was earning enough to pay for his addictions.

"At thirteen, I could not remember a time when I did not live in fear of this man, my own father," wrote Strawberry in his autobiography.

Darryl goes on to detail how he and his brothers and sisters forced their father out of the house one night for good. As can be imagined, it was a traumatic experience for the young man, made even more so when Darryl began exhibiting many of his father's qualities as he grew older.

In high school, Strawberry's ability was quickly apparent. He hit the ball farther—much farther—than any of the other kids. A pitcher, he threw it a lot harder than them too. Scouts across the country began to hear about him and started flooding into southern California. They saw the incredible talent. But they also heard about the attitude. They heard about how Darryl had quit the baseball team when his coach disciplined him for dogging it. They heard how Darryl did not seem to have a deep love of the game like other players. Was this concerning? Absolutely. But man, with a swing like that, how could you not see Major Leagues written all over this kid?

"I went to Crenshaw High when Darryl was a junior to watch Chris Brown," said Roger Jongewaard, the scout who found Strawberry for the Mets. "I saw Darryl, and I just felt like he was a natural. So I started following him, and I saw a lot of games, and he just got better and better."[23]

As the 1980 draft approached, *Sports Illustrated* was looking for a story. Since the Mets had the first overall pick, they reached out to Jongewaard and asked him who that might be. He rattled off a few names, including future A's general manager Billy Beane. Then he mentioned Strawberry.

"They said, 'Strawberry, is that his real name? That would be a natural. People would never forget that name.' So because of his name they really liked him," said Jongewaard. Without knowing much about who he was or what kind of player he was, *Sports Illustrated* went with Strawberry as the subject of their story. All because of that name.

The Mets took Darryl first in the draft. Strawberry, now an outfielder, burst through the Minors with the power and speed he had exhibited in high school. He won the 1982 player of the year award in the Texas League and was moved up to Triple-A Tidewater. Personally, however, the ride was not easy. He was still just a kid, surrounded by press and fans and hangers on, all looking for something from him. In the Minors, he had heard the worst kind of racial slurs when traveling through the South. It was all overwhelming, and at times, he had to be pushed into focusing on the game.

The ability, however, was too much to ignore. When the Mets got off to another horrific start in 1983, manager George Bamberger begged Cashen to bring Darryl up to the Majors. Cashen would have preferred another year of seasoning at Tidewater, but he relented. Strawberry came up on May 6. He was a smash, but the intensity of it all was too much for a twenty-year-old. Reporters were writing about him as if he, single-handedly, was going to rescue this abysmal franchise.

"Was I supposed to walk across the East River next? Actually that would have been easier than reading every day in the papers about the miracles I was expected to perform any minute now," said Strawberry.[24]

Darryl tried to live up to the hype. Instead, he struggled terribly. After a month in the big leagues, he was hitting .161 with just 3 home runs. Bamberger gave him a little rest on the bench, while coach Jim Frey taught him how to adjust to Major League pitching. It worked. Strawberry recovered and won the National League Rookie of the Year.

In 1984 the sky was the limit for Darryl. He hit for power. He hit for average. He stole bases. He was doing it all. Then came August. He went the entire month without hitting a home run. His batting average fell fifteen points. His play in the field was questionable. It could have simply been the struggles that go with playing a 162-game season. Players go into slumps at any given point.

Strawberry's teammates, however, did not see it that way. Darryl's home life was turbulent. He was frequently fighting with his fiancée and future wife, Lisa. And he continued to feel the pressure every day of having to perform under a microscope. What Darryl's teammates saw was a guy whose off the field problems took his mind away from the game. As a result, the guy simply did not try.

In time, Strawberry came to resent these attitudes. How come when he struggled it was because he was lazy and unfocused, but when a white player struggled it was just one of those things that happens in the game? But Darryl acknowledged that his 1984 performance could have been better, and he vowed to change things in 1985.

"I got down on myself and felt I let my teammates down," said Strawberry. "I have a different attitude this year. I feel like I am a veteran."[25]

THAT SENTIMENT WOULD NOT stand the test of time. For the moment, however, Darryl's teammates and Davey Johnson would certainly take it. Still nursing his sore wrist, Strawberry stepped to the plate against Franco and turned on a high fastball, drilling it just over the wall in right field. The Mets were now 4-0, with each win coming by a single run and three of the four wins coming in their last at bat. Despite a collective batting average of just .217 over that stretch, these guys were fun and incredibly exciting to watch. The late-game victories were creating a buzz perhaps never seen in the team's twenty-three-year history. But they were not resting on their laurels.

"This is a good start for us, but nothing to go crazy about," said Strawberry, in a hopeful sign of developing maturity. "It's a long season ahead of us. It's going to be a dogfight and we've got to keep pushing."[26]

Fans would disagree about the going crazy part, and the next day's game would encapsulate everything about the 1985 Mets that would be worth going crazy about. Closing out their opening home stand, Dwight Gooden gave the first indication of just how special his season was going to be. Against the Reds, he allowed only four hits, while striking out ten and going the distance for his first complete-game shutout of the year. It was still early, but Gooden's ERA fell to 1.80. It would never go above 2.00 for the rest of the season. Meanwhile, Carter hit another home run and drove in 2 runs, as the Mets won 4–0.

Afterward, the buzz—outside of the Mets' overall record—was about Gooden's performance. Pete Rose, just 88 hits away from breaking Ty Cobb's all-time record of 4,191, called Gooden's performance "terrific" and noted that even though Doc threw a good changeup, there was no need for him to use it because of how dominant his fastball and curveball were.[27]

"It's like sitting back in a rocking chair catching him," said Carter. "As the game wore on, you could see he got into his rhythm. No matter what [sign] you put down, he's in control of that pitch."[28]

There had been high hopes coming into the season for the Mets, but no one could have reasonably expected this: a 5-0 start, the greatest in team history, along with 3 home runs from Carter and a team ERA of 1.13. Sure, it was early, but the Mets were in first place and this was no fluke year where surprise performances could vanish at any moment. This was how they were supposed to be playing.

"It's like a dream," said Carter. "In all the games I played in Montreal, I remember only one curtain call, when I hit three home runs in one game. And we lost the game. I've had three curtain calls already this week. New York, New York. I love it."[29]

Moreover, the race for the soul of New York City baseball was already tilting in one direction.

"The Mets played five games at home and won all five, catapulting them well in front of the Yankees in the race for the attention of the fans and the news media," wrote the *New York Times'* Murray Chass. And while Yankees players were saying—probably truthfully—that they were not focused on the Mets' success, their owner most certainly was.[30]

"I guess when you get to the business side of it, Mr. Steinbrenner thinks about it," said Willie Randolph, before adding, "but the players don't."[31]

But as the year went on, it was going to become harder and harder for the Yankees to ignore the Mets, not just because of their owner, but because the press and the fans were getting swept up in comparing the two teams. Just a week into the season, stories noting the rise of the Mets and seeming fall of the Yankees were emerging. And the press was beginning to compare players on each side. When Yankees catcher Butch Wynegar hit a home run in his first home at bat of 1985, the press inevitably asked him about the similarities between his shot and Carter's opening day heroics.

"Gary Carter doesn't care what I do and I don't care what he does," Wynegar replied.[32]

Maybe he did, maybe he did not. But the press was going to keep asking questions like this, and fans were going to do the comparisons on their own anyway. It was going to be hard to ignore over the remaining 156 games.

THE YANKEES' OPENING DAY slaughter at the hands of the Red Sox put Steinbrenner on high alert. To The Boss, getting beaten that badly was a sin. Getting beaten that badly by the Red Sox was an almost unforgiveable sin. The second game of the season did nothing to alleviate Steinbrenner's concerns. Whitson, the Yankees' prized pitcher signing of the offseason, was set to make his team debut. As he suited up before game time, Whitson sat on the stool in front of his locker and bent down to pull up his socks. As he did so, he felt a pang in his back. It was not a crippling pain, but it was enough to cause Whitson serious discomfort. Still, he stormed ahead, intent on taking the Fenway mound on this sunny Wednesday afternoon. Anyone turning the game on after the second inning would not have known he pitched. Felled by bad defense, Whitson gave up 9 runs in an inning and two-thirds on the mound, leaving with his team trailing 9–1. Though the Yankees' offense managed to put up a few runs, the Red Sox came away with a 14–5 win.

In the history of baseball no team has gone an entire season without losing two games in a row. But these were the Yankees. This was opening week. And the team had a huge payroll with huge expectations. And so, George Steinbrenner panicked. After the game he held a press conference on the roof of Fenway Park. He expressed severe disappointment with the team and declared that the next day's game, only the third of the season, was "crucial."

Members of the press corps could hardly contain their amusement and bewilderment. Was he serious? It was the first series of the year, and the Yankees were without their best pitcher (Ron Guidry) and their prized off-season acquisition (Rickey Henderson). How could he call game number three crucial?

If The Boss was serious and meant the comment as a way to spark his club, he failed. The Red Sox beat the Yankees yet again, sweeping the season-opening series. Everyone sat and waited for Steinbrenner to explode. Many thought it was now a matter of counting down the hours until Berra was fired. Yogi was granted a reprieve, though things were about to get worse.

Most teams enjoyed a day off after the first series of the year. In theory, the Yankees did have the day off on Friday, April 12. But The Boss did not believe in days off.

"Miraculously . . . he's been extremely consistent in his ability to schedule either workouts, charity luncheons, or exhibition games on all our off-days early in the season," wrote Niekro.[33]

So the Yankees faced off against the Columbus Clippers, the

team's Triple-A affiliate, in a scrimmage match. It did not go well. The Clippers crushed the big league club, 14–5. Many of the players did not seem to give a shit. They openly laughed at on-field mistakes.

Steinbrenner was livid. Getting swept by the Red Sox was bad enough. But losing to the team's Triple-A affiliate was humiliating. It did not matter that the Yankees' regular players, the few Yogi had that were not injured, did not play. A loss to Minor Leaguers was a loss to Minor Leaguers.

The Yankees headed to Cleveland. Their season was only three games old, but they were seemingly teetering on the brink. Before the game, Don Baylor held a team meeting. Baylor was the de facto Yankees captain. The position had been left unfilled after Graig Nettles was traded to the Padres. Baylor was not the senior Yankee. In fact, he wasn't even close. Randolph, Guidry, Dave Righetti, Griffey, Dave Winfield, Wynegar, and Andre Robertson had all been in New York longer. But Baylor was a veteran player who was adored by just about everyone he played with.

Baylor was a large man, his frame perhaps more suited to football than baseball. In fact, growing up in Austin, Texas, Baylor had wanted to play at the University of Texas for legendary football coach Darrell Royal. But the Southwest Conference had almost no black players in the late 1960s, so Baylor gave up on football. He was drafted by the Baltimore Orioles and made a name for himself in Baltimore and then in California, winning the 1979 American League MVP with the Angels. He signed with the Yankees before the 1983 season.

"It was one of the best decisions of my Major League career to go there and play in New York. It was like you were on Broadway every night," said Baylor.[34]

That is not to say New York was not without its issues. After agreeing to the deal, Baylor took a red-eye from the West Coast for a press conference the next day. The whole thing was supposed to be a secret. The story, however, broke in the *Daily News* before he landed.

"I remember George saying the deal was off after I had got there. [But] it didn't come from us. When you leave Gene Autry [the Angels owner who was beloved by players and fellow owners], George Steinbrenner is the complete opposite."[35]

The Yankees' clubhouse was a bit of a problem too.

"We had some John Birch Society guys in baseball at that time," said Baylor, referring to the notoriously conservative and not especially diverse group. "The locker room was kind of set up [where] you had all the black players on one side. It was a little different that way. You just kinda rolled with it. You had Winfield, Griffey, Billy Sample, Randolph—all of us on one side of the locker room. It wasn't, I don't think, racism or anything. Just kind of the way it was."[36]

Baylor moved past those issues, becoming a force in the Yankees' lineup as designated hitter. Beyond his natural ability and strategic sense of the game, Baylor's frame could go a long way toward intimidating opposing pitchers.

"He was bigger than most human beings should be allowed to be," said Walt Terrell.[37]

Tough as nails, he hovered over home plate, never afraid to take a fastball in the arm or back. In fact, Baylor would eventually set the Major League record for being hit by pitches. He intimidated without ever being intimidated himself. Baylor would share words with opposing players if the need arose. He also had no issue taking a teammate aside if their effort on the field was lacking or if he felt they were putting themselves over the team.

"There was an incident where we had a scuffle with a team," recalled Guidry, who always referred to Baylor as "Mr. Respect." "Both teams emptied out on to the field. I got there first and all I was trying to do was get in there and protect my players. But when I got back in the dugout, he [Baylor] jumped all over me. He told me, 'Don't you ever go back out there again.'" Baylor did not want the team's ace pitcher getting hurt in some on-the-field fight.

But Baylor's frame and demeanor betrayed a teddy bear at heart. While vocal when needed, he was generally soft spoken and reserved. He raised millions of dollars to fight cystic fibrosis. He was generous with teammates, especially those new to the club. And he knew how to take charge without alienating or angering teammates, utilizing lessons he had learned in Baltimore from Brooks Robinson and Frank Robinson.

Baylor was a quiet leader only in that he generally did not make waves in the papers. He called a meeting of his teammates because it was time someone spoke up. It is time we get it together, Baylor told them. If we do not figure this out soon, we are going to be left in the dust by everyone else. Forget about the other stuff—like a know-it-all owner—just focus on the game. The talk seemingly worked, as they beat the Indians, 6–3, for their first win of the year. They even won the next game before heading home for Yankee Stadium.

IN 1985 YANKEE STADIUM was sixty-two years old. The outfield walls were still all blue and void of the advertising signage that would pop up a decade later. Alcohol was still served in the outfield bleachers. Right field remained friendly to left-handed hitters, with the foul pole standing just 310 feet from home plate. Left field, however, was referred to as Death Valley for its seemingly endless distance from home. While it was only 312 feet down the left-field line, it was 411 feet to left-center field, a nearly insurmountable distance for right-handed batters in the 1980s. What right field giveth, left field taketh away.

The stadium had received iconic status largely because of the many famous players who had called it home and the number of postseason games it had hosted. But much of that had taken place in the original stadium before it had been refurbished in the mid-1970s. The updated version remained iconic, with its navy-blue seats, steep upper deck, and inverted horseshoe shape. But in reality Yankee Stadium was a dump. The hallways were narrow, the seats uncomfortable, and it wasn't rare to pick up a whiff of urine while waiting online at the concession stand. The area around the park, located in New York City's South Bronx, had deteriorated over the years, following a national pattern of urban decay during the 1970s and '80s. Many fans simply did not think it was safe to go to a game there.

Still, the home opener at Yankee Stadium was always an event, and that day was no different. Fifty-three thousand fans filed in to watch Ed Whitson face off against the White Sox's Tim Lollar. They were treated to a back-and-forth contest that saw the lead change five different times before the ninth inning.

With the game tied at 4 in the bottom of the ninth, Baylor decided to do his best Gary Carter impression. Before he stepped to the plate, he told his teammates this was it, they were going home. One pitch into his at bat, he delivered, sending a drive into the left-field stands to end the game. Whatever the Mets could do in their home opener, the Yankees could do.

The euphoria over Baylor's home run was short lived. The Yankees won two of their next three games, but then the wheels quickly fell off. Not even an attempted comeback by the retired Bobby Murcer, who played two games at Single-A Fort Lauderdale before he called it quits, lifted the tension. Rickey Henderson rejoined the team on April 23 just in time for the start of a three-game home series against the Red Sox. But the outfielder immediately alienated the New York media when, before taking the field for batting practice, he declared "I don't need no press now." While it could be understood why Henderson might want to just get out on the field, the manner in which he told the press to go screw was not appreciated.

Henderson's rush to the field had taken place the day before the start of the Red Sox series, for an optional workout. Of course, in The Boss's world, optional meant mandatory. He had a long history of requesting such "optional" workouts, only to be incensed when most players did not show up. When many players did not show up to this workout, he let his displeasure be known.

"I thought they'd show more respect for Yogi," said Steinbrenner, in a statement that both chastised the players and attempted to show that Yogi could not instill discipline.[38]

"Players are just getting settled in, setting up accounts, maybe even locating apartments," noted Hernandez in his journal after hearing press accounts of the latest Yankees drama. "Steinbrenner is, once again, way off base. Without taking a poll, I'll bet there's not one Met who would rather be performing in Yankee pinstripes."[39]

To The Boss, the fact that so few players showed up was a clear sign that Yogi was losing control of the clubhouse, if he had not already lost it completely. Steinbrenner was of a football mental-ity. Discipline, workouts, and game-day speeches were what won games. Yogi appeared to be failing on all those fronts. Now, the wheels in Steinbrenner's head were spinning. He needed some-one who could whip these players into shape.

The day after the workout, the Yankees lost a heartbreaker to the Red Sox in extra innings. In his first game as a Yankee, Henderson hit into a crucial double play in the eighth inning. The following day, they lost again, dropping them to 5-7 and last in the Ameri-can League East. Perhaps not coincidentally, word leaked out the same day that Steinbrenner had had a conversation with retired former Orioles manager Earl Weaver about managing the Yankees. Weaver declined, though just a few weeks later he would come out of retirement to take over the struggling Orioles. The leaker of the story was most likely Steinbrenner. It was another common tactic from The Boss. Perhaps the players would now step up their game knowing Yogi's job really was on the line. It was also an opportu-nity for Steinbrenner to float an idea publicly and gauge reaction. And the media, who by now simply did not trust Steinbrenner on anything, still appreciated a good story.

A win by Niekro kept the Yankees from getting swept again by Boston and bought Berra a little more time. But the noose around Yogi's neck was tightening as the team headed to Chicago for a three-game weekend series with the White Sox. Chicago had already played host to some bizarre moments in Yankees his-tory. It was where Babe Ruth had allegedly called his home run during the 1932 World Series (though that occurred at Wrigley Field, not Comiskey Park). In 1978 Billy Martin had uttered the famous words about Steinbrenner and Reggie Jackson—"one's a born liar, and the other's convicted"—at O'Hare Airport in Chi-cago. Now Chicago would play host to another odd episode in team history: the firing of Yogi Berra.

It began on Friday night, April 26. Whitson, who had yet to find his groove early in the season, took a no-hitter into the fifth inning. Then in the sixth, with two outs, he gave up a single, a walk, and a 3-run home run to Harold Baines. The Yankees never recovered, stranding fourteen runners in a 4–2 loss. Their record fell to 6-8 and they remained in last place.

The next day was an even bigger heartbreaker. The Yankees blew a 2-run ninth-inning lead, on national TV no less, and were forced into extra innings. After taking a 1-run lead in the eleventh, relievers Bob Shirley and Dale Murray gave up five straight singles, and a 4–3 lead turned into a 5–4 defeat. Some felt the constant threat of losing his job was impacting Yogi.

"Yogi was just not at his best today," noted Niekro in his book. "In fact, his nerves are fuckin' shattered. The constant pressure had finally gotten to him. . . . It almost seemed as if he subconsciously wanted to lose the game, just to get all this shit over with."[40]

As the players gathered on the team bus, none of them knew that Berra's fate had already been sealed. Steinbrenner had been talking to an old friend about coming back to the organization . . . and the old friend had accepted.

SUNDAY, APRIL 28, 1985, was Berra's last day as a big league manager. And it was an unfortunate ending for the Hall of Famer. The Yankees blew leads of 1–0 and 3–1 and lost in the bottom of the ninth inning when Joe Cowley walked in the game-winning run. As the players filed back into the clubhouse, something seemed amiss. General manager Clyde King walked into Yogi's office and asked the assembled press corps to leave. King informed Yogi that he was fired.

"Some full season," Yogi responded.

Eventually word spread around the clubhouse about Yogi's dismissal. His crime? The Yankees were in last place. Even worse for Steinbrenner, Yogi seemed to be soft on his players. He did not push them to attend workouts, and he did not seem to punish them for any infractions. The Boss could not have that anymore. He needed someone who would put the hammer down on his players. A guy who didn't give a shit what they thought about him. The Boss believed he had found such a manager . . . for the fourth time. Billy Martin was returning to the Yankees.

The player reaction was a mixture of frustration over Yogi's ouster and anger over Martin's return. Mattingly, who had become a batting champion under Berra's tutelage, was livid. He began screaming in the locker room, eventually hurling objects across the shower. Baylor, no fan of Martin's, kicked a trash can across the locker room.

"I guess most of the guys around here just don't like ole' Billy," noted Niekro.[41]

Cowley, who had given up the game in the ninth, was devastated. Sitting at his locker, sobbing, he felt personally responsible for Yogi's firing.[42] In reality, the decision to fire Yogi had already been made the night before when Steinbrenner finalized the details with Martin and his agent, Eddie Sapir.[43] Steinbrenner had all but pleaded with Martin to return and instill some discipline. "The team needs me," Martin reported Steinbrenner as having told him.[44]

Dale Berra, Yogi's son and whom the Yankees had traded for that offseason to help play third base, walked into the clubhouse unaware of what had occurred. He asked Mattingly what all the commotion was about.

"They just fired your dad," Mattingly replied.

The younger Berra was stunned. Only Henderson seemed pleased. He had played for Billy during his early years in Oakland. He loved Billy's style. Rickey began whistling and singing in the shower as some of his teammates gave him angry glares.[45] Meanwhile, a press release was handed out to all players announcing the decision. One after another, each player either ripped it up or crumpled it into a ball and tossed it aside.[46]

Amazingly, Yogi was rather calm, seemingly taking his dismissal in stride. He told Dale not to worry. He had known Billy since he was a kid. All he had to do was play hard, and he'd be fine.

"I'm gonna go play golf," Berra told his son.

It was especially hard news for Dale, who had loved playing for his father. When he tried calling him "Skip" instead of "Dad" so as not to give the appearance of any favoritism, teammates like Baylor, Griffey, and Guidry told him that was ridiculous. Call him "Dad."[47]

Eventually the players got dressed and headed for the two team buses to take them to O'Hare International Airport. Yogi had wanted to take a cab to the airport, but King encouraged him to jump on one of the buses. It was a quiet ride. Once they got to O'Hare, the bus sidestepped its scheduled route to make a quick detour. Instead of heading for the terminal where the Yankees would be flying to Texas, it veered toward another terminal where a flight headed to Newark Airport in New Jersey would take Yogi home. The bus stopped, and Berra rose to grab his things. As he walked down the bus steps, everyone on the team rose and gave him a standing ovation. Some players had tears in their eyes. They watched as Berra, who hours before was manager of the most successful franchise in baseball history, walked into the terminal by himself, bags in hand.

"I remember looking out the window [of the bus] at this forlorn figure of Yogi, carrying his own bag and walking into the terminal to get a flight back to New York while we continued on to the United terminal where we had a private charter taking us on to Texas," recalled Bill Madden, a team beat writer for the *New York Daily News*.[48]

It was the last time Berra would have any connection to the Yankees for fourteen years.

Eventually, the team and the traveling media boarded their plane and took the two-and-a half-hour flight south across America's heartland before arriving in Texas. Few, if any, players were happy, and the media, though always down for a good story, was getting tired of the Billy Martin–George Steinbrenner show. But when they got to the team hotel, what awaited them let them know that the circus was back in town

THOUGH THE METS LOST their first game of the year in Pittsburgh following their 5-0 start, they took the remaining two games from the Pirates. In one game, Darling and Orosco combined for a one-hitter, the first such combined effort in Mets history. Naturally, however, the hard-luck Darling did not get the win, making it ten out of his last eighteen starts stretching back to 1984 where he did not factor into the decision. That game featured yet another last at bat win when Hernandez drove in Mookie Wilson in the top of the ninth, sealing a 2–1 victory.

The next day they won what Hernandez called the "worst game in baseball history."[49] Though it was a sloppy performance on all fronts, the Mets still persevered, 10–6. They didn't just win the pitching duels, they won the messes as well. After Pittsburgh, they headed to Philadelphia, where in the first game of a three-game series, Gooden tossed eight shutout innings. Unfortunately for Doc, Steve Carlton kept the Mets scoreless as well. Then in the top of the ninth, with two outs and several hundred Mets fans in the stands, Hernandez singled in Backman and the Mets ran their record to 8-1, with five of those wins coming in the team's last at bat. It was the best start in franchise history.

After the initial victory against the Phillies, some chinks in the armor began to show. They lost the remaining two games in Philadelphia, despite the offense coming to life and putting up 12 total runs. But the starting and relief pitching blew leads in both of those games. On their first trip of the year to St. Louis, they won the first game, 7–6. But the pitching continued to struggle, with the team nearly blowing a 6–0 lead, including allowing the Cardinals to put the tying and winning runs on base in the bottom of the ninth with only one out.

"This has got to stop," said Hernandez, who had tied a club record that night by driving a run in for the seventh consecutive game. "It would have been awfully deflating to lose the lead in this one too."[50]

The pitching, however, kept faltering, and the team also faced its first serious injury of the year. In the second game against the Cardinals, Berenyi, who had pitched well for the team after being acquired for the Reds in the middle of 1984, left early with right-shoulder discomfort. He never pitched again in 1985.

The Mets lost that game and the next one, dropping the series to the Cardinals. They returned to Shea for a quick home stand and promptly took two out of three from the Pirates. Darling, forever getting no decisions, threw a five-hit shutout in the first game, drawing a backhanded compliment from his manager.

"Sometimes, Ronnie thinks he is an overpowering pitcher because in college he overpowered everybody. But he's a complete pitcher," said Johnson, who clearly had grown weary of Darling throwing too many fastballs, instead of mixing in sliders, curves, and changeups.[51]

In the third game, the Mets scored 4 runs in the first on a Strawberry grand slam, and did not score again until the bottom of the eighteenth inning, but it was enough to win, 5–4. The thirty-six thousand fans in attendance received free chocolate sundaes, and booed loudly when the new manager of the Yankees was announced.[52]

On the last day of the month, Gooden outpitched Joe Niekro, brother of the Yankees' opening day starter, beating the Astros 4–1. As April came to a close, the Mets were the hottest team in the National League. Sure, they had stumbled in the previous few games, but they were still heading into May with a 12-6 record and tied for first in the National League East with the Cubs.

Gooden was 3-1 with 1.38 ERA. Hernandez was hitting .309. Carter, hampered by a series of small injuries, had slowed down, but his numerous clutch hits in the opening week had given him collateral for the rest of the month. Strawberry had 6 home runs and 12 RBIS. The bullpen, though struggling, still accounted for half of the team's twelve wins.

The Mets were winning offensive outbursts and pitching duels. They won sloppy games and defensive gems. Not only were they winning, but unlike the Yankees, their focus was on the field. During the entire month, not a single hint of clubhouse tension or controversy appeared. Was there concern about the health of some players? Sure. But that was part of any season. This Mets team, however, was not getting distracted by what happened off the field. They were one, cohesive unit operating on all cylinders.

New Yorkers took notice. Through their first nine home games, the Mets averaged 30,894 attendees a game, over 12,000 more than their first nine home game average of 1984.[53] And there is little doubt that the owner of their cross-town rivals noticed that it was almost 5,000 more fans a game than his team was drawing.

The Mets were the toast of the National League. Moreover, they were the toast of New York City. But May would bring about its own challenges for the Metropolitans.

# 5

# Billy and George, a Love/Hate Story

MICKEY MANTLE ONCE SAID that Alfred Manuel Martin was the only person he knew who "could hear someone give him the finger."[1] Perhaps no quote better sums up the life and times of the man hired in April 1985 to be the Yankees' manager. Like George Steinbrenner, he traversed all sides of the spectrum: at times, overly charitable and caring; at others, confrontational, mean, and clearly vulnerable. The two were so similar they seemed like a natural fit. But Martin spent years vying for George's adulation. He never got it.

When Alfred was born on May 16, 1928, in Berkeley, California, his father had already abandoned the family. He had been caught cheating by his wife and tossed out of the house. Alfred would be a teenager before ever laying eyes on the man. Instead, he was raised by his mother Juvan and a stepfather, Jack Downey, whom she married mere days after the infamous stock market crash of 1929. Alfred's grandmother began calling him *bellissimo* or *bellino*, Italian for "beautiful." Eventually, this transitioned into "Billy."

Billy's stepfather was a kind man, but there is no doubt that the major force in his upbringing was his mother. Known as "Jenny" she was strong and determined, and perhaps most importantly during the course of her son's life, she never shied away from a fight. Jenny was a stereotypical Italian woman straight out of a cartoon. All she needed was the rolling pin to bash someone over the head with. Maybe not with a rolling pin, but bash she did, pummeling Billy's father, his father's lovers, and anyone else she felt had wronged her.

"Don't take shit from nobody," she was known to say throughout her life.[2]

It was a lesson her son would live out to the hilt.

At an early age, Billy was enamored with baseball and the New York Yankees. He often snuck away to nearby Kenney Park in West Berkley to take part in games. Influenced by the play of his brothers, he proclaimed he wanted to be a baseball player when he grew up. To many, it seemed like a pipe dream. Billy was small, and his physical coordination did not match that of a ballplayer. Though ballplayers could hail from anywhere, the nearest Major League team was in St. Louis, halfway across the country. The Pacific Coast League, an independent league of various teams that played in the west, had some incredible talent. But it was not at the status of the Majors. Billy's dream seemed more like wishful thinking than an achievable reality.

As he would do for the rest of his life, Billy set out to beat the odds. As a teenager, he took part in ballgames at Kenney Park that pitted him against players twice his age. He honed his ability and skills against these bigger and supposedly better players. He could hit, and while he was not the smoothest fielder, he charged as hard as a person possibly could to get to every ball remotely close to him. Moreover, even at an early age, Billy showed the spark—the anger and drive—that would come to define his career and life.

"Billy showed his temper, but it was a winning temper," said childhood friend Bruno Andrino. "He wanted to win, wanted to beat you, and he did. He was a winner."[3]

Billy was not only sharpening his skills, but as he approached adolescence, he began to notice societal aspects of Berkley that would also shape his life. Billy's family, like many in Depression-era California, had little money. At times, they had to rely on charity for food. As he got older, Billy began to take notice of those who wore better clothes than he did, those who had while he had not. It created resentment. Moreover, he grew increasingly defensive about his body, both his small physical stature and his nose. This resentment, matched with fisticuffs skills inherited from his mother, led to fight after fight after fight in his youth. Some were typical teenager scuffles. Others were Billy and his friends going around the neighborhood literally looking for someone to beat up.

In high school, Billy became an All-Star-caliber player. His on-the-field talent was matched by his on-the-field encounters. In one game during his senior year, Billy punched a spectator who had been heckling him about his nose. He then punched the umpire when he tried to break up the fight.

After high school, he landed with the Oakland Junior Oaks, an affiliate of the Oakland Oaks of the Pacific Coast League, about as close to the Major Leagues as someone in California could get at the time. It was there that Billy fell under the tutelage of perhaps the second-most important person in his life, after his mother: Casey Stengel. Stengel, the Oaks' manager, took an immediate liking to Billy's hardball style of play. Martin, by now a second baseman, was scrappy, tough, and, perhaps most importantly, he loved baseball as much as Casey did. It was the beginning of a father-son relationship whereby Billy was known as "Casey's Boy."

In 1950 with Stengel now managing the Yankees, Billy realized his dream of playing for them. Martin saw limited playing time in 1950 and '51, but the Yankees were in the midst of winning five straight championships under Stengel. Billy may not have been playing much, but he was learning a lot by watching Casey manage. He became the team's regular second baseman during the 1952 season, and though his regular-season numbers were never much to brag about, he excelled in the World Series. (The expanded divisional postseason format did not exist until 1969. Until then, the best teams in the American and National Leagues met in the World Series after the regular season ended.) Billy, a career .257 hitter, hit .333 over five World Series, winning four of them. He also showed a rare streak of power, hitting 5 World Series home runs in just under one hundred at bats. Most famously, his catch of a Jackie Robinson pop-up in Game Seven of the '52 Series is often noted for having saved the game—and the championship—for the Yankees.

In New York, Billy could afford to be an average player, thanks to his postseason heroics and his do-or-die attitude. He wasn't especially fast, but he out hustled everyone. He wasn't especially strong but found a way to muscle out home runs in big situations.

But as it would so many times in his life, Billy's attitude led to his ultimate undoing.

Martin never backed down from a fight. Ever. And it did not take much to get him to engage in one. Martin's autobiography, *Number 1*, is filled with instances where he justifies his physical engagements. In almost all instances, it was the other person's (or persons') fault. And in almost all instances, Billy justifies it with some form of "What was I going to do, let the guy . . . insult me? challenge me? talk to me like that?"

His scraps had started at a young age and continued into his playing days. The feistiness of his mother, matched by the lingering resentment and insecurities of his youth, made Martin a near unstoppable force when he engaged in a fight. He almost always won, no matter the size of the other guy. Martin's first well-known fight in the Majors occurred in 1952 when, after the two traded insults before a game, he met Red Sox outfielder Jim Piersall underneath the stands at Fenway Park. At a bar in Tampa in 1960, Billy punched out a patron who had thrown a beer in his face (Martin had bought the guy the beer). Later that year, while playing for the Reds, Billy punched Cubs pitcher Jim Brewer in the face. During the ensuing melee, Brewer had his face caved in by one of Martin's teammates. Martin, however, took all the blame, later being sued by Brewer and the Cubs and having to pay several thousand dollars in judgement.[4]

Martin, like many of his teammates, stayed out after curfew and partied hard. In particular, he drank more than most human beings should be capable of, and he did it often. Yankees management began to feel that Martin was a bad influence over stars like Mantle and Whitey Ford.

Then, on a May night in 1957, Martin and several Yankees teammates and their wives went out to celebrate his birthday at the Copacabana, a popular New York nightclub. As several of the players later stated, a man in the crowd started yelling racial epithets at entertainer Sammy Davis Jr. Hank Bauer, Martin's teammate, followed the man to the bathroom and, according to the man, knocked him out cold with a punch. Bauer swore that it never happened and that bouncers at the club were the guilty parties. Either way, the altercation became huge news, with the players in attendance being questioned by police, brought before a grand jury, and eventually fined by the club.

Though everyone there agreed Billy was in no way the instigator of the fight, Yankees management blamed him anyway. They were getting tired of his tough-guy act. Shortly after the incident at the Copa, Martin was traded to the Kansas City Athletics. He was devastated, and harbored a grudge against Casey Stengel, which lasted until Stengel's death in 1975, for not stopping the trade.

Billy played for six teams over the next four years, but it was never the same for him. He retired after the '61 season and spent the next few years scouting for the Minnesota Twins. Eventually, he became the team's third-base coach and then, in a move that changed baseball history in countless ways, was offered his first managerial position with the Twins' Triple-A affiliate in Denver. It was in Denver that Martin's managerial style emerged: intense, inventive and driven by winning, purely and simply.

Billy was unlike anything most players at that level had seen. He screamed. He yelled. He got in your face. He demanded you give everything you had on that field, just as he had done. But he also took risks. He hit and ran. He bunted. He stole, including home. He tried every conceivable measure he could think of to win a game. And it worked. Denver excelled under his leadership, enough that Billy was brought up to manage the Twins in 1969.

It was there, in Minnesota, that a pattern developed that would, almost literally, encapsulate every single Major League Baseball managerial opportunity Billy had over the next twenty years. Martin took a team that won seventy-nine games in 1968 and turned them into ninety-seven-game-winning, American League West Division champions in 1969. Though they were swept in the American League Championship Series by Davey Johnson's Orioles, Minnesotans were ecstatic about Billy.

The Twins were young and exciting, and had the most skillful tactician in the game. But winning wasn't all that came with hiring Billy. There was also the fighting . . . always the fighting. Martin got into an altercation with the Twins' traveling press secretary on one of the team's flights. Then, in August, he punched out one of his own pitchers, Dave Boswell, outside a Detroit bar. Boswell suffered a concussion as a result.

There was also the yelling at the catchers.

Martin, a severe micromanager on the field, would second-guess any pitch that did not result in an out. It wore down nearly every catcher that played for him.

"Anytime a guy got a hit against us, it was the catcher's fault," said Rick Cerone, who played one full season under Martin in New York.[5]

Despite the Twins' incredible turnaround, Billy was fired almost immediately after the '69 season ended. The winning just wasn't worth the headache for management. In 1971 the struggling Tigers gave Martin a shot. Again, the turnaround was immediate. The Tigers went from fourth to second place in one year. Then, in 1972, Martin led them to the American League East Division title. But with that winning came the fighting and the yelling. In '72 he got into an altercation with a fan. Then he butted heads with Tigers management over playing time for Willie Horton. Finally in 1973, after being suspended for suspicion of having his pitchers throw at hitters, he was let go by the Tigers. Again, the winning just wasn't worth the headache for management.

Shortly after being let go by the Tigers, the struggling Texas Rangers brought Billy in at season's end to lead the team. As with the Twins and Tigers, the turnaround in 1974 was immediate and incredible. The Rangers went from fifty-seven wins to eighty-four wins and a second-place finish, the highest the team had ever placed. But with that winning came the fighting and the yelling. Billy slapped the team's traveling secretary and was constantly bickering with management over personnel decisions, even talking about it openly with the press. He did not make it through the '75 season before being fired.

Then along came George Steinbrenner. The Boss had been impressed by Martin's ability to turn teams around. The Yankees certainly needed it. The once-proud franchise had not made the postseason in over a decade. Their team was a mish-mosh of used to be's or never were's. Attendance had plummeted as the team's aging stars, one by one, either retired or were traded away. Two weeks after Texas fired Martin as manager, Steinbrenner fired manager Bill Virdon. Steinbrenner believed he could reign in Billy's less-endearing qualities, while at the same time take a crop of high-end free agents and up-and-coming talent and turn them into champions. Billy was hired in late '75 with the purpose of looking over the team as it was, then deciding what changes needed to happen to make them competitors in '76.

It should have been, on paper, a match made in heaven. Both men were incredibly driven, wanting to win at all costs. They detested perceived stupidity and anyone who did not appear to care as much as they did. They wanted to win, and they wanted to be surrounded by others who wanted nothing but to win. They both could be unimaginably cruel to anyone who did not perform to their standards. At the same time they were incredibly charitable and performed random acts of kindness without flaunting it to the media.

But it did not work. Even with success, it did not work. Steinbrenner could never relinquish complete control over what happened on the field, meddling in the smallest of game-time decisions. He second-guessed managers the way Billy second-guessed catchers. George, the rich kid from Cleveland, was a wannabe athlete who thought Billy could teach him the intricacies of the game and ingratiate him to athlete, clubhouse culture. Billy, the poor kid from Oakland who struggled and fought for everything he had in life thought George could bring him into the high-class, upper echelon life in New York City. No matter how many times they tried though—and try they did—it never worked.

As had happened four previous times as a manager, Billy came in and immediately turned the Yankees around. In his first full season at the helm, Martin led them to the World Series. Moreover, Billy largely behaved himself. He put up with Steinbrenner's calls and the panic attacks that would often ensue if the team lost more than two games in a row. But Billy kept any anger to himself. After winning the pennant, the Yankees promptly got swept by the Reds in the World Series. After Game Four, as Martin sat in the trainer's room crying over the loss, Steinbrenner stormed in. The Yankees—who most people did not think had any chance of reaching the playoffs, much less the World Series that year—had embarrassed their owner by being swept. The Boss warned Martin that he had better win the whole thing next year.

Steinbrenner did not sit back and hope that Billy would do so on his own. That offseason, he landed the biggest free agent in the game, outfielder Reggie Jackson. Billy was put off by the way Steinbrenner heaped lavish praise on Reggie and seemed to treat him with kid gloves. The three would quarrel all season, with Billy and Reggie nearly coming to blows on national television during a game in Boston. The Yankees, however, overcame internal turmoil to win the World Series, the team's first championship in fifteen years. In the clubhouse afterward, champagne flowed as the pain of a long season disappeared in the euphoria of a title. It did not last.

Winning a championship in '77 only put that much more pressure on Martin to win it all again in '78. But the clashes between him and Reggie, and him and Steinbrenner continued. Injuries decimated the Yankees and by midseason, they were in a tailspin. In an extra-inning game at Yankee Stadium, Martin asked Jackson to bunt with a runner on. Jackson was incredulous and thought Billy was trying to embarrass him. After Reggie squared around, but did not bunt, Martin removed the bunt sign. Reggie defiantly ignored the new sign and tried to bunt. He popped the ball up for an out. Martin was irate and, finally, lost control. Even though Reggie was suspended for his actions, Billy let loose on both him and Steinbrenner in comments he deliberately, and most likely under the heavy influence of alcohol, provided to *New York Times* reporter Murray Chass.

"They deserve each other," he told Chass. "One's a born liar and the other's convicted." The convicted line was a reference to Steinbrenner's having been convicted of illegally donating to President Richard Nixon's 1972 reelection campaign.

Rather than surely be fired by Steinbrenner, Martin, fighting back tears, read a statement of resignation to the team's press corps at the Crown Center Hotel in Kansas City. Citing his mental health and well-being, he said he was resigning. He apologized to Steinbrenner, going so far as to say he never made the remarks that Martin himself had made sure Chass had taken down and then published.

Martin's life was about patterns. Join a team. Turn the team around. Ruin it all with drinking and fighting. Steinbrenner also followed patterns, especially when it came to Martin. As would happen several more times over the next decade, immediately after Billy left the team, Steinbrenner felt guilty about what had happened. He was also concerned about fan reaction, which was swift and brutal against the owner. So, just a few days later, he flew Martin to New York for a secret meeting. There, he said he wanted to bring Billy back to manage for the 1980 season. Martin, heartbroken that he had to leave the only job he really wanted in the first place, agreed. Less than a week after resigning, the Yankees announced in the middle of Old Timer's Day that Martin would return in 1980, and the Yankees' current manager, Bob Lemon, would stay as manager through 1979, then move up to general manager. It was a coup. A piece of theater the always media-conscious Steinbrenner reveled in pulling off.

The Yankees won the title again in 1978, but just two months into the '79 season, Steinbrenner let manager Bob Lemon go. The Yankees, hurt by injuries, were playing sloppy baseball in The Boss's mind. Lemon, recovering from the death of his son that spring, just did not seem as concerned with baseball as Steinbrenner liked. So, needing a spark, he brought Martin back ahead of schedule to manage a second time. When catcher Thurman Munson, whom Martin treated like a son and absolutely adored, died in a plane crash in August, the team was devastated. Martin sobbed uncontrollably throughout the day of Munson's funeral. Already far behind in the standings, losing Munson was just too much to overcome, even with Billy as manager. The Yankees finished in fourth, missing the playoffs for the first time in four years.

Just weeks after the '79 regular season ended, Billy's familiar patterns emerged again. In Minnesota for a hunting trip, Billy and a friend stopped at the hotel bar for a few. While drinking, they were recognized by other patrons, including a man named Joseph Cooper. As they talked baseball, Cooper mentioned how he thought Dick Williams and Earl Weaver deserved to be named manager of the year in their respective leagues. Martin, who intensely disliked Williams and did not care much for Weaver, told Cooper that they were both assholes, and that Cooper was an asshole "for saying it."[6] After informing Billy that he made his living as a marshmallow salesman, Martin challenged Cooper to a fight outside. Billy would pay Cooper $300 if Martin hit him and Cooper was able to get up. As they made their way outside, according to Cooper, Billy sucker punched him, knocking him out.

News of the fight broke almost immediately. It was too much for Steinbrenner. Under the guise of trying to protect Martin from his erratic drinking and violent behavior, The Boss fired him a second time. Not fit to simply fire him, Steinbrenner began incessantly spreading news of Billy's drinking problem, which wasn't really news to most people. In turn, Billy said he was through with the Yankees as long as Steinbrenner was there. Martin kept his word . . . for three years.

Billy did not stay unemployed for long. Like so many teams before, the struggling A's came calling shortly after Martin was fired by the Yankees a second time. Oakland had finished 1979 with a 54-108 record, dead last in their division. They averaged fewer than four thousand fans a game. Then Billy came along and, as he always did, transformed the team. The A's won eighty-three games in 1980, with a core of young kids whom Billy molded into Bay Area stars. Their exciting style of play under Martin led to the moniker "Billyball," which defined an aggressive style of baseball that brought fans back to the Oakland Coliseum. From 1979 to 1980, attendance shot up over 250 percent. Then in 1981, Billy led the A's to the American League Championship Series, where they were swept in three games (the Championship Series was a best of five at the time) by the Yankees.

In 1982 the A's fell substantially, losing ninety-three games. Blame fell on Billy, with many claiming he was abusing his young pitching staff and ruining their pitching arms. Billy's personal life was in chaos. He was seeing a woman, Heather Ervolino, and her family lived in his Oakland home, preventing him from being at ease there. His unease may also have been due to his ongoing affair with Jill Guiver. Either way, Billy wanted nothing more than to get out of Oakland and go back to the Yankees. Luckily for him, the Yankees were in chaos too. In the three seasons since he had been fired a second time, the team had had five different managers. George needed stability: he needed Billy. At some point during the 1982 season, Steinbrenner told Martin he wanted him back and to get out of his A's contract, which, if it had ever been proven true, would have constituted a serious violation of baseball rules against tampering. Those who watched Billy during the last months of that season seem certain he was trying to get fired. Sure enough, after the season was over, he bickered with management over money. That—and according to some, his not so quiet affair with Jill—led to his prompt dismissal.

Like a married couple who thinks bringing a child into the relationship will solve all their woes, for a third time, Billy fell into the waiting arms of Steinbrenner. At a memorable (some would say awkward) press conference introducing him as manager, Billy and George pretended to argue, with George threatening to fire him. For many in attendance, it was not funny: it was sad. The same promises about working together and a greater understanding of each other were made. And as he had always done, Billy took a team that won only seventy-nine games in 1982 and got them to ninety-one wins in 1983. It was not enough, however, and as always, Martin's behavior during the regular season became so bizarre and brazen that beat writers hesitated to report it, knowing it would lead to his termination. In one incident in particular in Milwaukee, Martin (now married to Heather) sat on the top steps of the dugout while Jill, his mistress, sitting in the front of row the stands, passed notes to him with her toes.

Steinbrenner, hesitant to make a move lest he draw the ire of fans, instead waged a war of subtle attrition against Martin. He fired pitching coach Art Fowler, a longtime Billy companion, who showed up on every team Martin managed. He began, as an unnamed source, calling into question Martin's mental state. He said Billy was losing control of the team, a favorite tactic of the football-minded Steinbrenner. He dropped hints that the manager would be fired and replaced by Yogi Berra. And there were always the phone calls directly to Martin questioning his managerial abilities. Martin was already an alcoholic, but Steinbrenner's incessant bullying only drove him to drink more. And when he drank more, his behavior became more erratic. Shortly after the end of the '83 season, Martin was fired a third, and what many thought would be final, time as Yankees manager.

BILLY WAS NOW BACK to manage the Yankees a fourth time. And like so many times before, there were promises upon promises that everything would be just fine. The first signs were ominous enough. After leaving Chicago, the players and writers landed in Texas and headed to the Arlington Hilton. Once they got there, they found the elevators were out of order. Everyone had to carry their bags up over a dozen flight of stairs.[7] After getting settled into their rooms, the writers were called up to Martin's and Eddie Sapir's suite. There was a small spread and alcohol for all to indulge. Many of the writers, groggy from the flight and the trek up the stairs, still needed to file their original stories on Yogi's firing (the stories had been written in a rush to get to the team flight in Chicago and thus, in the pre-computer age, many were not yet filed), passed on the liquor and began taking notes.

"This time it's going to be different," said Sapir. "Billy and George really understand each other now."

"That's right," added Martin. "George and I have talked a lot and we have an understanding. The main thing is we both want to win."[8]

For many in the room, the words, which had been spoken before, felt incredibly hollow. Even more oddly, Sapir noted that Martin was going to be grooming Yankees bench coach Lou Piniella during the season to eventually take over as a manager. Billy would only be around for one or two years, then move into an upper-management position with the team. Few could remember a situation where a manager was brought on board just to groom someone else to be a future manager.

There was more to it than that though. Billy and George had, in fact, made a separate side deal. Angered over the lack of discipline and Yogi's being too friendly with the players, Steinbrenner agreed to never enter the Yankees' locker room—something he was fond of doing when he wanted to give inspirational speeches that often alienated specific players—in exchange for Billy enforcing certain rules.

"Shirts and ties on the road, no jeans on the plane," Martin told Murray Chass the night he was reinstated as manager. "Curfew three hours after a night game, 1 a.m. after a day game. If you're out, you know you're going to be fined—$500 the first time, $1,000 the second, the third time $1,000 and maybe suspension. No playing golf on game days. No public appearances on game days. I'll give them an additional warning on drugs. I really hate drugs. On the bus, all radios must have headsets."[9]

It was exactly the kind of meddling bullshit Martin had despised in his earlier Yankees managing days. But now, desperate to get back in the game, he agreed to do Steinbrenner's bidding. It cost him a tremendous amount of respect among players and writers. For the beginning of Billy IV was no love fest. The only four people on the planet who were happy that Billy was back appeared to be Steinbrenner, Martin, Sapir, and Henderson. The writers—many of whom had long covered the team and grown weary of both The Boss and Martin, even if they were good copy—were savage in their criticism. In many cases, they wondered if Billy's return was not meant to improve the team, but just to draw some attention away from the surging Mets.

"Martin once upon a time was innings and moves ahead of most other managers," wrote Chass. "But uniformed personnel who had watched him manage in previous tenures and who saw him in 1983 were amazed at the change in him, and his inability to concentrate on the games. Which Martin will the Yankees have this time? Does Steinbrenner care? The owner has appeared to be obsessed with the amount of attention being paid in the New York news media to the Mets. Is the Martin move an attempt to grab back some of the attention?"[10]

"Even if the rumors pouring out of New York hadn't been clouded with predictions of his return, you could have sensed that every bad dream you ever had about baseball was about to come true. For Billy Martin is the game's reigning nightmare, a 56-year-old juvenile delinquent who has mastered the art of sucker-punching and never shown an ounce of remorse for the careers he has ruined," wrote nationally syndicated sports columnist John Schulian. "All you can do is wonder whether Martin is Steinbrenner's last best hope for battling the Mets at the box office or just a symbol of King George's pathetic lust for attention."[11]

"Should Yogi have been fired? Of course not, not in the logical world," wrote the *Star-Ledger*'s Moss Klein. "But Steinbrenner had reached the panic stage. The team has been losing, first place was becoming more and more distant, people were talking about the Mets, about Gary Carter and Dwight Gooden. In the world of Steinbrenner, the instant-trend was that people were going to lose interest in the Yankees and loss of interest is one thing which Steinbrenner cannot tolerate."[12]

The *New Haven Journal-Courier* ran a contest where readers could submit their guesses as to when Billy would eventually be fired. The winner would receive four tickets to a Yankees game, "presumably to see the first game managed under Martin's successor."[13]

The players were resigned to their fate, but not all moved on as if this was just another managerial firing. Mattingly, in homage to Yogi, sported a T-shirt underneath his uniform that read, "It Ain't Over 'Til It's Over."[14] Several players ignored their new manager on that first day. Others continued to stress their disappointment with the situation. Ken Griffey, now serving under a sixth different manager in just four seasons, offered up no comment. In a way, it said more than any comment could have. Yankees fans in Arlington even had a banner ready. It simply stated, "YOGI."

To no one's surprise, both Steinbrenner and Martin showed no apathy toward the players. On the contrary. Steinbrenner blamed them for his making what was at the time one of the most unpopular managerial firings in New York sports history.

"I could care less what the players think," said Steinbrenner just before the team's first game under Billy IV. "They're in last place. Four and a half games back and slipping. They're the ones who cost Yogi his job."

The Boss even went a step further, hoping to appeal to working-class Yankees fans, many of whom were getting tired of his act.

"Today's players have changed because of long-term, guaranteed contracts," said Steinbrenner, perhaps overlooking the irony of himself having offered many of those long-term contracts. "Players have soft jobs and they're lazy. I keep hearing about this guy and that guy being unhappy. Well, if they're not happy, let them get jobs as cabdrivers, firemen or policemen in New York City. Then they'll see what it's like to work."[15]

Martin piled on.

"Remember," he said right around the time Steinbrenner was calling his players lazy, "George Steinbrenner didn't get Yogi fired. Billy Martin didn't get Yogi fired. The players did. They didn't do their jobs. If they did, I'd still be in Arizona right now soaking up some sun."[16]

After all the talk, however, there was still five months' worth of baseball to play and a season to save. The Yankees needed to start winning immediately if they wanted to stay afloat in the American League East. But they didn't. In fact, in the first game of Billy IV, everything that could go wrong went wrong. The Yankees blew leads of 4–0 and 5–3 despite having their ace, Guidry, on the mound. With the score tied in the eighth inning and a runner on, Martin replaced Guidry with John Montefusco, who promptly surrendered a 2-run home run to Larry Parrish. It was Parrish's third home run of the game. Perhaps the worst part, however, occurred in the fourth inning. With two runners on, Bobby Meacham sent a shot over the wall in left. But Meacham, not thinking the ball was going out, ran full speed out the box, watching the flight of the ball the entire time. In doing so, he passed Willie Randolph who stayed at first base to see if the ball would be caught. Meacham was called out for passing Randolph, turning a 3-run home run into a 2-run single.

The next night, Phil Niekro was shelled for 8 runs in five innings. After the game, Martin noted that the Yankees needed a left-handed power hitter in the lineup and were working on getting one. That left-hander was Seattle's Ken Phelps, who would not be traded to the Yankees until 1988.

Many thought two straight loses, under frustrating circumstances, would bring out the worst in Martin. They were waiting for the guy who yelled, cursed, threw objects, and picked fights. It never happened. Martin remained calm and focused on righting the ship. Billy even passed on getting drinks after the game.

"The Billy Martin that I've heard so much about would've never skipped a chance to have a few drinks after a game," wrote Niekro. "This guy we've got managing our club has to be an imposter!"[17]

The next night, Martin won his first game, stopping the team's five-game losing streak. Billy, who had tinkered with the lineup in each of his first three games, finally pushed the right buttons. Giving Don Baylor and Winfield a rest, he put catcher Ron Hassey in the lineup. Hassey went 4-4 with 4 RBIS. Martin brought Dave Righetti in in the sixth inning. Righetti pitched four innings, picking up the save and giving Ed Whitson a much-needed win.

The Yankees, after a grueling road trip that saw them lose five games and their beloved manager, were heading back to New York with a 7-12 record, just shy of being in last place in the American League East. When they got back, the team got its first taste of the discipline deal their manager had agreed to. Instead of an off day before the start of the home stand, there was a mandatory workout at Yankee Stadium. Rain cancelled the workout, but the fact that it had been scheduled to begin with added to the already growing resentment of the players toward their manager and owner.

Then, as had occurred nearly every single time Billy took over a team, it happened. The turnaround started.

ON MAY 1 THE Mets sat tied for first place in the National League East. They had been dinged up in the past few games, both in terms of score and some injuries. But overall, life was good in Flushing. The first game of the month, however, left something to desired. Ron Darling pitched well, but suffered behind a poor defensive effort, leaving the game trailing 5–3 in the seventh inning. With the score the same in the top of the ninth inning, Doug Sisk gave up 5 runs, putting the game out of reach. Sisk had continued to struggle after opening day, giving up 8 runs over three mid-April appearances. Now, against the Astros, he suffered his worst performance yet. His sinker, so devastating when it was on, simply was not moving.

In addition, Ron Gardenhire, who had alternated between backup and starting shortstop in April, suffered a hamstring injury in the second inning. He missed almost all of the next three months. Carter, playing through pain for much of April, was diagnosed with a cracked rib suffered during a collision in the eighteen-inning marathon against the Pirates. Mookie Wilson hurt his shoulder. George Foster hurt his knee. Ray Knight hurt his elbow. It seemed to go on with no end.

No one was crying for the Mets, though, as they headed into Cincinnati for a quick three-game series with the Reds. The lesser-known players and a crop of new talent were going to have to step up. Danny Heep, relegated largely to pinch-hitter duty despite leading the team in batting average during spring training, took over for Foster. In the first game against the Reds, he drove in a career-high 5 runs.

Leading off that same game for New York was a scrawny, hard-nosed kid who, once a game was over, tended to look more like Pig-Pen from the *Peanuts* comics than a baseball player. With Mookie nursing a sore shoulder and Gardenhire out with a bad hamstring, the Mets decided now was the time to get Len Dykstra into the lineup.

Dykstra, after just getting into Cincinnati from Tidewater, saw he was leading off in his first big league game. He had one thought in mind.

"Before the game, I said if I don't do anything in this game, I at least want to get on first base and talk to Pete Rose," said Dykstra.[18]

He eventually got his wish. In his second big league at bat, Dykstra hit a 2-run home run off Mario Soto. Dykstra practically ran around the bases, he was so giddy with excitement. In his next at bat, he singled, which gave him a chance to talk to Rose.

"Now that you're up here do your best to stay," the soon-to-be hit king told him.[19]

The efforts of Dykstra and Heep gave the Mets a 9–4 win. Two days later, with the team ahead by 1 run and the tying and winning runs on base, Dykstra dove to make a one-handed head-first grab of a Rose shallow fly ball, preserving the win. The victory pushed Gooden to 4-1, with a 1.57 ERA.

The team then returned to New York for a quick five-game home stand, with two against the Braves and three against the Phillies. In the first game, Carter, still suffering from the cracked rib and now dealing with a bruised left ankle that required hours of treatment, ripped an eighth-inning grand slam to left field. It was Carter's fifth home run, four of which were game winners.

"The fans went crazy and, of course, called Carter out of the dugout for a curtain call," said the *Star-Ledger*. "Carter obliged like nobody else had since the tradition began, thrusting his right fist into the air and taking in the exultation."[20]

In the ninth inning of that game, with the Mets up 5–1, Atlanta scored 2 runs. The Mets would not give up another run for twenty-nine innings. Lynch started it all with a complete-game shutout, the first of his career, as they took both games against the Braves. Then on Friday, May 10, over forty-six thousand came to see Gooden against Steve Carlton and the Phillies. The matchup of what seemed like two destined Hall of Famers did not disappoint, at least not for Mets fans. Gooden took a no-hitter into the seventh inning before giving up a two-out single. He struck out thirteen Phillies, which would not even be his highest single-game total for that month, on the way to pitching his second shutout of the year. Foster hit a 2-run home run, and the Mets won 5–0.

"He [Gooden] had the scariest curveball I had ever seen at that point, and when I say scary, I mean he was the type of pitcher that could embarrass you," said Phillies outfielder Von Hayes.[21]

"Dwight Gooden is moving closer to that inevitable no-hitter," wrote Rich Chere of the *Star-Ledger*, who was off by eleven years and four days.[22]

After Gooden, it was Sid Fernandez's turn to throw a gem. The big Hawaiian was about to become just one of numerous fan favorites at the ballpark that summer.

"I nicknamed him Dukey after Duke Kahanamoku, who was a world-class surfer from Hawaii," said Carter. "Dukey was kind of a free spirit. Laid-back kind of guy. The hang-ten type thing with the sign that Hawaiians do."[23]

Laid back, yes. Maybe a little flaky? Sure. After all, it became legend that Fernandez thought professional wrestling was real. But on the mound, there was no question he had talent. His fastball was not overpowering like Gooden's. But Fernandez used his size, which was also nothing like Gooden's, to hide the ball in the windup. And while not quite sidearm, he threw at enough of an angle that his fastball seemed to go higher and higher as it approached the plate. The laws of science tell us that there is no such thing as a rising fastball. Rather, our eyes only trick us into thinking the ball is going up. But talk to hitters who faced Dukey, and they will swear to you that the ball looked like a rocket boosting into outer space. And his curveball? Forget it. Hitters could not pick it up in enough time to swing.

Acquired by the Mets before the 1984 season, Sid was called up in July and won his first three starts. But spring training in '85 had been rough for Fernandez. Despite high hopes, he had posted an 0-4 record with an 8.38 ERA. That performance was enough to earn him a trip to Tidewater. But Sid dominated at Triple-A, allowing half as many hits as innings pitched and striking out more than nine per nine innings. The one issue that plagued him, however, was his control. And when he lost control of his pitches, he became flustered on the mound.

Problematic or not, Dukey was being asked to come to the rescue of a team riddled with injuries and in need of another starting pitcher. He did not disappoint, allowing only one hit over six innings, while striking out nine. Roger McDowell got the final nine outs, and the Mets had a 4–0 win. Despite hitting only .225 as a team—a batting average lower than Gooden's at that moment—the Mets had baseball's best record at 18-8.

Their performance was a sharp contrast to "the Bronx vaudeville act" being performed by the Yankees. The Mets had seen their share of injuries, and endured subpar performances from players they were counting on.

"But unlike the reaction at Yankee Stadium when the team there is struggling, the Mets show no symptoms of pique or panic," wrote Dave Anderson of the *New York Times*. "For those who enjoy baseball for baseball's sake, the Mets offer baseball, as opposed to the Yankees combination of the worst of both show biz and soap opera."[24]

Though their shutout streak ended in the final game of the home stand, the Mets won 3–2. They had taken all five games at Shea, while averaging over thirty thousand in attendance for each game. They left New York up by one game in the division and with baseball's best record. Their 19-8 mark was just one win shy of their best opening; only a 20-7 mark in 1972 was better.

Almost everything had gone perfectly, with one huge exception. During the Fernandez game, Darryl Strawberry had made a diving catch on a ball in right field. In the process, he jammed and rolled over the thumb of his right hand. Immediately, he came up in pain. Straw had torn ligaments and was going to miss at least seven weeks.

Though he had been struggling at the plate, Strawberry was still the team's main source of power, and his injury was a big loss.

"He [Strawberry] is very depressed and I think understandably so," said Frank Cashen after announcing the severity of the injury.

The rest of the league took notice. While certainly not wishing any one player ill health, they saw this as an opportunity to make up some ground on a wounded team.

"They have to miss him," said Cubs manager Jim Frey. "Let's face it, he's a guy who can hit 30 or 35 home runs. Danny Heep can't do that."[25]

It may have seemed like an innocuous quote, but make no mistake: with Strawberry out, National League East teams smelled blood in the water. The question was whether they would move in for the kill.

HURT AND HAMPERED, THE Mets pressed on. They left New York for a quick four-game road trip in Atlanta and Houston, splitting each series. Heep, stepping up in Strawberry's absence, went for 4-14 and hit his first home run of the year. Gooden, pitching in Houston, struck out the first batter of the game, then did not strike out anyone else before being removed in the seventh inning. Before that start, he had never struck out fewer than three batters in any Major League game he'd pitched. Nevertheless, he picked up the win, moving his record to 6-1.

The Mets returned home still one game up with the West Coast teams headed into town. Despite losing third-base coach Bobby Valentine, who accepted a job as manager of the Rangers before the home stand (Bud Harrelson replaced him at third), things started out well enough. But the Mets were struggling with their third base options.

In fact, the Mets had struggled with third base options since their first game in 1962. Seventy-seven different men had played at the hot corner in just twenty-three seasons. Felix Mantilla. Charlie Neal. Ed Charles. Wayne Garrett. Bob Aspromonte. Lenny Randle. The names stretched on and on. Not until 1981 had the team found a stable long-term third baseman in Hubie Brooks. Now, with Howard Johnson and Ray Knight platooning, they had their seventy-eighth third baseman in just twenty-four seasons.

Knight did not start out as a third baseman. He was drafted by the Reds in 1970 as the second baseman of their future. That changed when the team traded for future Hall of Famer Joe Morgan.

"When the deal for Morgan was made, I was switched to third base," said Knight.[26]

Knight showed tremendous promise, hitting .318 in his first full season, helping Cincinnati reach the playoffs in 1979. He followed that up with one of his strongest offensive seasons in 1980, making the first of two All-Star Game appearances. While not hitting for power, Knight continued to hit for average after being traded to the Astros in 1981. But in 1984, he encountered a series of injuries that wrecked his season and called into question whether he could continue in the big leagues.

It started in early May, when an inner ear infection gave Knight vertigo. He gazed up at a pop fly one night and became nauseous.

The problem was so severe he had to be hospitalized. Shortly after being discharged, he suffered through a kidney stone. At some point, he injured his shoulder. By the end of August, he was hitting just .223 with only 2 home runs. Houston shipped him to New York just before the trade deadline. The move seemed to rejuvenate Knight, who played well that final month. But the injuries had stunted his true capabilities.

"I just was a shell of myself physically because I was hurting, and I didn't want to tell anybody," said Knight. "I just didn't really recover. I had Achilles tendon surgery after that season ['84] on an injury that had scarred over. I go to spring training, and they had acquired Howard Johnson that year at the end of '84. I still thought I was going to be the everyday third baseman. Never dawned on me that I wouldn't be."[27]

The start of the '85 season was not kind to Knight. In addition to platooning with Johnson, injuries began to plague him early, though he played through the pain. It was no surprise. Knight, while not built like a prototypical power hitter, had the strength of a horse. Ray knew how to use that strength better than your average bar-fighting patron.

"My dad had me start boxing when I was 8 years old, and I was 17-0 in junior Golden Gloves until this southpaw broke my nose when I was 16 years old, and I told my dad I was done fighting," said Knight.[28]

Ray was not someone to be messed with. He avoided many of the vices his teammates were known for. He was deeply religious, his faith being a key part of his life. But Knight would not—and did not—hesitate to defend himself or his teammates when challenged on the field. He was not someone to be trifled with, and though his teammates often ribbed him for being married to world famous pro golfer Nancy Lopez, they certainly respected his willingness to use fists when the situation called for it.

Howard Johnson, while not a Golden Gloves boxer, was certainly strong. Born and raised in Clearwater, Florida, just blocks from where the Phillies held spring training, the switch hitter had the power to become a dangerous threat in the lineup. At least that was the thought when he was coming up through the Tigers' system in the early '80s. To them, HoJo, as he was called, was the third baseman of the future.

Johnson, however, had not been especially happy in Detroit. His playing time was limited—he'd had only one at bat in the 1984 World Series—and manager Sparky Anderson would often question Johnson's ability to come through in the clutch. He welcomed his trade to New York, even though the Mets already had a third baseman in Knight. But now the Mets had two third basemen suffering through abysmal early season slumps. Outside of the occasional bullpen hiccup, the third base situation was, by far, the team's biggest shortcoming on the field. As the new home stand began, over a month into the season, Knight and Johnson combined were hitting under .150 with 1 home run and 8 RBIs. It looked as if the third base issues that had plagued the Mets since their inception were destined to continue.

But the opening series against the Giants brought a glimmer of hope. Knight, hitting .186 for the season, came up in the seventh inning of the first game and hit a 2-run home run to tie the game. In the bottom of the twelfth, Carter—who else—smacked a two-out single to score Wally Backman with the winning run. After losing in ten innings the next day—their first extra-inning loss since July 30 of the previous year—HoJo came up in the bottom of the seventh in the final game against the Giants. He entered the game hitting .139 with 1 home run and 4 RBIs. With the bases loaded, two out, and the Mets trailing 2–1, there was possibly no hitter in baseball who needed a hit more at that moment than HoJo.

This time, he delivered. Johnson smacked a single into right field, scoring the tying and go-ahead runs. Roger McDowell closed it out, and the Mets had a 3–2 win.

"It may be a unique situation since we both play the same position and we're fighting for playing time, but we really do pull for each other," said Knight after the game about Johnson's big hit. "Honest to God. I actually said a prayer that he would get a hit in that spot."[29]

Despite having one of the worst offenses in the league, the Mets had baseball's best record at 23-12 and had opened up a two-game lead on the Cubs. After eighteen home games, their total attendance stood at over 553,000, an increase of over 50 percent compared to the first eighteen home games of 1984.[30]

But the next day, Monday, May 20, began a stretch of four games where anything that could go wrong did go wrong. First, the Padres' LaMarr Hoyt shut them out on a four-hitter, handing Gooden only his second loss of the season. That same day, Fernandez was diagnosed with tendinitis in his left leg.

"They don't need a manager here," said Davey Johnson, clearly exasperated by the never ending string of injuries. "They need a doctor."[31]

"I think I have seen a lot of disability over the years," said Cashen, "but never so many this early in the season. They usually catch up to you in August. But our guys are falling by the wayside at the start, and I've never seen anything like it."[32]

That same day, Doug Sisk, who had been demoted to the Minors to work on his pitching issues, was recalled. Though he did not enter the game, Doug was booed as he warmed up in the bullpen.

"I know they're waiting for me, that I'm going to get it," said Sisk with customary honesty. "The players gave me earplugs for this occasion."[33]

On May 21 they had a 4–0 lead over the Padres heading into the sixth. They lost the game in extra innings. On an off day, they flew down to Tidewater for an exhibition game against their Minor League affiliate. The good news was that Fernandez felt good enough to pitch in the exhibition, in which the Mets' staff threw a no-hitter. The bad news was they still managed to lose the game, 1–0, on two errors. It got worse.

Back at Shea the next day, Rafael Santana hurt his wrist and Knight's vertigo grew so bad he had to be removed from the game and sent home. The Mets used sixteen players in a 4–3 loss to the Dodgers. For the first time all season, they had lost three games in a row. Then Gooden was handed his third loss of the year when the team faltered to Fernando Valenzuela. In the first inning of that game, the Mets managed back-to-back hits for the first time in four games. The loss knocked them out of first place.

The Mets managed to salvage the home stand by winning the last two games against Los Angeles. In the final game, homers by Hernandez and Knight marked the first time the team had a multi-home run game in nearly three weeks. The home run was especially satisfying for Knight, who had driven in 4 runs while still dealing with his myriad health issues.

"I don't want to be thought of as a hypochondriac," said Knight after his big day. "I don't want any negative labels. So that home run was more than important to me. It got rid of some doubts for me."[34]

In addition to the offensive "outburst," McDowell had also picked up his fifth win in relief. The rookie reliever, like so many of his teammates, was exceeding expectations. Originally drafted by the Mets as a starting pitcher, McDowell had badly injured his pitching elbow in 1984. After having twelve bone chips removed, he missed almost the entire season, throwing only nineteen innings in the Minors.

"There were doubts," said McDowell. "Would I come back strong? Would I throw as hard? Would my sinker drop as far? But I had an optimistic outlook, and a lot of faith."[35]

McDowell's faith paid off. The chips were a blessing in disguise. Now moved from starter to the bullpen to help protect his arm, McDowell honed a devastating sinker with the help of his pitching coach, Greg Pavlick. It made him a deadly weapon when opposing teams put runners on base. When it was on, McDowell's sinker was nearly unhittable. As he wound up, McDowell seemed to whip the ball toward the plate, more than throw it. The sink was so dramatic that a hitter had almost no chance of making solid contact. Instead, they were forced to chop the ball into the grass for the inevitable ground ball out.

"The thing that freaked me out about Roger was that I caught a lot of guys with good sinkers," said Ronn Reynolds, the team's backup catcher that year. "But normally, when you catch a guy throwing mideighties with that sinker it feels like you are catching a cue ball. But Roger's was light and it still dropped off the table. It was funny. Obviously it was different because for a while nobody hit him constantly. But it was the most unusual sinker that I ever caught."[36]

His performance in spring training was so impressive—one walk in twenty-eight innings—that on April 1 Davey Johnson called him into his office to tell him he had made the big league club. "I asked him if it was an April Fool's joke," said McDowell.[37]

McDowell was more than just a great relief pitcher though. What made the 1985 Mets so much fun was not just their play, but their personalities. The team had someone for every stereotypical personality you would expect on a winning ball club. The grizzled veteran leader in Hernandez, the camera-hungry star in Carter, the moody prima donna in Strawberry, the young phenom in Gooden, the shy recluse in Foster. And in McDowell, they had their eccentric . . . and then some.

Roger studied commercial art, made charcoal sketch drawings in his spare time, and enjoyed fishing with his father-in-law. And he loved to play jokes and pranks. Loved it like few who have played the game before or since. The full extent of McDowell's repertoire—the hotfoots, the firecrackers, the wigs and masks, the second spitter—would have to wait. But 1985 was already providing a glimpse of what was to come. McDowell was . . . different. For example, few pitchers not only chewed bubblegum out on the mound, but blew bubbles as they were pitching.

"It's just a nervous habit," said McDowell. "They can call me the Bubble Gum Kid if they want. Maybe I'll start wearing a sweater that covers half my face like Bazooka Joe."[38]

Now, the sinker baller was the single most important piece of the Mets' bullpen. He was the bridge between the starting pitchers and Orosco, or he was the long man in relief, or he was the guy who came in to pitch out of a big jam. McDowell did it all.

"If anyone is our savior, he is it," said Hernandez about McDowell after he pitched four plus innings of scoreless relief to get his fifth win. "He's pitching like a 10-year veteran. He's pitching like a Bruce Sutter, a Rollie Fingers. If we don't have him, we're in big trouble."[39]

McDowell and company gave the Mets hope as they headed out to the West Coast for eight games. Moreover, no team in the National League had drawn more fans than the Metropolitans. It was quite a statement for a club that used to draw so few people to the ballpark that you could hear the individual taunts of fans throughout the stadium.

The coast would provide the Mets with many highlights, but the month of June would test them like no other month that year, and nearly destroy their season in the process.

IT HAD BEEN ALMOST eighteen months since Billy Martin last managed a game at Yankee Stadium. In that game, Don Mattingly knocked in Ken Griffey for a walk-off, bottom of the ninth win against the Red Sox. Despite being out of the 1983 playoff race at that point, there were few better ways to end a game.

Martin's return was not nearly as exciting as that late September 1983 game. In fact, it is doubtful that many of the twenty thousand fans in attendance when the Yankees returned on May 3 to play the Royals even remembered that moment. What they knew now was that their beloved Yogi had been fired, their owner was driving them crazy, and their crosstown rival was playing some damn exciting baseball.

Fans let their feelings be known when Martin brought out the lineup card before the start of the game. Though he received a mostly warm ovation, there were many audible boos, something that previously would have been unthinkable.

"A witness . . . would have thought Martin was MacArthur returning to the Philippines," wrote the *Bergen Record*'s Mike Celizic, referring to when Billy had replaced Bob Lemon in 1979. "Friday night, it was more like Jimmy Carter marching back to Georgia [after losing the 1980 presidential election]."[40]

"I happen to like Billy a lot as a manager," said fan Bob Schiffer, in attendance at Billy's fourth homecoming. "But I think they're making a joke of the organization by bringing him back. They give him a five-year contract and think they can hire him five times over."[41]

Any lingering anger was eased when, in the first inning, the Yankees scored a run that was pure Billy Ball. Rickey Henderson singled, then went to third on a hit-and-run single to the opposite field by Mattingly, whom Martin had moved to the number-two spot in the order. Henderson then scored when Winfield hit into a double play. Martin employed the hit and run again later in the game for another run. Behind a complete game by Dennis Rasmussen, the Yankees won Billy's return, 7–1. It was the first time in two weeks they'd won two games in a row. After the game, Martin announced he was moving bullpen coach Jeff Torborg to first base coach and reassigning Stump Merrill somewhere else, which meant Merrill was fired. Martin moved pitching coach Mark Connor to the bullpen and brought in twice-fired manager Gene Michael to coach third.

Also, with no lack of irony, Martin brought on Willie Horton, the same player he had tangled with and essentially lost his job over with the Tigers years earlier, to be assistant hitting coach. With each passing day, Billy made more and more certain that this was his team. Moreover, he was fully cognizant of his previous history.

"I think I will leave it like this," said Martin, looking around at his managerial office, which had nothing up on the walls. "Every time I get it lookin' pretty, I ain't here no more."[42]

The Yankees beat the Royals the next day then, thanks to home runs by Billy Sample, Henderson, Mattingly, and Griffey, gave Niekro career win number 288. It was their first three-game sweep of the season, and all of the sudden, many of the players had gotten over the firing of Yogi.

"It's completely opposite to what it was 10 days ago," said Baylor, perhaps referring to the trash can he kicked across the clubhouse when Yogi was fired. "It's Billy Ball, and it's working."[43]

"Playing for Billy is easier than playing for any other manager," said Henderson, always a cheerleader for Martin. "I know Billy so well that I understand what he wants from me: We have no prob-lems—no ups and downs, no disagreements."[44]

Not everyone, however, was overjoyed. Ken Griffey had had his fill of managerial changes and turmoil over his three previous seasons with the team. An All-Star member of the Reds' "Big Red Machine," Griffey had come over to the team in 1982 as part of the Yankees speed movement. He hit well, but never matched his Cincinnati numbers. Moreover, Griffey hated the clubhouse atmosphere in New York. In 1983 Martin had chased Griffey's two sons out of the clubhouse, an incident that still bothered Griffey two years later (and would sit with his son, Ken Griffey Jr., during a twenty-year baseball career that saw him murder the Yankees every chance he got). Griffey's playing time was cut, as he saw less and less action against left-handed pitchers. He had asked for a trade in 1984, but his contract and nagging injuries prevented any team from acquiring him. By 1985 he was telling friends he wanted to go back to the National League. When Billy returned and immediately began platooning Griffey with Sample, his mind was made up.

As the Yankees were sweeping the Royals, Griffey met with General Manager Clyde King and asked for a trade. All sides, including Martin, agreed there was no malice involved. Griffey simply wanted to move on. The kumbaya lasted only as long as it took Steinbrenner to find a reporter.

"We don't believe a man earning a million dollars a year should tell the boss what he's going to do," said Steinbrenner about the trade request.[45] It was a petty comment that gave the standard insight into The Boss's mind: I pay you well, therefore, you do as I say. And apparently King took his cues from his boss.

"I've now gone through this process of trying to trade Griffey two years in a row," said King in a statement just days after saying there was no bitterness involved. "Ken Griffey has two choices: He can discount his salary ($1.1 million a season for each of the next two years) to make him more marketable, or he can keep quiet and play when and where the manager wants him to."

The statement was clearly driven, if not directly written, by The Boss. Despite the vitriol, Griffey remained a Yankee until the middle of the next season.

Joe Cowley, the flakey right-hander, was upset when, after pitching poorly in his first start under Martin, the manager moved him to the bullpen.

"A pitcher who was behind almost every hitter, walked five guys and didn't pitch guys according to the reports we had. That's not a good pitcher," said Martin, ever so undiplomatically about Cowley.[46]

Willie Randolph was also upset. A veteran of the Bronx Zoo years, he had just about seen it all in his time in New York. He had been through every version of Billy, heard every possible slight from The

Boss, seen the highs and the lows. As much as he loved playing in New York—after all, he had grown up in Brooklyn—eventually the whole atmosphere broke down every player. Randolph was no different. He had been moved down in the batting order to the sixth spot. Willie understood that with Henderson on the team, he was no longer going to be their lead-off hitter. But the move so far down the order did not sit well with him.

"I don't like batting where I am. I'm not happy at all about it. But you're not going to hear any complaints from me. I'm not going to gripe about where I am right now," said Randolph, who was griping about it to reporters.[47]

The Yankees' second baseman for the last decade said he would abide by Billy's lineup and just play ball.

No one appeared less thrilled, however, than Yankees fans. Winning would help take away some of the sting, but many had grown leery of Steinbrenner's ways. In that Sunday's sports section of the *New York Times*, their anger came ripping through the pages.

"It is about time we loyal fans of the Yankees tell Steinbrenner where to go and stop going to see the Yankees play. The sooner we get rid of him, the quicker we will return," wrote one. Worse for Steinbrenner, these fans were not just mad, they were ready to make the switch to a more exciting, more stable team.

"I never thought I would say this, but Met fans, make room. It is better to catch the rising stars than to watch foundering over-paid ones," wrote Roger Greiner of Stamford, Connecticut. "I have had more than I can take of the Steinbrenner managerial circus. When I want a circus, Ringling Brothers–Barnum & Bailey does it much better. When I want baseball, I will be going to Shea Stadium."[48]

Whether their fans moved over to the Mets or not, the Yankees still had a lot of baseball left to play. After sweeping the Royals at home, they flew out to Minnesota for a brief two-game series with the Twins. Under the grayish roof and glaring lights of the Metrodome, the Yankees lost several fly balls, and dropped both games by scores of 8–6. More notable about the series, however, was that both Martin and Steinbrenner were in complete agreement on something: the Metrodome was a horrid place to play baseball.

After dropping the first game, Martin said the ballpark should be banned and referred to it as "an abortion." Before the second game, he filed a protest with American League president Bobby Brown, saying the Metrodome was simply not suitable for play. Steinbrenner supported Martin, saying the lights were actually too bright and needed to be used more before they would dim. It was all too ludicrous to be taken seriously and their protest went nowhere.

The Yankees moved on to Kansas City, taking two of three from the Royals. But even that was marred by news that the Pittsburgh grand jury was about to come out with indictments in baseball's drug scandal. Steinbrenner, in response, announced he was hiring two former FBI agents to trail his players. This was for their protection against any pressure to do drugs, he said rather unconvincingly. Perhaps Steinbrenner was on to something. Country Club Plaza—where Yankees hitting coach Lou Piniella just happened to be part owner of a bar—was a popular shopping area in downtown Kansas City. Around midnight the night before the first game against the Royals, Mattingly was relieving himself on a corner in the plaza when he was arrested and charged with indecent conduct. Just two nights later, Dale Berra was relieving himself in a parking garage in the plaza when he was stopped by a security officer. Incredulous that he was about to be arrested, Berra broke free from being handcuffed and, according to the guard, attempted to punch him but missed. Berra was eventually arrested and charged with indecent conduct and assault. Both Mattingly and Berra were fined $1,000 by the team. The charges were eventually withdrawn.

"Oh that was a fun thing," said Berra. "Went behind a dumpster . . . in an alleyway behind a dumpster. Obviously not in anybody's sight. We [him and Mattingly] were just targeted by a cop. And I found out that the area we were in in Kansas City, they arrest like fifty people a night doing it or some ridiculous number."[49]

Back in New York, the Yankees looked like they were about to suffer their most humiliating defeat of the year. Whitson had gotten smoked for 5 runs in just one inning of work. The bullpen quickly gave up 3 more, and before they could bat in the second inning, the Yankees were down 8–0. The fifteen thousand–plus fans at the park were not amused, and in an act that could have only enraged Steinbrenner, many of them began chanting "Let's Go Mets." Rather than have it spook them, the Yankees used it as motivation. They put up 5 runs in the sixth and entered the ninth inning down 2. With two runners on and two out, Mattingly faced former Yankee Ron Davis.

"I was still thinking about them when I got up there," said Mattingly, referring to the chants supporting the team from Flushing. Up in the count 1-0, Mattingly turned on a fastball and drilled it into the right-field stands for a walk-off 3-run home run. Rather than a horrific loss, it was now their most dramatic win of the year.

The next day, trailing 7–3 heading into the in the bottom of the seventh, Griffey hit a grand slam—off a left-handed pitcher—to give them a 9–7 lead they would not relinquish. Despite his friction with the front office, Griffey was all smiles in the dugout after his huge blast. The Rangers then came in for two. The Yankees won the first game on a tenth-inning error and trailed by 1 run in the eighth inning of the second game when Don Baylor tied it with a home run. In the bottom of the ninth, a bases-loaded groundout by Dave Winfield won the game. It had not been pretty, but two straight walk-off wins put the Yankees over .500 for the first time in almost a month. Martin was now 10-5 since taking the helm, and the Yankees were becoming a fun team to watch, at least on the field. They moved to the West Coast and won the first two against the Angels, giving them a season high six-game winning streak. Just weeks after publicly registering their unhappiness, Cowley and Randolph shared nothing but praise for their manager.

"Good move," Cowley told Martin after he took him out of a game against the Angels. "He knew I was tight."

"I like this style of baseball," said Randolph when the winning streak reached six. "We're aggressive and we're taking it to our opponents. I've said before, clubs that are aggressive on the base paths keep you on your toes."[50]

There was even some light-heartedness. Pitcher Bob Shirley, who had not been used in nearly three weeks, decided to sit in the stands at Angel Stadium during one of the games.

"I was just trying to get a better view of the game so I could relay what was happening to the other pitchers," joked Shirley, a funny guy who would spend most of the season wondering why Martin never used him.[51] Players joked that Martin probably thought Shirley was a coach. When his streak of no appearances stretched past twenty games, there was even talk of starting a Shirley Lottery, with prizes going to whoever could correctly guess the next time he would get in a game.[52]

The Yankees, however, could not manage to escape the coast without some bizarre incident. Henry Cotto served as a backup outfielder. In limited duty, he managed to hit almost .300 and provided the occasional rest for any of the starters. As the Yankees were on their way to a 13–1 victory over the A's, Cotto sat on the bench in the Oakland Coliseum cleaning his left ear with a Q-tip. As he did so, Griffey accidentally bumped into him, causing Cotto to jam the cotton swab deep into his ear. Cotto punctured his ear drum. He was sent back to New York ahead of the team to have it examined. Cotto eventually went back down to the Minors and did not get into another big league game until September.

As May came to an end, the Yankees returned home and took five out of seven versus the Angels, Mariners, and A's. It put them four games above .500 and moved them up to third place in the division. They were now 19-11 with Martin at the helm. The results seemed good enough for Steinbrenner.

"Some people might say it's Don Baylor's leadership or Dave Winfield's leadership that has turned this team around. Baloney, it's Billy Martin. He's a helluva manager," said The Boss.[53]

Steinbrenner even praised the performance of Winfield, with whom he often feuded, and said he was not concerned about the perpetually struggling Whitson. As the Yankees headed into the last month of play before the All-Star break, things finally seemed to be settling down.

THERE WAS ONE ISSUE, however, looming over both teams. In fact, looming over all of baseball. Since the advent of free agency a decade earlier, the tension between the owners and the players had become nearly unbearable. Owners, upset over the continuously growing strength of the players' union and escalating salaries, were doing everything in their power to stymie the impact of free agency. The players, after years of being tied down by the reserve clause—which forbid a player from playing for any other team unless he was traded or released—did not believe anything the owners had to say or offer.

It was a toxic situation. In 1981 a midyear strike nearly caused the cancellation of the entire season. Though it was resolved in time to save the year, it did little to ease tension between the two sides. Now, with the collective-bargaining agreement having expired at the end of 1984, negotiations were going nowhere fast. The owners wanted a salary cap. That was unacceptable to the players. The owners wanted changes to the arbitration process, which allowed a player to seek a salary increase through an arbitrator after two years of service. They felt that three years before arbitration was more fair, and that no player should be awarded more than double his previous salary. That was not something the players were eager to accept. Why should they not make whatever they were entitled to make? The players wanted the owners to contribute more than the $15 million a year they had been contributing to the player's pension fund. The players wanted $60 million. The owners thought $25 million was a fair enough number.

On May 23 with both sides making little headway, the executive board of the Major League Players Association authorized a strike. No date was set, and the action was in some ways standard procedure. It was an attempt to show ownership they were serious about negotiations and would not be pushed over. But it was also a brutal reminder of the 1981 work stoppage, which nearly crippled the game. Fans, not in love with either side, just wanted them to figure it out. Now that a strike had been authorized, it cast a pall over the rest of the season. Because now, no one knew what the rest of the season would actually be.

# 6

# The Russians Attack Atlanta

SAN FRANCISCO'S CANDLESTICK PARK was hardly anyone's idea of heaven. It was dreary and lifeless and possessed brutal wind currents that could knock players off their feet. Even on the hottest summer day it could still feel like you were playing an April exhibition match. A transparent outfield wall sometimes made it difficult to determine if a fly ball had landed before or over the fence. But for two days toward the end of May in 1985, Candlestick Park was heaven on earth for the Mets.

The team began their eight-game, three-city West Coast trip with a thrilling, come-from-behind win against the Giants. Trailing 3–0 in the eighth at a sun-splashed Candlestick, they strung together five hits, including a big two-out double by Gary Carter followed by a George Foster single to take a 4–3 lead. Roger McDowell closed out the game, and with the Cubs losing, the Mets, who had lost a few games in the standings when they had faltered at home, were now one game ahead of Chicago for first.

They closed out the short two-game set with a 2–1 win the next day, highlighted by the return of Dwight "Dr. K." Gooden, who, having lost two straight starts, took out his frustration on a Giants lineup that was overpowered and overmatched. Deftly mixing his blazing fastball with a devastating curve, Gooden struck out fourteen and went all nine innings as his parents sat in the stands. As they had the day before, Carter and Foster provided the big offensive hits, and the Mets picked up half a game over the idle Cubs. They were signs of fire in the team when Davey Johnson, still upset over Keith Hernandez getting ejected from the previous game over a third-strike call, was thrown out for arguing a foul ball. Johnson ended up missing the bottom of the ninth, when Gooden struck out the side, but the ejection showed his players he would stand up and protect them at all costs.

"I'll tell you this," said Giants catcher Alex Trevino of Gooden, "it's no fun to face him. His fastball looks great when it's coming in but then it winds up higher than you expect it to be."[1]

The team flew to San Diego, where Doug Sisk took a hard-luck loss in the first game. The loss, played on the last day of May, gave the Mets a 27-16 record heading into June, along with a half-game lead over the Cubs. People had expected the Mets to be good this year, but this may have even exceeded their expectations. They needed to keep the momentum going in June, and it looked like they would. On the first of the month, they overcame a 2-run deficit to come back and beat the Padres. McDowell—yet again—came in to rescue the team from a jam, providing two and one-third innings of solid relief. In the process, he did give up a run for the first time in twenty-three innings. He was tied with his teammate Gooden for the longest scoreless streak in the Majors that year.

Sisk got into the act when he saved the final game against the Padres.

"Sure, there was concern when Doug came in," admitted Hernandez. "There had to be."[2]

But Sisk preserved the victory—giving the Mets their first series win in San Diego in eight years—and the team moved on to Los Angeles.

After dropping a tough extra-inning loss in the opening game, Gooden faced off again against Fernando Valenzuela. Unlike their previous matchup at Shea, Gooden did not falter. With the score tied at 1 in the bottom of the eighth, he loaded the bases on two singles and a walk. In front of him stood three consecutive left-handed hitters: Greg Brock, Mike Scioscia, and Terry Whitfield. Rather than wilt, the twenty-year-old reared back and fired nine straight fastballs, striking out all three for his ninth, tenth, and eleventh k's of the game. It was the single most exhilarating pitching performance the Mets had seen in over a decade.

"This is the first time in my career I've ever seen a pitcher fire up an offense," said Hernandez. "But when we came in after the eighth, you just knew we were going to score. He had us all pumped up."[3]

Feeding off Gooden's energy, the Mets scored three in the top of the ninth, one off a Gooden single, to take a 4–1 lead. Gooden came out for the ninth, struck out one more Dodger for good measure—his twelfth strikeout of the game—and finished off his fifth complete game of the year. He now stood at 8-3 with a 1.72 ERA. Gooden's numbers were incredible, but what truly amazed everyone was the poise of this kid who still was not old enough to legally have a drink. Gooden never seemed to panic; rather, he appeared as if he knew he would simply pitch out of any jam by providing something his opponents had not seen yet.

"He's always got something on his hip, in his pocket, and he can reach back and get it. I've never seen anyone who could reach back so late in a game," said Davey Johnson after Gooden's performance.

The Mets lost the last game in Los Angeles, 2–1, but by winning five of eight, they had completed their most successful West Coast trip in ten years. While 5-3 may not seem overly impressive on its face, it was important to keep in mind that from 1979 to 1984, the Mets were 31-67 in games played in San Francisco, Los Angeles, and San Diego. Even for teams as bad as the Mets had been, a .316 winning percentage was especially horrific. The West Coast had been a place where the Mets flew to get their heads kicked in. This road trip showed that was all over. The Mets, struggling offense or not, were not only going to put up a fight, but now more often than not, they were going to win that fight. But as the Mets headed back east, they quickly realized they may have been better off playing the rest of their games in the pacific time zone.

FROM JUNE 7 TO June 16, the Mets played eleven games, four at home and seven on the road. They lost all but two of them. Returning home, they began a four-game series with the now streaking Cardinals. This was a different St. Louis team than the one they had played just a few weeks before. The Cardinals were now running—literally and figuratively—on all cylinders. Despite having only one legitimate power threat in the lineup, first baseman

Jack Clark, the Cardinals came to Shea leading the league in runs scored. Their team batting average, .273, was 45 points better than the Mets. Even though the season was not yet two months old, they had already stolen over one hundred bases, led by rookie Vince Coleman. Coleman and teammate Willie McGee were first and second in the league in stolen bases and runs scored.

The Cardinals had lagged early because their pitching had not yet come together. Now that was changing too. Joaquin Andujar, John Tudor, and Danny Cox were all finding their stride at the right time. As the Cardinals came to Shea, they trailed the Mets by five games.

Meanwhile, the Mets had persevered through a struggling offense and injuries thanks to solid pitching. But that could only last so long. Heading back home, their offensive numbers suggested a team more reminiscent of the '62 Mets than a team fighting for first.

"With one-third of the season gone, they [the Mets] started the weekend hitting .225 as a team, and only the San Francisco Giants had a worse average in the National League," wrote the *New York Times*' Joseph Durso. No regular was hitting .300, and three weren't even hitting .200. Gary Carter, the cleanup man, had gone twenty-six days without hitting a home run. Darryl Strawberry was hitting .215 when he tore ligaments in his thumb and went on the disabled list for two months. George Foster, a man with 321 home runs in his career, was batting .216. Ray Knight stood at .188. Howard Johnson, imported from the Detroit Tigers because of his bat, was swinging at .168.

The first game against the Cardinals could hardly have gone worse. With the score tied at 1 in the bottom of the seventh inning, Danny Heep hit a deep fly ball to right field. Thinking it was a home run, he began a slow trot around the bases. But the ball hit the fence, where right fielder Andy Van Slyke quickly turned and nailed Heep at second base. The score remained tied into the thirteenth inning. Sisk entered the game and promptly gave up 5 singles and a walk, eventually allowing six runners to score.

"Those who remained for the 13th inning . . . had a field day booing Sisk."[4]

The Mets fell 7–2, falling out of first place. The next day they were shut out by Tudor, putting together only three hits. They dropped a game and a half behind the Cubs. Playing a doubleheader that Sunday, only another solid performance by Gooden prevented them from being swept. Doc won the first game, improving to 9-3, only to watch teammates Terry Blocker and Heep collide in the fifth inning of the second game while chasing a Terry Pendleton fly ball. The bases, which had been loaded, cleared and Pendleton came all the way around for an inside-the-park grand slam. The Cardinals ended up taking three of four, gaining two games on the Mets.

Off the Mets went to Philadelphia, for what should have been a rejuvenating four-game set against the lowly Phillies. Philadelphia, just one full season removed from being National League Champions, were already fifteen games under .500, sitting second to last in the East. In theory, the Mets had an opportunity to beat up on a weak team and gain some lost ground. Instead, they limped out of town losing three out of four, including a historic beat down that no Mets team—not the '62 Mets, not any of the horrific late '70s or early '80s clubs—had ever endured.

The first game featured a single highlight: for the first time in almost two months, the Mets hit more than 1 home run in an inning. But it was not enough to surpass 6 runs from the Phillies against Sid Fernandez and Sisk. The second game featured a bevy of highlights, none of them for the Mets.

AS CLINT HURDLE DUG in to lead off the top of the third inning, the scoreboard at Veterans Stadium flashed a surreal sight: Mets—0, Phillies—16. It was not a mistake. The scoreboard guy had not hit the wrong button. The Phillies, thrashing the Mets in a manner not seen in decades, already had fourteen hits in the first two innings, more than the Mets had had in any single game in the '85 season. Von Hayes, entering the game 6 for his last 52, led off with a home run. Eight batters later, with the bases loaded and two out, Hayes hit a grand slam in nearly the same exact spot his lead-off home run had landed. To that point, there had been twenty-one times in baseball history where a player had homered twice in the same inning. But none had ever done it in the first inning, until now.

Almost more incredibly, Hayes had hit both home runs with a bat he had borrowed from teammate Jeff Stone. After hitting the second, Hayes found the bat had had a slight crack in the handle the entire time. Moreover, when Hayes dropped a fly ball later in the game, he still heard boos from the crowd. Such was life in Philadelphia.[5]

The beat down did not end there. Tom Gorman, having given up 6 runs, and reliever Calvin Schiraldi, having given up 10, were already out of the game when Hurdle came to bat. Schiraldi saw his ERA rise from 6.23 to 9.78 in a matter of minutes. The Phillies as a team hit for the cycle in the first inning and came a home run short of doing so again in the second. Before Hurdle had his first at bat of the game, Hayes was already 3 for 3 with 5 RBIS and 3 runs scored.

It kept going. The Phillies tacked on 10 more runs. Every starter in the lineup, including pitcher Charles Hudson, had at least one hit and 1 run scored. Including pinch hitters, only one player in the Phillies' lineup failed to reach base at least once. Dave Rucker, a relief pitcher who replaced Hudson in the sixth, went 2-2, accounting for 40 percent of his career hit total in just two innings. When Heep grounded into a double play to mercifully end the game, the scoreboard flashed: Mets—7, Phillies—26.

It was the worst defeat in franchise history—since eclipsed by a 25–4 defeat to Washington in 2018—and the worst beating any National League team had taken in over forty years. The Phillies, a franchise over one hundred years old, had never had that many hits—twenty-seven—or runs in one game. Naturally, a game with so many records and oddities would not be complete without some irony: The Mets recorded a season high thirteen hits, and the team's best pitcher that day was Sisk, who tossed two and a third innings of scoreless ball.

"I feel as though I've been through World War III," said Frank Cashen afterward. "I spent the last six innings writing imaginary headlines for the New York tabloids."[6]

"I have never been involved in anything like that in my life, not in Little League, not in sandlots, never," said Wally Backman. "It was like taking a bunch of six-year-old kids and beating them."[7]

Lamenting his team's loss to the Blue Jays that same night, Niekro noted there might be some saving grace for The Boss.

"But all wasn't bad for George today, 'cause the Mets lost to the Phils by a score of 26–7. I'm sure that the only disappointin' aspect of that game for George was that it wasn't on national TV."[8]

Davey Johnson was certainly not amused. He closed the door to the clubhouse after the game to address his team. Calmly standing in the middle of the locker room he told his players that this moment should serve as a wake-up call.

"Gentlemen, I know you are better than this," he told them. "When you play tomorrow, carry this game onto the field with you. When you go out on the field tomorrow, do not forget what happened here tonight."[9]

For one day, it looked like Johnson got his wish. The Mets came out the next day and smacked eighteen hits, a season high, along with 3 home runs, and won a big extra-inning game to stay three games out of first. But Jesse Orosco gave up a two-out, 2-run home run to Glenn Wilson in the eighth inning of the series finale, giving the Phillies the win and three out of four games in the series. The loss dropped the Mets into third place, now trailing both the Expos and the Cubs, with the Cardinals right behind them.

The team landed in Montreal early the next morning and arrived at the hotel at 3:00 a.m. Only a few hundred feet away sat the Chez Paris, one of the more upscale topless clubs in the city. Many players decided to undergo grief therapy in the club that night.

Carter was almost certainly not one of them. This Montreal series was supposed to be a feel-good return for Gary, instead of the team clawing to remain relevant in the East. Still, the focus remained on Carter as the Mets flew north of the border. There was not a person in baseball who was not aware of what Carter's former teammates had said about him. They had not even bothered to keep the grumblings private anymore. In spring training, someone cut out a newspaper article about Carter and posted it on the bulletin board in the Expos' clubhouse. Someone had taken a blue pen and underlined each time "I" or "me" appeared in the article. The total was eighteen.[10]

Stars like Tim Raines and Andre Dawson publicly expressed their joy at having seen "Teeth" shipped to New York. Carter's confidence, injected with joie de vivre, was seen as arrogance in Montreal. In New York, however, it was seen as the attitude of a winner who stuck it to opponents with his style of play.

"I came here from St. Louis in '83 with a bad rep, so I understand his situation," said Hernandez. "I think he's great. Nobody plays the game harder. His aggressive style is really appreciated here."[11]

Carter said all the right things. He did not think about what his former teammates said. He had no hard feelings about Montreal management. He was focused on the Mets and winning the division. But there were few people, if any, who felt Carter did not want to go back to Olympic Stadium and put a pounding on the team that seemed so ungrateful for all he had done.

Surely Expos fans still appreciated the effort of their former All-Star catcher. When Carter came up in the top of the second inning, his first at bat as a visiting player in Montreal, he received a standing ovation. Carter responded with a single, then singled his next two times up and walked his final two times up: 3 for 3 with two walks in his return home. Not bad.

"I appreciated their salute," said Carter. "The more I got on base though, the more annoyed they became."[12]

Carter's performance, however, was marred by the continuing struggles of the bullpen. Holding a 4–3 lead in the bottom of the ninth, Sisk walked the first two batters. Schiraldi came in and gave up a game-tying single. After inducing a double play, he was replaced by Orosco, who gave up a bloop hit to end the game. It was a crushing loss, costing Gooden his tenth win and, more importantly, they failed to pick up a game on the Cubs.

Sisk, now 1-5 with a 7.68 ERA, sat at his locker after the game, shaking his head. Davey Johnson, annoyed at a string of late-game, blown-save situations, made his displeasure known.

"My patience is wearing thin," said Johnson, referring to any reliever whose name was not McDowell.[13]

Johnson's lack of patience and mistrust of his bullpen, combined with an ankle injury to McDowell, contributed to the Mets' defeat the next day. Johnson relied on his starter to get him through the end of the game, but Sid Fernandez gave up a game-tying home run in the eighth inning. Then, in the ninth, with two outs, Fernandez allowed a double to Dawson and single to former teammate Hubie Brooks, giving the Mets their third straight defeat in an opponent's final at bat.

It was a jarring loss. Brooks, at first trying to shake it off as just another hit to win a game, quickly fessed up that it was more than just that.

"Well, it's gratifying to do something good against the Mets. A lot of people questioned my ability there," said Brooks.[14]

Revenge was sweet. Even sweeter in this instance because Brooks's hit knocked the Mets into fourth place in the division, now trailing the Cardinals, Expos, and Cubs.

Shortly after Dawson scored the winning run, Davey Johnson was on the phone to Cashen. "I was calling for help," said Johnson. "We can't keep going like this." Johnson then recounted everything wrong with the state of his bullpen. He paused, and, after drawing a deep breath, noted, "I'm not in the ideal situation out there, and that's a gross understatement."[15]

The Expos completed the sweep the next day, bashing Rick Aguilera for 6 runs in his first Major League start. The win, coupled with a Cubs loss, put the Expos in first place. At 1-5, it was the worst road trip in two years for the Mets and marked the first time during the season they were swept. Carter went 4-11 in his return to Montreal, but it was overshadowed by the losses, and the fact that Brooks now had more RBIS on the season than he did.

The Mets limped back home for a four-game series with the Cubs. Weeks earlier, this series had the makings of a playoff-style matchup, with the Mets looking to avenge their disastrous four-game sweep of the previous season. Now, with the Mets in fourth and the Cubs in second, the whole thing had lost some of its luster to the press and fans.

The Mets, however, viewed this series as critical. They were three and a half games out and on the bottom end of a four-team race for first. They had to start winning games. And if the bruising they had just taken in Philadelphia and Montreal was not enough, they were given new motivation in the form of Cubs starting pitcher Rick Sutcliffe.

Sutcliffe, who never shied away from commenting on, well anything, had been traded to the Cubs in June the year before. He proceeded to go 16-1, leading Chicago to the division title over the Mets, and winning the National League Cy Young Award despite pitching two months of the season in the American League. Confident in both his own and his team's ability, he was quoted in a story comparing the Cubs and Mets heading into the matchup. He predicted the Cubs would sweep, before adding that he would not trade the Cubs' catcher, Jody Davis, for Carter. Nor did he think the Mets were the team to beat in the National League.

Whether he was truly offended or merely looking to spark his team, Davey Johnson acted as if Sutcliffe had committed a grievous outrage against his club. He pinned the story to the clubhouse bulletin board.

"The Sutcliffe thing was an offense. I hung it up. It was better than any speech I could give," said Johnson.[16]

The year before, the Mets had been confident but possibly still unsure if the run for first was real or a flash in a pan. A year later, they were more than confident. They were now cocky. Almost any one of them could have given a similar interview saying the same kinds of things, and they would have viewed it as truth. Whether it insulted a player or a team was not their concern. But when someone did this kind of thing to them? Well that would not do at all.

So in response, the Mets went out and beat Sutcliffe and the Cubs in the first game, 2–0. Sure enough, Carter took Sutcliffe deep in the fourth for the eventual winning run. Jody Davis, meanwhile, dropped a throw home in the fifth, allowing the second run to score. Ron Darling went the distance for the shutout. Though he did not feel the Sutcliffe incident made any difference in his performance, Darling did not hide his feelings for Sutcliffe.

"Sixteen and one doesn't make him God," said Darling after the game.[17]

Then Ed Lynch stepped up with a complete-game win of his own, as Carter drove in 2 more runs for a 5–1 win. Not to be outdone, in the third game, Gooden threw his third shutout of the year. The starters were stepping up big time to give the beleaguered bullpen rest. Moreover, despite their recent slide, 51,778 fans came out to see Doc dominate the Cubs, the largest crowd at Shea in eight years.

A grand slam by Foster—with former President Nixon watching from the stands—sealed a victory in the final game, and even gave Foster the chance for a rare curtain call from the fans. After the game, Nixon visited the clubhouse with his grandson and took a few pictures with the players.

"You certainly know how to handle the press," the former president told Carter. "I didn't know much about that."

Hernandez, to whom Nixon had sent a copy of *Lee and Grant* the previous year with an inscription thanking him for his "indispensable leadership," asked the team's traveling secretary to set up a dinner with him. "We're both Civil War buffs. We'll talk about it and baseball," thought Hernandez.[18]

The Mets' four-game sweep of their rival—their first four-game sweep of the Cubs in fifteen years—put them in second place, just a half game behind the Cardinals, who had leapfrogged everyone to get the top spot. The four games had drawn over 172,000 people, the most for any one series in the history of Shea Stadium, and put attendance at over 1 million fans for the year. It was the earliest, by far, the team had achieved that mark. For the seven total games at home, they would draw over 306,000 fans, which was 41 percent of what the Yankees had drawn for the entire season.

Sure, the Mets had struggled, but the fans loved them, and they were loving them a whole lot more than the Yankees. And with pitching like that and the occasional big hit by Carter, they were fun to watch on any given night. On average, they were seeing 33,000 fans a game, 7,000 more a game than what the Yankees were drawing. At this pace, it was not unrealistic to think they might break the 3 million attendance mark.

"If the Mets attract three million customers, they will probably outdraw the Yankees by more than a million—an embarrassing difference that would make George Steinbrenner squirm more than usual, if not inspire the principal owner to new heights of hauteur," wrote Dave Anderson of the *New York Times*.[19]

The Expos came into Shea, and the Mets took the first game, with the crowd even cheering Sisk after a strong performance that gave him his second win of the year. It was an especially needed moment for Sisk, who was undergoing the kind of brutal treatment that would only be surpassed by a crosstown starting pitcher throughout the year. Doug was getting hate mail after hate mail, with one letter "written like a prescription. Take one Tylenol and one cyanide capsule—per day."[20] Sisk handled it in stride, especially because his win helped move the Mets into a tie for first. But it was short lived, and they would not see first place again for another six weeks. Montreal took the final two games, knocking the Mets all the way back to third place, two games out.

JUST AS THINGS SEEMED to be coming together for the Yankees, the armor started to chip. They reached five games over .500 with a June 3 win against Oakland. Then they lost eight of the next ten games, including three out of four in Milwaukee and two of three to the first place Blue Jays, who were surprising many by quickly overtaking the Tigers as the team to beat in the American League East. An off day on Thursday June 13 should have been relatively peaceful. It wasn't. So far, Billy Martin had lived up to his end of the bargain with Steinbrenner: off days saw team workouts. It was satisfying to the owner, and it kept Martin in his good graces. But the players were tiring of it.

"I disagree with all these workouts," said Don Mattingly. "The guys need a day off. They need to step back and rest for a day. It's a good time to look at things and get your head together. It's like getting a new start. You come here and you don't want to be here, and you get lazy in the field. You get into bad habits. Besides, it's too late to be working out. If guys don't know what do by now, then we have a real problem here."[21]

Mattingly's comments, while likely reflecting the feeling of most of the team, were almost immediately met by a stinging rebuke from Steinbrenner.

"If he's [Mattingly] fed up with these off-days it's too damn bad," said The Boss. "He ought to talk to the taxi drivers, to the steel workers and to the farmers in Indiana that are being laid off and losing their farms. Last year I thought he was a fine All-American boy. This year, with the incident in Kansas City, I've re-evaluated my opinion. He may not realize it, but his lack of hitting has killed us."[22]

It was an all-too-familiar tactic of Steinbrenner's. Trying to manipulate fans with some workingman-hero image. By now though, that shtick had backfired. Sure, there were many fans who thought players were paid far too much money. But Steinbrenner—born into money and privilege—just wasn't the right person to be delivering that message. Moreover, given the ridiculous kinds of contracts he had handed out over the last few years, few thought The Boss had a leg to stand on when it came to griping about money. Plus, Mattingly, while not matching his numbers of 1984, was hitting .288 with 44 RBIs by the first week of June. Steinbrenner considered someone on pace to drive in over 150 runs to be killing the team.

Not content to let Steinbrenner blow hot air alone, Martin got into the act as well.

"A lot of things have to be corrected here," said Billy, still bitter over a blown ninth-inning lead the night before. "We need to work on a lot of little things—rundowns, cutoffs, pickoffs. The other day, I asked the guys if they went over plays with the infield playing in and they said no. Well, what did they do in spring training? Can anybody tell me?"[23]

Martin, realizing how his comments were an obvious shot at his friend Yogi Berra, blamed this lack of spring-training prep work on Clyde King. It was hard to believe that he would blame the general manager for what drills the manager may or may not have conducted in spring training.

That, however, is exactly what Martin wanted the press, the players, and the fans to believe. When they did not, the next day he instituted a new rule: he would begin carrying a tape recorder with him, so every word he spoke he would have an accurate account of. Of course, the accuracy of his words was never really in doubt. And many of the beat writers had recorders as well.

That same day, not satisfied with browbeating the reigning American League batting champion, Steinbrenner shifted his focus to the other side of the diamond. Referring to the platoon of Dale Berra and Mike Pagliarulo at third base, The Boss called it the "biggest mistake of my life. I got two guys down there that have 11 errors between them and can't catch a cold with their bats. I'm beginning to feel now that I should have kept Toby Harrah."[24]

There was no denying that Berra, hitting .258 with 1 home run and 7 RBIS, and Pagliarulo, hitting .173 with 2 home runs and 16 RBIS, were struggling in their platoon situation. But the hyperbolic nature of Steinbrenner's comments was so ridiculous one would almost have to believe it was intentional. Somehow, his failed venture into the ABA, making illegal campaign contributions during the Watergate scandal, allowing Reggie to leave as a free agent, hell, even the trade to acquire Harrah (who put up worse numbers than Berra and Pagliarulo in his one season in the Bronx), all were lesser mistakes than this current platoon situation.

Yankees fans may have been bitter, but they still showed up. On Saturday, June 15, 55,623 attended a nationally televised game against the Tigers. It was the largest regular-season crowd since the stadium had been renovated in the early 1970s. Unfortunately for them, they saw the Yankees lose 10–8, dropping them below .500 again. It was, however, the last time the team would sit below that mark in 1985. With exactly one month to go before the All-Star Game, the Yankees put together a four-week stretch that made true believers of the baseball world.

IT STARTED WITH A walk-off win against the Tigers. Then they moved to Baltimore where it became the Rickey Henderson Show. In three games at Memorial Stadium, Henderson went 10-13 with 4 walks, 5 runs scored, and 5 stolen bases. Henderson, flourishing under Billy again, raised his average from .313 to .344. The Yankees, outscoring the Orioles 26–4, swept the series, their first three-game sweep in Baltimore in ten years.

"They're kicking me out of this town," said Henderson. "I've done enough damage here."[25]

In the process of sweeping the Orioles, Bob Shirley, forced into the rotation due to injuries, was named player of the week for his two impressive starts. At the hotel in Baltimore, his fellow teammates mockingly asked him for his autograph.

Though they lost three of four in Detroit, Henderson continued his tear, going 7-15 with 3 home runs and 4 stolen bases. Returning home, the Yankees swept the Orioles again. Henderson went 5-10 with 6 stolen bases. For the entire month of June, Rickey stole 22 bases while only getting caught once, and raised his batting average from .293 to .354. For his seven-game performance in Baltimore and Detroit, where he batted .607, he was named American League Player of the Week. There was still another half of the season to play, but Rickey was looking more and more like an MVP candidate with each passing game. Moreover, he was saying all the right things.

"I didn't come to the Yankees to win a batting title or set any stolen base records," Henderson said in the midst of his hot streak. "I came here to play on a winner and get to the World Series, that's all. If I win those titles and we win the World Series, fine. But the titles don't mean anything if we don't win."[26]

After sweeping the Orioles a second time, they took the first game against the Brewers at home. Ron Guidry, who pitched seven strong innings for the win, was gradually turning the season into his best in eight years.

Born in Lafayette, Louisiana, and known as "Louisiana Lightning" or "Gator," Guidry's career began with a bit of serendipity. Growing up an only child—his brother was not born until he was ten—Guidry's mother would not let him walk to a nearby playground by himself. One day when he was seven, he decided to sneak out, telling his mother he was visiting his grandparents, who lived across the street. He got to the playground to find a local team practicing. A misplayed fly ball ended up rolling all the way out to a snooping Guidry deep in left field. With everyone telling him to throw it back in, he heaved a toss that sent the ball all the way to the backstop.

"So when I looked up, the coach was running towards where I

was standing and I thought I had done something wrong. So I took off running," recalled Guidry.[27]

The coach turned out to be a naval reserve friend of Guidry's dad, who now wanted Ron to play baseball. The rest is history. Guidry, though not especially big by Major League standards, threw hard, eventually learning a slider from Sparky Lyle that was so devastating the Major League Baseball Network would later rank it as the greatest in big league history. After spending a couple of years pitching for the University of Southwestern Louisiana (now the University of Louisiana at Lafayette), the Yankees drafted Guidry in 1971. He made his big league debut in 1975 and appeared in a handful of games—all as a reliever, save one—for the next two seasons. But during the summer of '76, Guidry nearly quit the game for good.

He had made the team out of spring training, only to be sent down to the Minors just as they were about to leave Florida to start the season. The Yankees had just made a roster move that day and no longer had space on the club for him. Throughout the rest of the year he was called up only to be sent back down multiple times. After one demotion, he told his wife he was not going to report to the Minors. They were headed home. Guidry was tired of the back and forth, but worse, he was tired of not being given a chance to pitch when he was dying to get out on the mound.

As he and his wife were driving, they literally approached a crossroads: heading west on 1-80 in Pennsylvania, they could turn north on 1-81 to Syracuse, where the team's Triple-A club was playing. Or they could take 1-81 south and make their way back home to Louisiana. Guidry's wife, explaining she had never seen him quit anything in his life, convinced him to turn right and head north to Syracuse. A few weeks later, Guidry rejoined the Yankees, this time for good.[28]

Guidry emerged as one of the league's best starters in 1977, winning sixteen games as the team won the World Series. But in 1978, he put together one of the greatest individual seasons of any starting pitcher in the game's history. He went 25-3 with a 1.74 ERA, 248 strikeouts, and 9 shutouts. He set the franchise record for strikeouts in a season as well as a single-game franchise record when he struck out eighteen Angels in a June start. In his three losses, the team scored only 2 runs combined. He picked up another two wins in the postseason as the Yankees won the title again. At season's end, he easily won the American League Cy Young Award.

The succeeding seasons were good for Guidry but not as great. He was still pitching well, but as the quality of the team declined, he saw fewer wins. In 1983, he finished 21-9, leading the league in complete games. What seemed like a harbinger of more good things to come was derailed in '84 when he tore a rib muscle but pitched through the pain. He suffered his first losing season as a starter.

Heading into '85, Gator looked to utilize the lessons he had learned from teammates like Catfish Hunter and Tommy John on how to change speeds when necessary.

"What I started doing probably after '81, '82, '83 was I didn't rely so much on just raring back and throwing as hard as I could," said Guidry. "I learned how to kind of harness some of the power that I had. Not that I was throwing any slower. I was still topping out at ninety-four, ninety-five. But I didn't have to throw ninety-four, ninety-five every time I threw a fastball. I learned how to throw some ninety miles per hour, I learned how to throw some at eighty-five miles per hour. Not really changeups, just what we call dead-fish fastballs."[29]

The dead-fish fastballs were working. Guidry was now 9-3, showing that '78 form but without the strikeouts. Moreover, the win against the Brewers put him out 71-22 under Martin and 70-43 under all other managers. Guidry did not think that was a coincidence.

"He didn't just yank you out at the first sign of trouble," he said about Billy. "And when you have those tests, you learn how to get out of them. So, consequently, you might be losing a game 2–0 and all the sudden you get the bases loaded and you give up another 2 runs and its 4–0. But instead of taking you out of the game, he'd leave you in there, and all of the sudden your team comes back and you end up wining 5–4. And that's what was good about Billy. Billy was a pretty damn good manager."[30]

Guidry was not just reverting back to being the ace of the Yankees' staff. As senior member of the team, fellow players, especially pitchers, looked up to him and sought to learn from him as he had learned from Sparky Lyle. And while not boisterous like Reggie or chatty like Joe Cowley, Guidry had his outlets.

"Very quiet, but he loved to play the drums," recalled Marty Bystrom, a teammate of Guidry's that season. "He used to play the drums underneath Yankee Stadium. They had two drum sets set up down there and before the games he would come in early and play."[31]

Though they lost the remaining two games to the Brewers, the Yankees took two out of three from the first-place Blue Jays in Toronto. At one point during the series, their record was a half game better than the Mets, something that did not go unnoticed by Billy Martin. It was the first time they could claim a better record since September 21 of the previous year.

The Twins came to town on July 4, and the Yankees proceeded to sweep the four-game series, including both ends of a double-header on the 7th. Former President Nixon, showing no favoritism, was on hand to watch Winfield's walk-off home run in the first game. In the second game, Griffey drove in 6 runs but, still unhappy with his situation in New York, told the press afterward he did not feel like discussing his day. Additionally, during the July 4 game, a woman sitting in the box seats along the first base line was shot in the hand during the sixth inning. The bizarre crime was never solved as police were not certain where the bullet came from, and no one could remember anything like it ever happening at the stadium.

The Yankees then took two of three from the Royals, with Guidry winning his tenth game in a row, before the Rangers came in for a four-game series before the All-Star break.

The Yankees decimated the Rangers, winning all four games by a combined score of 27–9. In the second game, Ed Whitson hurled a complete-game shutout, his best performance of the season. The win put the Yankees into a second-place tie with the Tigers, the first time they had been in second since September 9, 1983.[32]

The next day, Phil Niekro picked up career win number 292 on Old Timer's Day. The clubhouse, so tense all year long, seemed loose, even fun. As aging, retired Yankees walked about, Niekro's teammates asked him what it was like to pitch against Honus Wagner (who last played twenty-two years before Niekro was born). Joe DiMaggio, normally standoffish and distant, decided to get in on the act.

"Not even Phil Niekro was alive when I started playing for the Yankees," said the Yankees' legend.[33]

Guidry finished the first half with a complete-game win, his eleventh victory in a row. The Yankees finished the first half 49-36, in second place and just two and a half games behind the Blue Jays.

The Yankees were loose and having fun. Winning can have that effect.

"Once we won a few, got into a groove, all that other stuff—the controversy that's always around here—quieted down," said Willie Randolph.

"The controversy usually starts when we lose a few and it makes things worse. Now we have a more workmanlike atmosphere. We're coming to the ballpark thinking baseball instead of that other stuff. And we feel we can beat anyone."[34]

Great performances by Henderson, Winfield, and Guidry had helped propel the Yankees leading into the break. But emerging as perhaps the best player on a team stacked with talent was Don Mattingly.

Born and raised in Evansville, Indiana, Mattingly had excelled at baseball and basketball in high school. Ultimately, baseball won out, with the Yankees taking him in the nineteenth round of the 1979 amateur draft. There was little question that Mattingly had talent. But he was certainly not thought of as a power hitter in the Minors. He was more a line drive guy, who would put up a good average and give you a lot of doubles by spraying the ball to all fields. Defensively, he was as solid as they came. But the Yankees had several first baseman in the system and at the big league level. So Mattingly spent time in the outfield too.

He grabbed a cup of coffee in the big leagues toward the end of '82. In '83, after Bobby Murcer retired, the Yankees called him up for good. He split time between first base and the outfield. His numbers were not overly impressive, but they were good enough to keep him on the big league team. When Berra became manager in 1984, he let Mattingly know he was going to be his first baseman. Moreover, Donnie worked with hitting coach Lou Piniella on generating more power with his swing. A guy like him, with that kind of that swing, was tailor-made to drive balls over the short Yankee Stadium porch in right field.

It all came together. Mattingly led the league in batting average, base hits, and doubles. He popped 23 home runs and drove in over 100 runs, finishing fifth in MVP voting. And his defense at first was spectacular, surpassed only by the guy playing first over in Flushing. There were high hopes for Mattingly going into 1985.

The season, however, had not started off well for the reigning American League batting champ. The previous year's accomplishments had created high expectations, but a spring-training injury slowed him down once the year started. Henderson's being injured also robbed him of a top-of-the-order presence who could set him up with RBI opportunities. Plus, after a season in which he displayed enough to power to hit 23 home runs, Mattingly had gotten away from hitting the ball to the opposite field. His numbers through June 11—a .285 average with 6 home runs and 44 RBIs—were nothing to be embarrassed about but not what he expected of himself. They certainly were not what Steinbrenner wanted, and the first baseman and his owner tangled in the early going.

In mid-June, however, Mattingly adjusted his swing and began hitting the ball in all directions.

"Basically, I am seeing the ball a little better and I'm not trying to pull it as much," said Donnie. "I'm hitting the ball where it's pitched. . . . When I don't try to pull everything, I see the ball better and it works for me."[35]

From June 22 to July 12, Mattingly hit in twenty consecutive games, raising his average from .289 to .315. By the end of the first half, thanks in part to Henderson setting the table for him, Mattingly led the American League in RBIS with 69.

Despite all the turmoil, the Yankees were in great shape heading into the second half of the season. Henderson, Winfield, and Mattingly were headed to the All-Star Game. Guidry was pitching like it was 1978. Even Whitson seemed to have finally found his groove. Most importantly, despite some hiccups, Billy Martin had largely kept it together. There was little to no indication he was drinking to excess. He had not gotten into any fights. He had avoided any negative statements about Steinbrenner. The same reporters who had lamented his return just two months earlier were now singing his praises.

"You begin with Martin," wrote the *New York Times*' Michael Martinez, "a man whose style and temperament have made him less than beloved among many players, most reporters and some fans. But Martin, who is in his fourth tenure in the Yankee dugout, injected a daring and an aggressiveness that Berra's club lacked."[36]

THE METS, AFTER LOSING two in a row at home to the Expos, moved on for a six-game road trip: three in Chicago, three in St. Louis. If they stormed through these two cities, they could take back first place heading into July, where the remaining four series before the All Star break pitted them against some of the league's lesser teams. Even if they simply split the six games, they would still keep themselves afloat in the race.

Gooden appeared to set the pace with yet another complete-game win in the first game in Chicago. It was the Cubs' thirteenth consecutive loss. But the next day, Chicago came to life in more ways than one. They clubbed McDowell for 2 big home runs including a Ryne Sandberg shot in the seventh. When McDowell followed the Sandberg home run with an inside pitch to Gary Matthews—though just how inside was a matter of debate— Matthews threw down his bat and took a few steps toward the mound. The umpires prevented any further incident, but after

Matthews walked, Kelvin Chapman decided to inform him of just how not close the pitch was. The two started jawing and the benches emptied, though no fights ensued. The Cubs went on to win.

Matthews was clearly trying to fire up his team, which had gone two weeks without a win. While Davey Johnson seemed to know that, he still took the bait.

"If he thinks we were throwing at him, then he doesn't know a damn thing about baseball," said Johnson. "If I were the pitcher, I'd have burned him on the next pitch. His hat would have left his head, and he would have been flat on his back."[37]

Whereas outbursts like this from Billy Martin were getting tiresome, and seemed indicative of Martin's inability to simply walk away from a fight, from Johnson it was almost refreshing. The Mets, so long the doormat of the National League, needed this kind of fire in their belly. Still, in this instance, it was an overreaction, one that gave the appearance that it was the Mets who were just coming off a thirteen-game losing streak.

Sutcliffe beat them in the finale, giving the Cubs two out of three games for the series. The Mets fell two and a half games behind the Expos. Even Strawberry's return to the lineup in St. Louis did not do much to help the offense. The Mets scored 3 runs combined in the series, wasted yet another solid performance by Gooden, and were swept out of St. Louis. The offense, which for weeks had struggled to gain any momentum, only got worse. Over the five losses to the Cubs and Cardinals, they failed to send more than five hitters to the plate in any one inning. Their last nineteen hits were all singles. Perhaps worst of all, the one person who had been producing offensively, Hernandez, was now enduring the worst slump of his career. He was 2 for his last 25, and 7 for his last 57. Hernandez's average had fallen from .280 to .251 in just two weeks.

"I'm killing this team," said Hernandez after being swept by the Cardinals. "I'm in a dark forest, deep foliage, no sun."[38]

The sweep, coming at the end of June, knocked the Mets five games out of first. They were now in fourth place—behind the Cubs,

Expos, and first-place Cardinals—and their record had dropped to 38-34. The team was happy to leave June, a month in which they had gone 11-18, behind. They welcomed July, and a three-game home stand with the lowly Pirates, with open arms.

THE METS MAY HAVE welcomed July in theory, but the first game of the month just seemed like an extension of June. No offense, crippling injuries, and now, displeasure from the home crowd. Against the Pirates—the worst team in the National League—the Mets managed only 6 hits, and were shutout 1–0.

"Maybe it's time to do something illogical," said Davey Johnson after the game, referring to an offense that had scored 1 run—an unearned run—in their last thirty innings.[39] The team went twenty-three innings without an extra base hit, and had not stolen a base in eight games.

The fans, tiring of the lack of offense, booed throughout the night as the Mets continued to falter at the plate.

"It's like a morgue on the bench," added Johnson. "We're getting great pitching but it's just unbelievable the way things are going offensively."[40]

More bad news came. Mookie Wilson was undergoing shoulder surgery, putting him out for the next two months of the season.

The Mets' season was teetering on the brink. They were now just three games over .500, competing with three other teams for the top spot. Their offense, which included three players who would hit more than 300 home runs in their career, was failing in all capacities. How bad was it? The *Star-Ledger*'s Dan Castellano wrote a column wondering if the Mets may have been better off not making the Carter and Johnson trades. A Mets fan was quoted in that same paper saying, "Triple-A players have got to be better than [George] Foster and [Doug] Sisk anyway."[41]

The shine was starting to wear off, even if fans were still coming to Shea. Something had to give, or the Mets' season—so full of hope that opening day seemed like Game One of the World Series—would be over before the All-Star break.

Finally, in the second game of July, something gave. The Mets "exploded" for 5 runs, including putting together extra-base hits in the same inning for the first time in over a week, and beat the Pirates 5–4. It ended their six-game losing streak and prevented them from falling even further behind the Cardinals. The next night—even though it was a Wednesday—saw a crowd of 46,220 watch the Mets bash the Bucs again, 6–2. Foster led the way with a 3-run home run in the first inning and Lynch, the forgotten man in the rotation, threw a complete game. For the first time in nearly two weeks, the Mets won two games in a row. They ended the short home stand and flew out to Atlanta, where they began an eleven-game road trip to end the first half of the season. Little did they know on the plane to Georgia that not only were they about to start the most successful road trip in team history, but that they were about to play a game so bizarre it would end with residents thinking the Russians were bombing Atlanta.

BRAVES FANS HAD BEEN promised fireworks after the July 4 matchup between their hometown team and the incoming Mets. Atlanta, seven games under .500, was going through one of just many subpar seasons in the '80s. They had talent in players like Dale Murphy and Bob Horner, but for the most part, they were a team that provided wins for competing teams in the National League. In spite of that, here on the United States' 209th birthday, almost forty-five thousand had come out to Atlanta Fulton County Stadium, mostly to see those fireworks. What they got instead was one of the craziest regular-season games in baseball history.

It began with rain, and a lot of it. The start of the game, supposed to take place at 7:40 p.m., was delayed eighty-four minutes. When play finally began, both teams were off to the races. The Mets put up three singles, a double, and a walk in the top of the first, but they managed to come up with only 1 run. The Braves answered in the bottom of the inning when Claudell Washington led off with a triple against Gooden and scored on a groundout. Then, in the bottom of the third, the rain came pouring down again. Despite a runner on first, the umpires called out the ground crew and play stopped. The delay lasted forty-one minutes, long enough for Davey

Johnson to decide not to have Gooden go out again. He replaced him with McDowell. There had now been over two hours' worth of rain delays, and despite only being in the third inning, the game was almost into July 5. Moreover, parts of the field were so saturated that they would stop the ball dead in its tracks.

McDowell promptly gave up 2 runs, putting the Mets down 3–1. But in the top of the fourth, the Mets put up 4, retaking the lead. Meanwhile, as the game progressed into the eighth inning, Hernandez had already hit a double and a triple. Now, against Steve Shields, he lined a ball down the right-field line for his fifth home run of the year. The Mets' first baseman was a single short of hitting for the cycle.

But would Hernandez get the chance for that single? In the eighth inning, with the Mets ahead 7–4, Orosco walked in a run and left the bases loaded for Sisk, who gave up a 3-run double to Dale Murphy. Like that, the Mets trailed by a run going into the ninth. But they did not give up. With one out and two runners on, an infield single by Dykstra plated the tying run. When the Braves failed to score in the bottom of the ninth, the game moved to extra innings.

Through the first nine innings of the game, there had already been:

Two rain delays totaling more than two hours

Nine pitchers used by both teams, only one of whom did not give up a run

The one pitcher who did not give up a run (Sisk) was still charged with a blown save

A player who was a single short of the cycle

Four lead changes

A fly ball out that was never caught (Murphy slid for a Hernandez line drive that ended up behind him, but he fooled the umpire into thinking he had the ball the entire time)

A protest from the Mets over McDowell's placement in the lineup when he entered the game

Yet the craziest elements still had not taken place. Sisk and Braves reliever Terry Forster traded scoreless innings until the top of the thirteenth. With two outs, and the clock at the stadium showing 1:53 a.m. on July 5, HoJo drilled a 2-run home run to left field, giving the Mets a 10–8 lead. As he crossed the plate, Johnson embraced Ray Knight as if the two had just gotten through some sort of dramatic, life-threatening ordeal in which they had both come out alive. It was only HoJo's third home run of the season, and his first as a right-handed batter in almost two months. All the same, the Mets now had the lead and were ready to put this game behind them.

Tom Gorman came in to relieve Sisk and close things out. After a leadoff single then two quick outs, he had an 0-2 count on the Braves' Terry Harper. Gorman delivered a breaking ball over the heart of the plate. With the clock showing 2:03 a.m., Harper sent the ball flying into the left-field foul pole. The game was tied at 10.

"Threw an 0-2 forkball on him, and he hit it down the line," recalled Gorman. "High towering ball and it hits the foul pole to tie it up. So I was pretty pissed about that."[42]

They had to play on . . . and on . . . and on. The game reached the top of the eighteenth. Mookie Wilson, just out of the hospital after his shoulder surgery, had been home watching the game. At some point, he fell asleep. Waking up in the middle of the night and seeing baseball still on the screen, he assumed the game had been delayed, and they were showing a replay from another night. Or maybe his pain medication was making him see things.[43]

By this point, Hernandez had long since gotten his single, becoming the fourth Met to ever hit for the cycle. And it was no coincidence that Hernandez was crushing the ball this game. That morning, he had called his father, as he often did, to discuss hitting. Recently they had been trying to come up with ways to get Hernandez out of his slump. On this call, his dad told him he had found something after reviewing old tapes from the Cardinals years.

"He has discovered that my stance has gradually opened, until now, he believes, it's too open," wrote Hernandez. This means, in essence, that Hernandez was pulling away from the ball as he swung, rather than staying square toward it. His dad used to be able to see both digits of his uniform number on his back when he swung. Now he could only see the one closest to the pitcher.

Hernandez did not believe his father at first. He had his mechanisms down. At this point, it was muscle memory. He planted his feet in the box the same places he always had. His dad must be wrong. Nope, says his father. The tapes showed clearly he was opening up. "Do me a favor," says his dad. "Tonight, just try hitting with your right foot about one foot-length ahead of your back left foot." Hernandez agreed. The results spoke for themselves.

As exciting as that all was, it was now a mere afterthought. When Davey Johnson and Strawberry got ejected in the seventeenth, no one seemed to care, even the umpire. Strawberry disputed a third-strike call from home plate umpire Terry Tata.

"I turned to [Tata] and said, 'That was low,' as I started walking towards the dugout," Strawberry said. "He followed me and said, 'It's 3 a.m., that pitch is a strike.'"[44]

The Mets just wanted to get this thing over with and go home. When HoJo scored on a Dykstra fly ball to give the Mets an 11–10 lead in the eighteenth, it looked like finally—mercifully—the game would come to an end. When Gorman got the first two outs in the bottom of the inning, all that stood between the Mets and their hotel beds was Braves reliever Rick Camp. The pitcher had been a reliever, and at times a starter, for Atlanta since the late '70s. Camp was a good pitcher, and on a better team, he may have put up a few more wins than his record eventually showed. One thing, however, was indisputable: Camp was no hitter. In 167 career at bats leading up to this moment, Camp had ten hits. His .060 lifetime average, matched with an average of one strikeout per every two at bats, was, even for a pitcher, horrific.

But Atlanta had no position players, or even other relievers, on the bench to pinch-hit for Camp. Left no choice, they sent him to the plate, down 1 run and with two outs.

"If he hits a home run to tie this game," said Braves radio announcer John Sterling, calling the game for the Turner Broadcasting System (TBS), "this game will be certified as absolutely the nuttiest in the history of baseball."

Camp strode up to bat, and Carter stood up from the behind the plate and emphatically waved the outfielders in, as if Camp was the ninth batter in a Little League lineup. Gorman quickly got two strikes, making Camp look overmatched in the process. In the stands, though no one could count for sure, it appeared only a few hundred of the forty-five thousand now remained. The scoreboard showed 3:22 a.m. as Gorman wound up and delivered a fork ball. Camp waited, swung, and crushed the ball, sending a drive to deep left field. Almost immediately, Knight, playing third base and with a clear view of the ball off the bat, lifted his hands in disbelief. As it cleared the fence, left fielder Heep put both hands on top of his head, as if to exclaim what everyone watching was feeling: "I don't fucking believe this!"

The few fans left went crazy. Sterling screamed, "Holy cow! Oh my goodness! I don't believe it! I don't believe it. . . . That certifies this game as the wackiest, wildest, most improbable game in history."

Dykstra dropped to one knee in the outfield. Hernandez could not even bring himself to look in Gorman's direction. The Mets just wanted this to be over. How the hell could this happen?

"[The reporters in the press box] were like screaming in agony and laughing," said Bob Klapsich, covering the Mets for the *New York Post*. "It was alternating between sheer panic, like you couldn't believe what was going on, and in some weird way appreciating that this is a once-in-a-lifetime phenomenon that would never happen again."[45]

"Let me put it this way," said Gorman decades later. "I don't watch TBS on Fourth of July that much because every time I do I usually see myself and go 'don't throw that pitch!'"[46]

The game was tied, and they had to play on. Gorman got out of the inning, and they moved to the nineteenth. There, the Mets showed they finally had had enough. Knight, who to that point had left nine runners on base, doubled in a run. Heep knocked in 2 more, with a third scoring on an error. Before they were done, the Mets scored 5 runs, breaking out to a 16–11 lead.

But even a 5-run lead in the bottom of the nineteenth was almost not enough. The Braves scored 2 runs, and had two runners on when Camp came to the plate again as the tying run. This game had been so over the top ridiculous, that it was not improbable—in fact, at this point, it seemed highly likely—for Camp to hit yet another two-out, game-tying home run. Darling, however, making his first ever appearance as a relief pitcher, was not going to allow another magical moment. He blew Camp away on a high fastball to end the game at 3:55 a.m. The Mets had won the most bizarre, improbable game in regular-season history, 16–13. Even though their team had lost, the few fans still remaining stood and gave a standing ovation to the clearly exhausted players on the field.

Just how incredible was this game?

Gorman, who pitched six innings of relief to get the win, gave up 2 two-out home runs to tie the game. In fact, Gorman never actually maintained a lead he was given in his six innings.

Fourteen different pitchers were used, yet the only two pitchers who did not give up an earned run were the two pitchers with the highest ERAS of anyone who took the mound that night: Sisk and the Braves' Gene Garber.

Thirty-seven total runners were left on base.

The only players not used by the Mets were Ronn Reynolds, Fernandez, Lynch (who had pitched the day before), and Aguilera (who was pitching the "next" day).

Carter caught all nineteen innings.

Hernandez hit for the cycle, but Carter also had five hits—the first time in his career he had done so—as the Mets set a team record of twenty-eight hits.

Eleven players on both sides collected at least three hits, including someone at every infield position for the Mets.

The game itself took six hours and ten minutes to play, but if rain delays are included, it took eight hours and fifteen minutes from the scheduled start time to play the game.

No game in Major League history had ended later than this one.

Nielsen ratings indicated that when Camp struck out to end it at 3:55 a.m., 284,700 homes were still tuned into the game in the New York metropolitan area.

"It was the most unbelievable game I have ever seen or been involved in," said Hernandez. "At the 17th inning, I figured I just had to call somebody. I called my brother Gary and told him I just wanted him to know I was still out here playing."[47]

"I thought I had seen it all," said Gorman, referring to the Camp home run. "When you throw a pitch in the 18th inning that someone can hit out, it's embarrassing. But then, I've never pitched before at 3:30 in the morning."[48] Gorman had now won the opening day game, the eighteen-inning marathon against the Pirates, and this game.

The craziness of the night (and morning), however, did not end with the final pitch. Atlanta fans had been promised fireworks to honor the country's birthday. Granted, that day had now passed, but the Braves organization wanted to make good on their word. And so, at 4:01 in the morning of July 5, fireworks lit up the Atlanta sky.

Those still in attendance loved it. Those who had long gone to sleep and had no clue what had happened did not. The sudden explosive bursts so early in the morning caused some people to panic. This was, after all, a tense period of time in the Cold War. The threat of nuclear war, real or imagined, seemed real to millions of Americans. So when Atlanta residents heard loud booms rippling through their city, some assumed the Russians were attacking.

"Oh, fuckin' Atlanta," said Backman when asked about that night decades later. "I remember it very well. I played that whole god damn game."[49]

Approximately nine hours after the game was supposed to start, the Mets stumbled back to their hotel rooms.

"You were out partying, weren't you," said Aguilera as his roommate, Fernandez, walked in the door at 4:30 a.m. Aguilera had gone to bed early, resting up for his start the next day. He had no idea what had occurred.[50]

Just as the sun was rising, many of them fell asleep. After all, they still had a game that night.

Hours later, as players arrived at the field, the buzz was still about the previous day's game. Players stood around and swapped war stories about how crazy the night had been. Many had gotten little sleep that morning, but were still moving on the adrenaline of the game's events. If the Mets were tired at all, they certainly did not show it. They came out swinging, scoring 6 runs in the first three innings, one coming on Backman's first home run of the year. Aguilera, the only person on the team to actually get any sleep, went the distance, providing the bullpen a sorely needed rest. The Mets won their fourth in a row and moved to within three and a half games of first, jumping past the Cubs into third.

On Sunday, July 7, they took both games of a doubleheader, giving them a four-game sweep of the Braves. It was the first time the Mets had swept a four-game series on the road since September 1979. The offense, sluggish for so long, put up 34 runs in the series. It was led by the rookie Dykstra, filling in for the injured Mookie. In Atlanta, Dykstra reached base in 12 of 26 plate appearances, stealing 3 bases and scoring 5 runs. He was the sparkplug the top of the lineup had been missing for some time.

The only bad news was that Knight sustained a pulled groin. It was incredibly bad timing for Ray, who raised his average 26 points in the Atlanta series and looked as if he was finally finding his groove. He missed almost all of the rest of July.

The offensive explosion continued in Cincinnati. Strawberry hit his first home run since returning—his first since the end of April—a high shot over the wall in left-center. It gave the right fielder a boost of confidence he needed and was a hopeful indication that he would begin to carry some of the offense.

"When I got hurt," said Strawberry, "I think the other guys put too much pressure on themselves to try to carry the team. With me back, they can relax a little more."[51]

Hernandez, Johnson, and Foster also went deep, the first time in over two years the team hit 4 home runs in a game. The Mets won that day, and the next, and then the next, sweeping the Reds. In the process Gooden—despite losing eight pounds because of the Cincinnati humidity—picked up his twelfth win, Hernandez and Foster homered again, and the Mets added 20 more runs to their offensive output.[52] They had won nine straight, the longest streak for a National League team that season and the longest for a Mets team in nine years. Their seven straight road wins was something no Mets team had ever done on one road trip before. Nor had they ever swept a series at Riverfront Stadium.

The Mets moved to Houston for the final four games before the All-Star break. Their winning streak came to an end in the first game, noteworthy when Astros pitcher Nolan Ryan fanned Danny Heep for his four thousandth career strikeout. Though their streak was over, the Mets shook it off, taking the final three games through a combination of great pitching and the occasional big hit. Appropriately, Gooden finished off the first half of the year with a complete-game, 1–0 shutout victory. At 10-1, it was the most successful road trip in franchise history.

The Mets went into the break with a 50-36 record, sitting in second place just two and a half games out. Considering all they had been through, it was a minor miracle. They had lost numerous key players, including their biggest bat, and the offense had sputtered to '62 Mets proportions. But they were in the thick of the hunt. Foster, maligned by the fans throughout the season, led the team in home runs and RBIS. Carter, despite numerous dings and scrapes, had provided clutch hit after clutch hit. Hernandez, after enduring the worst slump of his professional career, was on fire. He won the National League Player of the Week award, hitting .519 with 2 home runs and 7 RBIS, before the break. And most impressive of all was Gooden.

Heading into the break, Doc's record stood at 13-3. He had not lost a game in nearly two months. His ERA of 1.68 was the best in the game. His 153 strikeouts, almost one per inning, led the Majors. His four shutouts also led the Majors and were the most by a Mets pitcher in one season in nine years . . . and it was still only the first half. Moreover, people constantly kept referring not just to Gooden's ability, but his composure and intelligence on the mound. He was not just a thrower: Doc knew how to dissect hitters—he knew how to pitch. Just before the final game of the first half, Hall of Fame pitcher Bob Gibson said of Gooden, "People keep comparing him to me, which is more flattering to me than Gooden. I didn't feel I knew how to pitch until I was 26. At 20, I didn't know anything."[53]

Gooden, Carter, Strawberry, and Darling were headed to the All-Star Game. Strawberry received the third highest vote total for any National League player, a testament to how good he had been in his first two seasons. Straw would reach base and score twice. Carter, nursing an injured knee, did not play in the game, nor did Gooden, resting after his start in Houston, or Darling. It was clear though: the days of the Mets having token representation in the All-Star Game were long gone.

THE PLAY OF BOTH the Mets and the Yankees had the city buzzing. The Mets had one more win than the Yankees, but the same number of losses. They were both two and a half games out of first place, but were nipping at the heels of the Cardinals and the Blue Jays. The Mets' mix of experience (Carter and Hernandez) along with youth (Strawberry and Gooden) was electrifying fans and sending them to Shea in record numbers. The Yankees' mix of experience (Winfield, Baylor, and Guidry) along with youth (Mattingly, Henderson) was reassuring fans that had grown tired of years of discord and a failure to win.

The Mets looked like a team ready to take the next step. But would they encounter another second-half collapse like the previous year? The Yankees looked like a team ready to make a postseason run. But would Martin keep his demons at bay long enough to guide them to the playoffs?

ON MONDAY, JULY 16, as fans were getting ready for the midsummer classic in Minneapolis, the Players Association made an announcement: if no agreement with the owners could be reached, a strike would commence on August 6. That was three weeks away. Three weeks for both sides to reach some resolution or risk crippling the game for a long time, perhaps forever. While both sides publicly stated they felt an agreement could be reached, in reality things had gotten no better. The owners still felt the players' demands were unreasonable. The players still did not believe the owners' claims of poverty. They had three weeks to figure it out.

# 7

# Hospital Management

THE BEGINNING OF THE second half brought hope to the Mets. For the second straight year, they emerged from the break in the thick of pennant race. But now, they were a year older and a year wiser, and had additional talent that had been lacking in 1984. The Cubs seemed to be fading fast, living up to Wally Backman's spring-training prophecy about several players having to repeat career years. The Expos, however, did not look like they were going away any time soon. And the Cardinals' style of ball, which could have come from the playbook of Billy Martin, was bound to make them the team to beat in the final two and a half months of the season.

In Flushing, however, the Mets were focusing on themselves. Something had awakened in this team. Some thought it was the marathon game in Atlanta.

"I truly believe it brought us closer together as a team," said Wally Backman. "The game was so crazy, to have gone through it and to wind up winning it got us on the right track."[1]

Others thought it was the return of Darryl Strawberry, helping alleviate the pressure on some of the other big hitters in the lineup. Whatever it was, the Mets were playing ball more cohesively and successfully than perhaps at any other time in their history. The start of their second half saw them face the same teams they had just run over on their previous road trip. Then they would welcome the Expos for a big three-game series to close out July.

Playing the Braves at Shea for the first four games, the offense showed no sign of reverting to its June slump. Trailing 4–1 in the first game, the Mets put together a 5-run rally through a series of walks, singles, fly balls, and errors. They were taking advantage of mistakes in a way that had eluded them just a month earlier. Ron Darling moved to 10-2, and they picked up a game on the Cardinals.

After a tough loss, they mashed Braves pitching in a 16–4 drubbing. Strawberry hit 2 home runs, including a grand slam, and drove in a career-high 7 runs. It was the team's fourth grand slam of the year, their highest single season total since 1973. HoJo, Danny Heep, and Clint Hurdle each added home runs, the first time in fifteen years and only the fifth time in team history the Mets hit 5 home runs in a game. Gooden's record moved to 14-3, and he became the first Mets pitcher in six years to win eight straight decisions.

The offense would not let up. The following day, they outslugged the Braves 15–10 in a sloppy affair played in front of over fifty thousand faithful at Shea. George Foster, perhaps feeling warmth from the fans for the first time in four years as a Met, drilled another home run and boosted his team-leading RBI total to 51. It was the first time the Mets scored double-digit runs in back-to-back games since 1976, and the most runs the team had ever scored in consecutive games. Moreover, the slugfest showcased one of the many feel good stories for the team that year in the person of Terry Leach.

OCTOBER 1, 1982. THAT was the last time Terry Leach had won a baseball game. The submarine style pitcher from Alabama had a happy-go-lucky way about him, and he needed it for the early part of his career. Drafted by the Red Sox in 1976, signed by the Braves as a free agent in 1977, released by the Braves in 1980, and signed by the Mets a few days later, he did not actually get to the Majors until 1981. He was a twenty-seven-year-old rookie on an incredibly bad baseball team. He pitched well, but not well enough to make the team out of spring training in 1982. Terry was called up in June, made a handful of appearances, and with the season long since over, made his only start of 1982 in the third to last game of the season. Against the Phillies at the Vet, Leach pitched ten innings of one-hit baseball, winning a 1–0 shutout. It is the only time in Mets history that a pitcher has thrown a ten-inning one-hitter. Even with that bit of notoriety, he did not see Major League action again for over two years.

In the time between that October 1, 1982, shutout performance and his July 21, 1985, start against Atlanta, Leach was traded by the Mets to the Cubs, then from the Cubs to the Braves, released by the Braves, and then signed again by the Mets. He had made seven appearances in relief before Davey Johnson tagged him to replace an ailing Ed Lynch against Atlanta, the team that had twice released him. Leach decided 1,024 days was long enough without a win.

"I'm in the two year and four month rotation," joked Leach after the game when asked if he would remain a starter.[2]

Taking three out of four from the Braves put the Mets within a half game of the Cardinals. But the momentum was tempered when the Reds came in and swept all three games, the first time that had happened to the Mets at home in '85. Mustering only 3 runs in the series, it looked for a moment as if the offensive woes might be returning. The fans certainly took notice, booing a team they had been lustily cheering for weeks now. When Kelvin Chapman, filling in for a resting Backman, made a few questionable defensive plays, chants of "We want Wally" went up in the crowd.[3]

Ron Darling referred to it as the "Jekyll and Hyde season." After being shut out by rookie Tom Browning, Davey Johnson was left shaking his head.

"Either feast or famine," he said. "You'd like to get something in between 15 runs and zero runs."[4]

As if to remind them of what they had just accomplished, in the middle of the sweep, Strawberry was named National League Player of the Week for his four-game performance against the Braves.

The sweep cost them three games in the standings, but a four-game series against the Astros provided a quick remedy. Gooden, despite allowing 2 home runs in one inning for the first time in his career, went the distance in the first game, moving his record to 15-3. Carter hit a big, late-inning home run to give the team the lead. A pumped-up Carter high-fived anything in sight after crossing home plate. The crowd wanted him back out of the dugout, in a scene that had played out countless times that year and would continue to do so for the rest of the decade. The curtain call had happened before in baseball, and certainly with the Mets. But in 1985 it became a requirement of any player after a big moment. Some did not like it and gave half-assed waves to the crowd before disappearing from view. Others, however, loved it. And no one loved it more than Carter. With the crowd beckoning him yet again, he jumped up the dugout steps and enthusiastically pumped his hand high into the air. It was easy to see, in that moment, why other players and even some teammates disliked Carter. It was also easy to see, in that moment, why hometown fans loved him. His was an energy not seen at the ballpark in years, perhaps ever.

In addition to Carter's heroics, Keith Hernandez picked up two more hits, moving his average up to .290. In the previous eighteen games, Keith improved his average 39 points, and it was no coincidence the team was 14-4 in that stretch. Carter, Strawberry, and Foster all provided the pop, but it was Hernandez that the Mets truly needed to make their offense run.

The second and third games, played as part of a Saturday doubleheader before fifty-one thousand towel-waving fans at Shea, saw the Mets pound the Astros, 16–4 in the first game and 7–3 in the second. It was the most runs the team had ever scored in a doubleheader. The ambush came with help from nearly everyone, as ten different players drove in at least 1 run over two games. Knight and Johnson, the third-base duo that had struggled so much throughout the season, drove in 6 runs. Perhaps the biggest hero, however, was Jesse Orosco. The lefty pitched three and two-thirds innings, striking out four and winning the first game while saving the second.

This kind of effort was no surprise to anyone who had been around Orosco long enough. Jesse had clawed his way into the Majors through grit and determination. A native son of Santa Barbara, California, like seemingly every Met, his father had been a semipro ballplayer. He started playing baseball with the kids of other players on his father's team. It did not take too long to notice he had talent. A hard throwing lefty with a good breaking ball was pretty much destined to make it to the Majors.

Drafted by the Twins, Orosco was one of the few players to be traded to the Mets in the 1970s who was actually happy about it.

"I wasn't really familiar with what was going on yet," he recalled about the trade. "I was still young, and my guess was the Twins don't like me, so we will see what happens with the Mets."[5]

The Mets tried making Jesse a starter, but it was not his comfort zone.

"They just felt like they wanted to have one more lefty [starter], so I told them I would give it a try, but I just wasn't built to be a starter and my record showed it," said Orosco.[6]

After a few years shuttling back and forth between the Majors and Triple-A, Orosco settled into the big leagues for good in 1982. His seminal moment came on July 8 when, after nearly blowing a late lead to the Cardinals, he shut down a potential rally to save the game. Jesse credits then-manager George Bamberger with boosting his confidence enough to stay in the Majors.

In 1983 Jesse was the surprise hit of the pitching staff. He won thirteen games out of the bullpen, and finished third in the National League Cy Young Award voting. His performance gave Frank Cashen enough comfort to deal Neil Allen away for Hernandez. Orosco followed that up with a career-high thirty-one saves in 1984. He averaged sixty-one appearances and almost one hundred innings over those two years, showing he was more than just a lefty-on-lefty pitcher.

"Heart as big as a lion," said Mel Stottlemyre of Orosco. "He wanted the ball in tough situations. He had an outstanding curveball, which the whole league knew. But it was such a big sweeper that it was very tough to hit. Nobody in the league during that period of time had a curveball like Jesse's, which made it real tough on the hitters."[7]

Jesse's role as closer was somewhat diminished with Roger McDowell pitching as well as he was. But that did not matter much to Orosco. Closer or not, he just wanted to do his job, whatever it may be.

THE METS LOST THE last game to the Astros. Despite taking three out of four games, they were no closer to first place. The Expos were up next, a big three-game series with the team right on their heels in the division race. Montreal was only a game behind the Mets and four and a half back of the Cardinals. They could come to New York and make a statement about who was really going to challenge the Cardinals for first.

A statement was certainly made, but by the Mets. The rookie Rick Aguilera took a shutout into the eighth inning in the first game, guiding the team to a 3–2 win. Aguilera, the guy called up to help fill in for a slew of injured players just seven weeks earlier, was now a vital component of the Mets' starting rotation. His latest effort gave him a 3-1 record and a 0.89 ERA in July. Not bad for someone who, when Davey Johnson managed him in the Minors, thought he might have trouble competing in the big leagues.

"He used to pace around on the mound, all jittery and nervous," said Johnson. "But he's all business now. And very early in things, he got over being intimidated by the league."[8]

Dwight Gooden took control in the second game, in more ways than one. Not only did he dominate the Expos, throwing a five-hit shutout while striking out ten more batters, but he sent a message that he would protect his teammates. In the fourth inning, Expos pitcher Bill Gullickson sent an 0-2 pitch high and tight to his former teammate, Carter. The pitch came close to hitting Carter in the head, though it missed him. The crowd was irate at this challenge of their beloved catcher. And while Gullickson said he was just doing what good pitchers do—owning the plate—it crossed the minds of more than a few people that it may have been a message from a club filled with players still annoyed with the behavior of their former teammate.

Gooden, though he possessed more composure than your average twenty-year-old New York baseball star, knew full well what he was supposed to do. No one was going to challenge his catcher like that, certainly not a team trying to catch them in the standings. Fortunately for Gooden, Gullickson was set to bat in the top half of the next inning. When he came to the plate with two outs, Gooden sent the first pitch, a ninety-five-mile-per-hour fastball, sailing just over his head. Both benches were immediately warned, and no further incidents occurred. But the message had been sent: this was not the old Mets. This was a strong, cohesive team that—even if not all the personalities exactly meshed—was going to protect one another. No questions asked.

"I go to my face a lot. Some moisture must have gotten on the ball. The pitch just got away," said Gooden after the game.[9]

Everyone knew the real story, and certainly no one in the Mets' clubhouse objected. Not only had Gooden tied a team record that night by winning a tenth consecutive decision, but he had earned the respect of his teammates and the trepidation of the rest of the league that had to face him.

The following afternoon, the Mets completed the sweep with a 5–2 win. Carter, with a badly aching knee, started the game despite having also caught the night before. He did not care. He just wanted to play and sent Davey Johnson a note before the game saying as much.

"I said in the note that I really wanted to play, and I said, 'please.' I signed it, 'Love, The Kid,'" said Carter.[10]

Though he would not admit it, certainly the chance to help sweep his former team, and after being thrown at no less, played a role in Carter wanting to play. His insistence paid off for the Mets. Carter's sixth-inning home run turned out to be the winning run.

The sweep brought an end to the month. The Mets' 21-7 record made for the best July in team history. They had started the month in fourth place, five games out. Now they were in second place, just two behind the Cardinals. Hernandez, mired in the worst slump of his career as July began, had had his greatest single offensive month ever. He raised his average 40 points, had 8 game-winning RBIS, hit safely in 24 of the 27 games he played in, and batted .517 with runners in scoring position. The effort earned Hernandez the National League Player of the Month, the first Mets non-pitcher to win the award in ten years.

The Mets' three-game sweep of the Expos all but eliminated Montreal from the division race. Carter's former team would never leave third place for the rest of the year. The Cubs, meanwhile, put up their second-straight losing month. Their season was all but finished. Their last gasp was a four-game series at Wrigley against the Mets to start off August. It was almost the same scenario as a year earlier when the Mets came to Chicago a half game out of first and left devastated by a four-game sweep. As the Mets flew to the

Midwest, certainly many of them were having flashbacks to that dreary August week. And if they were not, the press were certainly happy to remind them of what happened.

EVEN THE ALL-STAR BREAK, a three-day period in which he had nothing to do but sit back and relax, caused Billy Martin agita. Martin, who detested the game, watched only one inning of the '85 matchup between the American and National Leagues. It just so happened that inning was the fifth inning, when the Astros' Nolan Ryan came in high and tight to Henderson, sending Rickey to the ground. An inning later, Ryan did the same thing to Dave Winfield. Martin was incensed. "I don't like my guys getting decked by a .500 pitcher," said Martin, though at the time Ryan was 239-212 in his career. Martin may have also harbored some lingering resentment over Ryan's refusal to pitch for him in the 1977 All-Star Game.

Martin did not just target Ryan or the National League. He also went after American League manager Sparky Anderson for leaving Henderson in the game for five innings. Henderson had been bothered by a sore left ankle, and Martin did not want him aggravating it in an exhibition game.

"Rickey had a note from our doctor," said Martin. "I guess Sparky can't read. I wonder if Sparky ever got that note. I noticed that a couple of his players . . . didn't even go because of injuries."[11]

Two days later, the Yankees started the second half with a fifteen-game Midwest road trip. After losing the first game in Minnesota, Martin was back to blaming the Metrodome for his team's performance.

"If it wasn't for the kind of artificial turf they have here, the balls wouldn't have bounced that true and the runners would've have been safe," said Martin, laying blame on the stadium for the fact that four Yankees got thrown out on the base paths.[12] "I don't care if we win the next three games. I'll still stand here and say this is a shit ballpark."[13]

Shit ballpark or not, the Yankees won the next three, pulling them within a game and a half of first place. It would be nearly seven weeks before they were that close to first place again. The Yankees flew into Kansas City and lost all three games. Perhaps most disconcerting, Martin began to show signs he might be unraveling. The first sign was a standard tactic: publicly admonishing his starting pitchers.

Martin was seemingly infatuated with demonizing any pitcher who gave up a home run, or even a base hit, when it was an inopportune time to do so. He became obsessed with calling pitches from the dugout, especially for pitchers he did not trust. Rich Bordi, a reliever acquired from the Cubs that offseason, was one such pitcher, despite his having performed well overall. Martin became irate in June when Bordi gave up a first-pitch home run to Seattle's Al Cowens that ended up being the game-winning run. He would tell Bordi that "you think you have a good fastball, but you don't" and demand that Bordi throw sliders. "Every time you throw a fastball I am going to fine you $100," Martin told him. Bordi would ignore the directives, throw fastballs, and then, if they resulted in a hit, would claim they were sliders that he just left up.[14] Such was life as a pitcher under Martin: you had to lie about what kind of pitches you were throwing.

In the first game against Kansas City, Dennis Rasmussen endured the wrath of Billy by blowing a 3–0 lead. "I'm not very happy with what he did," Martin told reporters after the game.[15]

Like many of his teammates, it had not been an easy ride for Rasmussen. Growing up in Southern California, as a teenager he nearly lost his left foot in a bicycle accident. Suffering a compound dislocation of the ankle, Dennis would be forever grateful to Dr. Morris F. Skinner, the surgeon who was able to save his foot without amputation.

Rasmussen played forward guard for Creighton University's basketball team before committing full-time to baseball. Drafted by his favorite team, the Angels, he was playing winter ball in Venezuela in November 1982 when he read in the paper that he had been traded to the Yankees. A year later, Rasmussen was traded back to the West Coast in a deal that sent him to the Padres. Then, just at the end of spring training in 1984, he came back to the Yankees in the Graig Nettles trade. The team brought him up as part of its midseason youth movement, and Rasmussen performed well, winning nine games in twenty-four starts.

There were high hopes for Rasmussen heading into 1985. Like many of the young players, while he appreciated his manager's ability to make things happen on the field, he did not have the easiest time adjusting to Martin's style.

"I think he would have been happier playing the game without pitchers, or not ever having to deal with pitchers," said Rasmussen of Billy. "I don't think pitchers were his favorite guys."[16]

Rasmussen pitched well throughout the season's first couple of months but failed to generate much run support from his teammates. After blowing the lead to the Royals, his record stood at 3-5. While not representative of how he was pitching, his failure to keep the lead rankled Martin. Even worse, it rankled the team's owner.

Little did Billy know as he expressed his anger that earlier in the game, Howard Cosell, broadcasting the matchup as part of ABC's game of the week, announced that if Rasmussen failed to perform here, he was getting sent down to Columbus. Cosell, a confident of Steinbrenner's, no doubt heard about this possible demotion from The Boss himself. Word got back to Rasmussen, who promptly went out and surrendered the lead.

"Then when he gets into the clubhouse, the TV is on and he hears Cosell say that he's probably gone," recalled Phil Niekro.[17]

Rasmussen was banished to Columbus, yet again, the next day and would not to see Major League action for another eight weeks.

In the third game, Joe Cowley gave up 3 home runs on route to a 5-3 loss.

"He gets me mad," said Martin about Cowley. "I was asking him why he was letting them jack the ball out of the park. Then he'd get mad and strike a guy out to show me what he can do. Why doesn't he show me before they hit the homers?"[18]

But Martin's breakdown signals did not end there. The second sign was a common one: he began attacking the umpires.

"The umpire had a brutal night. A brutal night," said Martin about home plate umpire Nick Bremigan. "A guy who calls a game like he called tonight behind home plate isn't going to be around here much longer."[19]

The team moved on to Texas, where they lost two of three to the Rangers. A blown save by Dave Righetti in the final game ended Ron Guidry's twelve-consecutive-game win streak and pushed the team seven games back of first place. But that game was more notable for what was happening off the field. That Sunday morning, Martin had been complaining about back spasms. The Rangers' team doctor gave Billy an injection just below his right shoulder to help alleviate the discomfort. As the Yankees fell behind 7–0 in the second inning, Martin started having trouble breathing. At first, it seemed that the 105 degree Texas heat might be getting to him. But fearing something more serious, Martin left the dugout and was brought to a local hospital. There, they determined that the injection had actually collapsed Billy's right lung. The doctor, by his own admission, had misjudged the thickness of Martin's chest wall.

Billy's injury was not life threatening, but he was in severe pain. Most importantly, a change in air pressure could seriously harm him. That meant he had to stay behind as the team traveled to Cleveland for a rare five-game set with the Indians. Martin sat in an Arlington Memorial Hospital bed recuperating. In his absence, Lou Piniella would serve as acting manager.

It was certainly not how Piniella imagined he would begin his career as a big league manager. "Sweet Lou" had been a Yankees mainstay for years. The 1969 Rookie of the Year, Piniella was acquired by the team in 1974 and quickly became a fan favorite. A good hitter with occasional power, Piniella also had a temper and intensity to match anyone who had played on the Yankees before, including Martin. He was a key component of the 1977 and '78 championship teams, and hit over .300 in twenty-two World Series games. Piniella was not just a great player, he had the unique ability of both getting along with Steinbrenner and being able to joke with and about him where others would not dare. Steinbrenner, in turn, loved Piniella's intensity and his ability to live up to big pressure situations.

When Berra became manager in '84, he asked Piniella to become the team's hitting coach. Though still an active player, he jumped at the chance. Injuries had forced him to retire two months into the season, but they allowed him to focus full-time on coaching. He worked especially hard with Don Mattingly, getting him to use his lower body and lower batting hand to generate more pop. Mattingly hit 23 home runs in 1984, a burst of power few were expecting.

Players loved Piniella, but it was odd when Billy took over and said he would be grooming Lou to succeed him. Billy was essentially managing while training the guy who would take his job on how to take his job. Piniella, caught off guard, did his best to prevent any appearance that he was trying to force Billy out.

Now Lou sat in the visitors' dugout at Municipal Stadium—the depressing colossus on the banks of Lake Erie—ready to temporarily take charge. Only it was not that simple. With the Yankees, it never was. From 1,400 miles away, Martin was keeping tabs on the game by calling into the dugout every inning. He called Piniella before the first game and dictated the lineup to him. Butch Wynegar, on the disabled list with an injury, would pick up the phone, give Billy an update and relay any suggestions to Piniella.

The selection of Wynegar as the go-between was an odd one, given the contentious relationship between him and his manager. Martin was notoriously hard on catchers, but few earned more wrath from him than Butch.

"I had trouble with Billy because he was a master second-guesser," said Wynegar. "God rest his soul, you know I don't like talking negative about him. But if somebody hit a curveball, he is screaming and yelling it should have been a fastball. And if someone hit a fastball, he is screaming and yelling it should have been a curveball."[20]

Eventually, Wynegar confronted Martin in his office after a game against the Twins. He was tired of Billy's second-guessing and irrational behavior. From now on, Wynegar told him, you can call every pitch in the game. Martin, knowing better than to take the bait, backed down, but Wynegar believes the incident cost him playing time down the stretch.

A Winfield home run and another strong start by Ed Whitson gave the Yankees an 8–2 victory in the first game. Piniella was presented with the game ball afterward by the players.

The next day, the tri-state area papers were filled with the same picture of Wynegar, the receiver in his right hand while his left hand covered his left ear, listening to Martin's instructions.

"He called about eight or nine times [that first game]," said Wynegar, "usually about once an inning. If there was nothing going on, he'd say, 'Okay, I'll call back.' If there was someone on base or certain situations, he'd tell me to tell Piniella something."[21]

That process, arduous as it was, gave way to even more problems. Seeing what was happening and hoping to throw Martin off, Indians president Peter Bavasi decided to have some fun. He instructed the switchboard operator, anytime Martin called, to send him to the Indians' dugout instead of the Yankees. Bavasi's plan worked, but not enough to upset Martin.

"When the operator connected him with our dugout, he just called back a few minutes later," said Bavasi. "She said he was very polite. He just said, 'My dear, would you please connect me with the right dugout this time.' That doesn't sound like Billy. He must have been sedated."[22]

The Yankees won the first game of a doubleheader the next day. Then things went bad, fast. At some point in the middle of the first game, Martin could no longer get through to the Yankees. Others were doing it for him, claiming to be Billy and even, in one instance, Steinbrenner.

"It was people calling up the Indians, asking for the dugout and saying they were Billy Martin. I guess the circuits were so busy that he couldn't get through," said Cowley.[23]

But the real calls from Martin, when he got through, were far weirder than the fake ones. It became apparent that Billy had left the hospital and was calling from a bar.

"By the third day he is slurring on the phone to me," said Wynegar. "And we have a pitching change or a long delay and so I am just sitting there with the phone to my ear and not talking to him. So finally I hear, 'Butch?' and I said, 'Yeah Billy?' And there is a long pause like he is gathering his thoughts, and he goes, 'Why don't you like me too much?'"[24]

Wynegar explained he liked Martin, but Billy did not believe him. At one point, Wynegar could barely hear Martin over the loud music playing in the background. Then, when talking directly with Piniella, a clearly inebriated Martin asked why all the players on the team hated him.

The Yankees dropped the second game of the doubleheader and lost the next day as well. The crank callers were still reaching the dugout. Martin got through just in time to talk to Wynegar as the Indians' Pat Tabler laced a bases clearing, 3-run double.

"He wasn't too thrilled about that," said Wynegar. "That was the last time we talked to him."[25]

Players began to laugh at the insanity of it all, and Piniella saw that he had little to no control over the club. He was just four games into his managerial career and already overwhelmed by all of it: the calls; the crank calls; the postgame questions; wondering if Billy would be irate over some decision. Piniella wasn't even out of his first series yet, and he seemed to encounter all the carnival like attributes that came with managing the Yankees.

Cleveland, the worst team in the league, won the final game to take three out of five and drop the Yankees eight and a half games out of first place. As they stood at the baggage carousel at Newark Airport after getting back from Cleveland, Piniella told Moss Klein he was finished. Lou, prone as a player to making claims of quitting the game for good whenever he felt frustrated, seemed deadly serious. Klein told him to take the night to sleep on it. Piniella told him he meant it and that he would not see him at the stadium the next day for the start of their home stand. Piniella was finished with this circus.

True to his word, Lou was nowhere to be found the next day. When Steinbrenner called him at home, Piniella unloaded.

"I didn't sign up for this, getting caught up in this firestorm for four days in Cleveland," he told The Boss. "It became a joke and took all the fun out of the game for me."[26]

Eventually both Steinbrenner and Martin were able to talk him out of it, and Piniella's "retirement" lasted just one day.

Piniella was probably better off missing that day. The Yankees, minus a hitting coach, and badly battered after their 6-9 road trip, returned home to Yankee Stadium on Friday, August 2 for a three-game series against the White Sox. Before the start of the first game, Mark Connor was fired as pitching coach and replaced with Bill Monbouquette. Martin openly made it known it was not his decision. The Yankees pitching staff had given up 59 runs over the previous eleven games, and the team was losing badly. In yet another classic Steinbrenner move, someone had to pay the price for this performance. When it couldn't be a manager, it was always a coach. So the axe fell on Connor. It was the eighteenth pitching coach change under Steinbrenner's reign. It had been five years since a pitching coach even lasted a full season with the Yankees. And it was the first act of Billy IV committed by Steinbrenner that went against Martin's wishes.

Once the game started, it was the third-base coach, Gene Michael, who came into focus. The score was tied at three in bottom of the seventh inning. With Bobby Meacham at second and Dale Berra at first, Henderson drove a ball deep into the gap in left field. It looked like, at the very least, a 2-run double or even triple. But Meacham, who initially went back to second to tag, pivoted to instead go to third, and fell down. Berra, running on the play, came up right behind him, almost like it was a relay race. Rather than stop, Berra continued right behind Meacham as they both broke for third base. Michael tried sending Meacham while telling Berra to stop at third, but the two were so close to each other that they could not differentiate between signs. Instead, they both charged home. Michael threw his arms up in disgust. White Sox catcher Carlton Fisk received a perfect relay throw from Ozzie Guillen in plenty of time to tag Meacham, who, trying to pry the ball out of Fisk's mitt, merely grazed the catcher. Meacham went sprawling into the ground behind home plate. Fisk, the ball now in his bare hand, was temporarily spun around by the glancing blow, but with Meacham out of the way, he had enough time to set himself, stretch out, and tag Berra with the ball. Berra tripped over Fisk's left leg and joined Meacham on the ground. Both looked up in disbelief. It was your typical 8-6-2 double play, one that has been replayed time and again on highlight shows since that night in 1985.

"New York baserunners appeared to be filming a Keystone Kops comedy last night at Yankee Stadium," wrote the *Star Ledger*'s Rich Chere.[27]

Meacham went back into the dugout and awaited the storm he was certain was coming.

"I was shocked and I can remember getting back to the dugout and thinking Billy is going to kill me," said Meacham. "Just sit there and be quiet and just take it. He is just going to kill me. Billy was going crazy, and he was just screaming and yelling and he was yelling at Dale. And I am just waiting for it, thinking he was going to yell at me, and he never did."[28]

While fans booed Meacham and Michael, Martin put the blame squarely on Berra.

"The play was right in front of him and we've got our top hitters coming up. My God, you've got to do a little thinking on that play," said Martin.

Asked if he'd ever seen a play like that before, Billy replied, "No and I hope I never see one again. I've never even seen one like that in grammar school."[29]

Looking back years later, Berra did not agree with Martin's assessment.

"He got thrown out," said Berra, referring to Meacham, while also emphasizing that he loved his former teammate. "He was the lead runner and got thrown out. How'd that happen? He didn't run."[30]

The base-running gaffe would not have been so painful if the game had not remained tied and gone into extra innings. There, the Yankees eventually lost in the eleventh. A win the next day by Whitson only tempered the bleeding because the Yankees were about to commit the ultimate sin. They were about to be the victims of a historic day at the hands of one of the greatest Mets players of all time.

IN 1985 THERE WAS no greater pitcher in Mets history than Tom Seaver. In fact, there was no greater player. "Tom Terrific" was the 1967 National League Rookie of the Year. Then he won twenty-five games in 1969—a team record that still stands—and took home the Cy Young. It was first of three he won with the Mets. By 1977 Seaver held every single starting pitching record you would want to hold for the franchise. But he was a great player on a bad team. And he was feuding with ownership. At the trade deadline that year, he was shipped off to Cincinnati. An emotional Seaver cried as he addressed the New York media before leaving for his new team.

Seaver returned to New York in 1983, still a good pitcher, the Mets still a bad team. Regardless, it was the feel-good story of the season. His 9-14 record was more reflective of a lack of run support than his own performance. Tom Terrific could still pitch, and now he was only twenty-seven wins away from the magic three-hundred-victory mark. Though the Mets were moving more toward youth, what a story it would be for Seaver to win his three hundredth in New York. But an internal decision to protect younger players resulted in the White Sox nabbing Seaver as a free agent compensation pick. To that point, Tom had set half a dozen different pitching records, including most seasons with two hundred or more strikeouts and most season opening day games pitched and won.

In Chicago, Seaver put up fifteen wins in 1984. He had eleven more in 1985. Now, on Saturday, August 4, 1985, Tom Terrific, perhaps the most beloved member of the Mets ever, took the mound at Yankee Stadium, staring down the Yankees, George Steinbrenner, and history. He was sitting on 299 career victories. It was almost too perfect to be real.

Cowley, opposing him that day and trying to have fun, sent Seaver an autographed baseball before the start of the game. It read:

"Congratulations on winning No. 300 next week in Chicago."[31]

Over fifty-four thousand flooded into the stadium on a beautiful Sunday afternoon. By the time the game was over, it felt like most of them were Mets fans.

SEAVER WAS NOT ESPECIALLY sharp to start, giving up three hits and a hit batter in the first four innings. Down 1–0 in the top of the sixth, the Sox rallied for 4 runs off Cowley and Brian Fisher and staked Seaver to a 4–1 lead. Seeing that they were just twelve outs from history, thousands of people in the stands, many who were politely applauding for Seaver earlier, were now openly advocating for a Yankees loss. Seaver retired ten straight hitters going into the eighth inning, and with every recorded out, the crowd began cheering even louder for him. And every now and then, you could even hear the occasional, "Let's Go Mets" chant. In the eighth, when Seaver allowed two runners to get on base and faced the tying run with two outs, the fans actually booed when Sox pitching coach Dave Duncan went to the mound for a visit. They wanted Seaver in the game, and they wanted him to win it. It was an astounding display that previously would have been unthinkable. It certainly did not go unnoticed by a certain someone sitting in the owner's box.

Seaver got out of the eighth inning without any harm. Before heading back out for the ninth, he leaned out of the dugout so he could talk to his daughter Annie, then seven years old.

"Got to get three more outs, Annie," he told her.

"Good," she replied. "Then we can go home and go swimming."[32]

His daughter may not have been enthused, but just about everyone else watching was on the edge of their seat, including former President Nixon, who stood in the owner's box as the drama unfolded heading into that last inning.

In the ninth, Seaver allowed a single and a walk to bring the tying run to the plate with two outs. Don Baylor, pinch-hitting for Meacham, just got under the first pitch he saw. Rather than a dramatic game-tying home run, he sent a lazy fly ball to left field, where it was easily caught. Seaver crouched down with his rear sticking out toward the first base line, pounded his glove, and then was engulfed by his teammates. The crowd began chanting, "Sea-ver! Sea-ver!" Along the façade of the upper deck, someone had unfurled a sign reading "Tom is God."

Seaver was the seventeenth pitcher to win three hundred games. But more remarkably perhaps, the greatest pitcher in Mets history, the first to win three hundred games after pitching for that franchise, had achieved this historic moment while on the mound at Yankee Stadium, in front of throngs of cheering supporters, most of whom were Yankees fans. For a few hours, Yankee Stadium just as well could have been confused for Shea.

This love for Seaver and his historic moment ended at the entrance to the Yankees' clubhouse. Though the team had purchased an engraved silver bowl to present to Seaver after the game, Martin and Steinbrenner emitted nothing but misery after the historic event. Billy, who paced around the clubhouse afterward, attacked a favorite target: Cowley.

"He's got good stuff, but he's too timid," said Martin. "When you're on that mound, you've got to be aggressive. I'm disappointed because I think he should have won that game.[33]

If Martin was mad, Steinbrenner was apoplectic. His team lost; they were on the wrong side of history; and they were on the wrong side of history to the most prolific player the Mets ever had. But most of all, he was livid because of what he had seen in the stands: Yankees fans openly cheering for their team's loss, and all for the benefit of a former Met.

Rather than take it out on the fans, which The Boss would rarely if ever do, he took it out on his players.

"I respect the hell out of Tom Seaver but I don't like to lose," said Steinbrenner in the clubhouse afterward. "And I don't know if losing bothers all my players as much as it bothers me and Billy. I wish it did. I'll never accuse Dave Winfield of giving less than 100 percent but Mr. Cowley was certainly less than spectacular."[34]

The statement, full of anger and awkward praise, mixed with lashing criticism, was pure Steinbrenner. It lumped him and Martin together as the only two people on the planet who seemed to care about the future of the Yankees, a compliment that Billy could have either loved or seen as the kiss of death depending on circumstances. It praised Winfield, but just weeks later, Steinbrenner would bash him with one of the most memorable nicknames in team history. And it attacked a young pitcher who, though full of potential, was failing to live up to what was expected of him.

Fisher, who gave up 2 runs after relieving Cowley, was horrified when, after the game, Steinbrenner came storming into the clubhouse. He braced himself for a tongue lashing he was certain would end with his demotion to the Minors.

"He went right past me and started yelling at Joe, you know, not throwing strikes, blah blah blah, and he goes right past me. . . . He stops and goes, 'You are okay kid, just keep throwing good.'"[35]

According to Niekro, behind closed doors, Steinbrenner let loose on Martin.

"Let's go Mets! Let's go Mets! What the fuck, Billy? Your guys didn't even look like they were tryin' out there? And why, Billy, why does it always fuckin' happen here? Perry and fuckin' Seaver! Perry and fuckin' Seaver, Billy! I hate to be the fuckin' answer to some fuckin' trivia question!"[36]

Steinbrenner was referring to Gaylord Perry, a one-time Yankee, who had won his three hundredth game against them in 1982, though Perry did that at the Kingdome in Seattle, not Yankee Stadium.

But facts did not matter in that moment. What mattered was that the Yankees had now lost ten of their last fourteen games and were nine and a half games out of first place. The day after Seaver's historic moment, they beat the Sox to salvage a split of the four-game series. But with the strike deadline looming the next day, and the rest of the season left in uncertainty, 1985 was shaping up to be a disappointment on just about every level for the Yankees.

WOULD THE METS FALTER at Wrigley again? It sure looked that way when the Cubs won the first game, 2–1. Then the next day, clinging to a 1-run lead in the bottom the eighth, the Cubs successfully executed a suicide squeeze to tie the game. When Hernandez, fielding the bunt from Chris Speier, turned and flung the ball to first base, no one was there, and the go-ahead run scored. Hernandez returned to the dugout after the end of the inning and smashed several objects in disgust.

That play, however, revealed more about Hernandez than fans at home could see. Reading the situation before it happened, Hernandez had theorized that a bunt was coming. Rather than look at the third-base coach, he kept his eyes on Cubs manager Jim Frey.

When the count went to 2-1 on Speier, Hernandez noticed Frey ran-domly touch the bill of his cap with his right hand. The squeeze was on. There was no doubt in Hernandez's mind. Slowly he came in toward home. Davey Johnson told him to step back. Hernandez trusted his instincts, but decided to take one step back to placate his manager. Sure enough, the bunt came down.

"Davey and I are probably the only ones in the park who know that if I had held my ground before the play, instead of moving back that one step, I would have had [Richie] Hebner at the plate."[37]

It was quintessential Hernandez. Always analyzing. Always play-ing out the possibilities. Trusting his instincts over those of every-one else on the field.

Down to their last out in the ninth, it looked like 1984 all over again. The crowd, some of whom had pelted Orosco with debris while he was warming up in the bullpen, was exultant. They could feel another four-game sweep and a chance to get back into the race coming on. As Backman strode to the plate, Hernandez, standing in the on-deck circle and still smarting from the suicide squeeze, called out to him.

"Get on base, give me a shot," he told him.

Backman obliged with an infield single. Hernandez then drilled an inside slider from Lee Smith down the right-field line, scoring Back-man easily and tying the game. The crowd went quiet. To that point, it was the biggest hit of the season for the Mets. Had Hernandez got-ten out, it is possible the team would have gone in a completely dif-ferent direction over the remaining two months. Instead, they played on into the tenth. And with two outs in the top half, HoJo, the man accused of failing to come through in big situations in Detroit, hit a ball against the wind into the first row of the right-field bleachers. McDowell closed out the game, and the Mets had a 5–4 win.

"Last year, after blowing that lead in the eighth, we would have died on the vine," said Davey Johnson after the game, noting the clear difference between his '84 team and this one. "But we're a different club this year, a much more confident club. To come back against their ace [Smith], who was pitching in the shadows, and tie the game, we all just knew we were going to win."[38]

Confidence. It was a word that would come to define the Mets for the rest of the decade. By the time the '8os were done, it would have a negative connotation. It would be more about arrogance and, well, just being assholes, than about the feeling of actually being able to win. But here, in 1985, it was the first time that word could truly be used to describe a Mets team. Nineteen-eighty-four had shown them they had the talent to win. But 1985 was telling them more than that. They did not just have the talent to win, they *were* going to win. They were going to beat you, and there was nothing you could do about it. The offensive hiccups of June had been outliers. This was the real team. Gritty, gutsy, and in your face. You do not like the curtain calls? Tough shit. Do not give up a big home run then. You do not like a twenty-year-old pitcher throwing high and tight? Tough shit. Do not throw at one of our guys then. You are going to try and beat us with a suicide squeeze? Fine, we will just beat up on your ace closer and devastate you with a big hit in the tenth.

That confidence was further exemplified the next day when Gooden threw yet another complete-game victory. As Seaver was winning his three hundredth game back in the Bronx, Gooden broke Tom Terrific's franchise record by winning his eleventh consecutive decision. There was something beautiful about the symmetry of it all. On the same day, just hours apart, you had Seaver, the best pitcher in Mets history, winning his three hundredth game against the Yankees and Steinbrenner, while Gooden, the biggest pitching phenomenon the game had seen in decades, was establishing new club records against one of the team's most bitter rivals. Many people taking in events that day were certain that Gooden was destined to achieve that three hundredth win someday as well. As it stood now, he had not lost a game since May and had not allowed more than 3 earned runs in any game yet.

"Doc is in a class by himself. Nothing in either league is close to him," said Hernandez after the game. "If I could switch uniforms for just one day and face him, I'd love the challenge."[39]

Hernandez never did get that chance, but he was probably better off for it. Gooden was running away with the Cy Young Award, but more than that, he was putting together one of the single greatest seasons any pitcher had ever had.

Gooden's win, along with a Cardinals loss, put the Mets just a half game out of first place with one game remaining in Chicago and one day left before the strike could end the season. Having seen his friend and fellow star Gooden shine all season long, Strawberry stepped up in the final game in Chicago with a career performance. The lean, lanky outfielder hit 3 home runs, the last one a moon shot that almost left the ballpark in center. With a chance to make history in the top of the ninth, Strawberry lined a hard single to right field, completing a 4-4 afternoon. It was the fourth time in team history that a Met had 3 home runs in one game, the first since Claudell Washington did it in 1980. Strawberry's 5 RBIS helped give the Mets a 7–2 win and three out of four against Chicago.

The ghosts of August '84 had been exorcised. The Cubs, like the Expos, never recovered. From there on out, it was a two-way race between the Mets and Cardinals. And now, with a little help from the Phillies, the Mets were actually a half game ahead in the standings. It was the first time in exactly two months that they stood alone at the top of the division. The team flew out to Montreal in the hopes of staying hot. But as they flew off that Monday afternoon, the specter of another work stoppage loomed. They had made it back to first place, but it was entirely possible that it was all for nothing. If a strike happened and went on for weeks, the Mets' season would be just an asterisk.

ON TUESDAY, AUGUST 6, the Mets gathered in the lobby of the Le Centre Sheraton awaiting the latest news. They were stuck in limbo in Montreal. There they sat for more than five hours before Hernandez, the team's player representative, informed them the strike was on. "The association has instructed everybody to go home," said Hernandez, as his teammates began packing their things and heading to the airport.[40]

Davey Johnson, like many of his players, grabbed his things and headed for Dorval Airport. They had a 4:41 flight to catch to LaGuardia.[41] Johnson was going to head back to New York first, then hit the road with his coaching staff to observe the team's Minor League clubs. Might as well make the best of a bad situation, Johnson thought.

"I'll stick around New York and wait," said Fernandez. "There's no sense in my going home—I live in Hawaii."[42]

THE PLAYERS AND OWNERS had been unable to resolve their differences, even after the Players Association dropped its $60 million pension demand to $40 million. Meanwhile, the owners would not relent on changing arbitration.

"The clubs feel we have to start making changes in the system or baseball will go down the drain, so to speak," said Lee MacPhail, chief negotiator for the owners.[43]

Games were cancelled for Tuesday, August 6. Then they were cancelled for August 7. But on that day, there was a breakthrough. While owners would later grumble that he had compromised their position by telling the players he did not agree with a salary cap, Commissioner Peter Ueberroth was hailed as a hero for bringing all sides together to make a deal. The owners got their three-year-eligibility increase for arbitration. They would contribute $32.6 million annually to the pension fund, a substantial increase but nowhere near the original $60 million price tag. There would be no salary cap. The new agreement was for five years, expiring at the end of 1989.

All cancelled games would be made up throughout the remainder of the season, the only time a regular-season players' strike has not resulted in the loss of any games. Now that the strike was over—somewhat anticlimactically—it was time to get back to baseball.

DAVEY JOHNSON, MINUTES AWAY from boarding a flight to Orlando, got a call from the team front office. The strike was over and he had to get back to Montreal.

"It's the only time I've been happy about not going to Florida," said Johnson.[44] The Mets were scattered throughout various parts of the East Coast. Gooden had flown home to Tampa. Orosco was in Florida walking through a new home he had just purchased.

Ray Knight was in North Carolina watching his wife compete in a golf tournament. Carter had just gotten off a flight in LaGuardia and was trying to arrange a ride to Shea Stadium. In an era before cell phones or even pagers, each had to be painstakingly tracked down one by one. As they heard the news, players scrambled to find flights and get north of the border in time for the next day's game.

THE FIRST-PLACE METS TOOK the field in Montreal for a strike-shortened one-game series. After panic and concern about a season of hope wiped out over labor strife, the strike turned into a mere two-day opportunity to rest up. The Mets, looking to build upon their lead in the division, came out of the stoppage like a team possessed. They scored in each of the first five innings against the Expos, en route to a 14–7 win. Hernandez tied a team record with five hits—something he had done only one other time in his career—and in the process saw his average rise above .300. It was an incredible performance considering Hernandez had flown back and forth between Montreal and New York twice over the last two days. And when he was not in the air, he was meeting with the Players Association or keeping his teammates informed of any progress.

"He's a natural born hitter," said Strawberry after Hernandez's five-hit performance. "He can get out of bed and hit and, tonight, he practically did that."[45]

Carter, Foster, and Strawberry added home runs, and Leach provided four innings of scoreless relief. It was only one game, but the Mets showed the strike was not going to impact their play. Perhaps the only misfortune of the trip came when Davey Johnson found out his home had been robbed, including the theft of his 1966 World Series ring.[46]

The team returned to Shea where the fans showed no hard feelings over the stoppage; 132,000 plus came to Flushing for a three-game weekend series against the Cubs. Few left disappointed after their Amazin's swept Chicago out of the city. In the first game, every Mets starter except Darling got a hit and a late rally gave McDowell his sixth win of the year. The next day, Gooden won his twelfth consecutive decision, pitching a complete game for the fourth time in a row, something no Met had done in six years.

The win put the Mets at 65-42, the first time since 1969 the team had been twenty-three games over .500 at any point in a season. It also marked the first time in six years they won the season series over the Cubs. The Mets took the final game over Chicago, thanks to 2 Carter home runs. Carter, now with 16 on the season, set the team's all-time single season record for home runs by a catcher. That same day, home attendance surpassed that of 1984, despite the team having played twenty-three fewer games to that point.

"It's funny what has happened in New York City this year," wrote Hernandez. "[Mattingly's] numbers smother Darryl's, with or without the latter's injury; Mattingly leads the major leagues in RBIs. But Straw gets the greater acclaim. Rickey Henderson is having a super year too, but rather quietly. And Ron Guidry may win twenty games, but who other than a diehard Yankee fan is aware of it? Dwight in the only pitcher in town. The Mets are *the* team this year; we're outdrawing the Yankees by over 5,000 fans a game, even though the Yanks are in contention, playing good ball."[47]

The rise in attendance was clearly due to the exciting—and winning—nature of the team, and Gooden played a large part of that. When Doc took the mound, the average crowd at Shea was bigger by almost five thousand.

Gooden was not just a draw at Shea. He was bringing bigger crowds to television too. Richard Hussey, director of program planning for NBC's *Game of the Week*, said Gooden was worth half a rating point to the network. That was approximately 450,000 additional viewers who were tuning into a game solely because Doc was on the mound. When NBC decided to have the second game of the Cubs-Mets series as their game of the week, they did so not knowing if Gooden would pitch. When Davey Johnson announced Gooden would be the starter for that game, "We were surprised and delighted," said Hussey. "We scrambled around putting in advertisements saying Gooden was 'scheduled to pitch.'"[48]

Gooden was not alone in bringing excitement to the field. Strawberry, after struggling when healthy and creating a void when injured, was on fire in August. The right fielder was 11 for his last 28 with 4 home runs and 9 RBIS. His electric 3–home run performance at Wrigley had shown just what he was capable of when healthy and, perhaps more importantly, focused. That focus, that ability to zero in on the things he needed to do to be a better ball-player, was what was setting Strawberry apart this year from his previous two seasons.

"I'm different this year," said Strawberry. "I'm more relaxed. I'm coming to the ball park ready to play, mentally. Not letting things bother me on the field and off."[49]

It may sound simple, but that was no small accomplishment. Strawberry's moodiness, his inability to take personal issues and leave them out of the business at hand at Shea, rubbed many of his teammates the wrong way. In particular, some had grumbled in May when the offensively struggling Strawberry appeared to take his issues at the plate with him into right field. His work habits were called sloppy and his immaturity was only that much more pronounced next to the stoic, cool-as-ice Gooden.

"I was taking my concentration away from my offense to my defense," said Strawberry. "I had never been in that situation. You see guys picking on you, and you say, 'Oh, wow, what's this?' You go into a shell."[50]

The injury, however, allowed Strawberry to sit on the bench and just watch and listen. He felt it made him a better hitter. The results were clear as day. Strawberry was on fire. In a four-week period, Darryl had twice been named National League Player of the Week. Moreover, getting married and having a child seemed to even out Strawberry's personality, giving him a focus, even if it ended up only temporary in the long-term, that he lacked before. In July when Davey Johnson removed him from a game because his thumb became swollen, Strawberry told his manager afterward that he did not want to come out of games anymore.[51] It was not something that would have happened a year earlier.

With Strawberry, Hernandez, and Carter all clicking, the Mets' offense was virtually unstoppable. Each day brought more wins and more individual or team records. No one was hotter than the

Mets. Unfortunately for them, however, the second hottest team in the league seemed to be the Cardinals. The Mets won seven in a row, but their lead in the division peaked at only one game. In fact, over the next two weeks, at no point would any team lead the division by more than a single game. The Mets did not just have to win games to hold on to the lead, they had to win them just to stay afloat. Any slip could be the difference between going to the postseason and going home.

Case in point, their next series against the Phillies. The Mets took three out of four from Philadelphia. Sid Fernandez joined the now long list of players taking a curtain call by throwing eight plus solid innings in the first game. The crowd booed Johnson when he took Fernandez out of the game, and began chanting in unison, "We want Sid!" after the pitcher reached the dugout.

It was a proud moment for the pitcher, who spent the first part of the season dealing with self-doubt on the mound.

"A walk here and a bloop hit there often unsettle the timid Hawaiian," wrote the *Bergen Record*'s Jack O'Connell.[52]

Davey Johnson had tired of this routine early. It came to a head in the early August series at Wrigley when Fernandez lost his composure after walking his fourth batter of the game in as many innings. Johnson took him aside and, in so many words, explained to him the importance of poise on the mound. Both noticed an immediate change after. Now, with Sid able to keep things together mentally on the mound, he was becoming a dangerous man to face in the batter's box.

Even when Gooden turned in his worst performance yet in the concluding game against Philadelphia, the Mets' offense bailed him out. Three first-inning home runs off former Met and '69 hero Jerry Koosman—the first time the Mets had hit 3 home runs in one inning since 1974—led to a 10–7 win. By all accounts the series was a triumph. But that one loss, just that one loss, hurt. It hurt because the Cardinals kept winning. Instead of making up ground by winning three of four, the Mets found themselves now tied for first. All because of just one loss.

The Pirates, bottom dwellers of the east, were supposed to provide a remedy for that. But the Mets lost two of three to Pittsburgh. This time, however, it was the Cardinals turn to slip. They lost two of three to the Expos, and both teams remained tied. New York flew to Montreal for a quick makeup game. Darling, who lost a filling on the plane ride from Pittsburgh, took a three-hour nap before making the start, waking up just in time to warm up and take the mound. He threw seven shutout innings and the Mets won, 1–0. It put them a half game up in the standings.

They headed back to New York for a home stand against the West Coast teams. To that point, it seemed like there was almost nothing left for Gooden to do to prove just how dominant a season he was having. But in the first game back, he showed there was more, much more, to be seen. In his best start of the season, he struck out sixteen Giants without allowing a run. But the numbers cannot do justice to how electric the ballpark was that night. The players, the fans . . . everyone there knew they were witnessing something incredible.

"He threw me a fastball that I saw leave his hand and didn't see again until it hit Carter's glove. Never happened to me before," said Giants third baseman Chris Brown.[53]

"You're looking at something special," said Davey Johnson. "You probably won't ever see anybody at his age who dominates so completely."[54]

As Gooden began compiling more and more strikeouts throughout the night, "the crowd of 31,758 got into the act, cheering every pitch and even booing a couple of times when Giants managed to hit the ball into outs when a strikeout seemed imminent."[55]

The sixteen strikeouts put Gooden over two hundred for the year, the first time any National League pitcher had struck out two hundred or more batters in their first two seasons. His record moved to 19-3, and the Mets jumped out to a one-and-a-half-game lead over St. Louis. The 31,758 fans that night put the season attendance mark over 2 million, the first time that had happened since 1972. And there was still over a month left in the season.

GOODEN'S PERFORMANCE, HOWEVER, WAS one of the last high-lights of August for the Mets. The next night, Bob Brenly, hitting only .214 for the year and hitless in twelve at bats against Mets pitching, hit a one-out, 2-run home run in the top of the ninth to give the Giants a 3–2 lead. The Giants, 1-63 when entering the ninth inning trailing, stole one away from New York. It cost them a game in the standings.

Terry Leach provided a bit of stability—and levity—the next night. Leach was sitting in the clubhouse doing a crossword puzzle just as the game was about to start. Davey Johnson approached and told him he was starting because Fernandez was having dizzy spells and could not get on the mound. Leach got up, got ready, then went out and threw a complete-game shutout, his second in four career big league starts. His performance kept the Mets from fall-ing out of first place. But only for a day. The Padres entered Shea and split four games with New York, dropping the Mets a game behind the Cardinals. The only thing that prevented them from falling two games out was Gooden, who in the series finale picked up his twentieth win of the year. At twenty years, nine months, and nine days old, Gooden was the youngest pitcher in history to win twenty games in a season.

His performance drew praise from across all facets of baseball, including the Yankees.

"He's one of those pitchers who comes along once in a long while. You can start calling him great now," said Guidry.

"That's a lot of ballgames, especially for a young man, only 20. I've never seen a pitcher with a future ahead of him like Gooden has," added Niekro.

The praise did not just come from contemporaries either.

"That fastball and those curves of his just whiz by the bat-ters. Sometimes he doesn't look as though he is for real," said Burleigh Grimes who, at ninety-two, was the oldest living Hall of Famer in 1985.[56]

"Years from now I can tell everyone I saved Doc's first 20-win season," said McDowell. "I know there'll be a lot more of them, but it's great to be a part of his first."[57] Little did McDowell, or anyone for that matter, know at the time that it would be Gooden's only 20-win season.

The euphoria of Gooden's twentieth win was spoiled by the Dodgers, who won both games of a short two-game series. Each loss was near crippling, because the Cardinals just kept winning. The Mets dropped three games out of first place. Meanwhile, the Mets' abundance of confidence, the curtain calls and pumped fists, were starting to wear thin for the rest of the league.

"Maybe when a team is so used to patting itself on the back it forgets there are other good teams out there," said Dodgers second baseman Steve Sax after Los Angeles took both games.[58]

The Mets went 4-5 on their home stand. While not the kind of performance they would have wanted, it would not, in most other situations, have been viewed as catastrophic. But the Cardinals went 7-1 during that same stretch, costing the Mets three and a half games in the standings. The team was not panicking, but they were looking forward to the upcoming West Coast road trip, which would start on the final weekend of August.

"I just think we're a more relaxed club on the road," said Hernandez. "We have a lot of young guys and I think we may press more here. New York fans are good fans, but they're also tough fans. When a guy is going bad and they get on him, they do a good job of it. That makes a guy press."[59]

Hernandez could have been referring to any of a number of players whom fans were booing. In this case, he was most likely referring to Knight, whose struggles at the plate had gotten so bad that fans booed him every time he made an out. In the excitement of the season, the hometown crowd had come to expect nothing but success from each of the players on the field. When that did not happen, especially for those players for whom much was expected, the fans were merciless. Knight, HoJo, Foster, Doug Sisk. The list was almost as endless as those who had been asked for curtain calls.

These ten games on the West Coast were critical. After the trip was over, the Mets would return home for a three-game series against the Cardinals. If they faltered in California, that series could mean nothing more than a chance for the Cardinals to put the final nail in the Mets' coffin. But if the Mets could prevail out west, that series could mean a chance for them to surge ahead into the post-season for the first time in twelve years.

PERHAPS IT WAS THE two-days' rest. Or maybe it was just that moment in a season where everything falls the right way. Whatever it was, when the Yankees came back from the strike, they embarked on one of the greatest thirty-four-game stretches in team history. By the time their run was over, they would be on the cusp of the American League East division lead, and all of New York would be talking about a subway series.

The run began with the first two games after the strike. Hosting the Indians, the Yankees swept a doubleheader by a combined score of 15–7, with Winfield and Mattingly each hitting 2 home runs. They picked up a game on the Blue Jays in the process. But naturally the wins and the return from the strike were not without controversy.

Mike Armstrong, a relief pitcher who had fallen out of favor with Martin, had journeyed back and forth on the "Columbus Shuttle" between New York and the team's Triple-A affiliate. As the strike was set to begin, Armstrong was with Columbus. But if he stayed in the Minor Leagues, and was thus not considered a striking player, the Yankees were on the hook to pay him nearly $2,000 a day in salary. So on the Monday afternoon before the strike began, the Yankees suddenly decided they wanted Armstrong's services in the Major Leagues again. He was now on strike and thus, not eligible to collect his salary. The move was so transparent that Armstrong did not even bother hiding his disgust.

"I would like to get out of the organization," he said while sitting at his home during the strike. "It doesn't really matter to me how. . . . They really can't do anything else to me as far as punishing me. It stinks."[60]

The Yankees did not grant Armstrong his wish. He remained with the organization for another season and a half.

Armstrong was not alone in his misery. Henderson had flown home to Oakland that Wednesday in anticipation of a long strike.

It wasn't out of the ordinary. Most players had gone home. But when the strike was quickly resolved, possibly before Henderson's plane even landed in Oakland, he informed management he had a personal matter to tend to before he could get back to New York. Henderson did not make it back for the doubleheader, infuriating Steinbrenner. The Boss immediately attacked Henderson, relying on the money argument he always felt would gain him support from the fans.

"He won't be suspended but he will be fined and the fine will be heavy," said Steinbrenner. "It bothers me very much that he wasn't on the red eye last night. I would like to count the number of times I've ridden the red eye on the same day I went to the Coast—when I wasn't making $10,000 a game."

The Boss went on to say Henderson had to learn about responsibility, a comment which could easily have been interpreted as having racial overtones.[61]

Henderson, capable of making a bad situation worse when he felt he was being slighted, made clear he would not be pleased with a fine. At the same time, he was equally clear he wanted to get back to playing baseball.

"Whatever he wants to say is his story," said Rickey, referring to Steinbrenner's comment. "He's doing all the talking now. I'm here to play ball, that's all."[62]

In the end, Henderson was fined for missing the two games. The controversy moved on quickly though, if for no other reason than because the Yankees were winning.

Henderson rejoined the Yankees in Boston for a three-game series with the Red Sox. He collected two hits in his first game back and stole his fifty-first base. The Yankees scored 22 runs in a three-game sweep, their first sweep at Fenway in five years. In the process, they picked up another game on the Blue Jays, putting them seven back. From Boston, they moved on to Chicago, their first trip there since Berra's firing in April. They took two of three, giving them eight wins in their last nine games.

Everything that could go right was going right. Mattingly was named American League Player of the Week after hitting .542 with

3 home runs and 5 RBIS. Mike Pagliarulo, who struggled for much of the first half to get his average above .200, was 3-8 in Chicago with 4 RBIS. "Pags" as he was known, who had just 1 home run against a left-handed pitcher all year, hit an 0-2 pitch against a lefty to the opposite field for a home run. It was his first home run in over two weeks, and it ignited a power streak that saw him hit 6 more home runs and drive in 13 runs over the remaining two and a half weeks of August.

The hot streak came at a great moment for the third baseman. Pagliarulo grew up in Massachusetts as a Red Sox fan. The Yankees had high hopes for him after drafting him out of college. He came up as part of the Yankees 1984 youth movement after the season appeared lost. Pags excelled early on but began slumping after the league clearly figured out his weaknesses. Pagliarulo had rejected advice from Piniella after he came up, thinking he was doing just fine. Now, desperate to get on a hot streak, he implemented the adjustments in his swing Piniella had called for. In his first at bat post-adjustments, a pinch-hit appearance against Milwaukee's tough left-hander Bob McClure, he lined a triple. In the next game, he had three more hits. Whatever it was Piniella suggested, it worked.[63]

Though his average dropped toward season's end, the team had high hopes for Pags going into '85. But he struggled throughout most of the first four months, prompting Steinbrenner to regret having him and Berra playing third. Now, he was playing like the third baseman the Yankees had hoped for.

The winning, however, was momentarily disrupted by two events. After taking the last game in Chicago in dramatic fashion, with 4 runs in a comeback ninth inning, Martin announced the team would not conduct a workout at Yankee Stadium the following off day. It was the first time Martin had defied Steinbrenner on their discipline pact. Steinbrenner warned that if the Yankees ended up missing the playoffs (which one would have to assume would be because of a single canceled workout) there would be consequences.

"If you're running a corporation and your vice president tells you he can meet the month's quota without having his guys work overtime, that's fine. But if he doesn't meet the quota, then he's not the vice president much longer," said The Boss, who also could not resist adding yet another line about salaries. "I want total dedication for the next six weeks. That's not asking too much when you have guys making $7,000 and $8,000 a game."[64]

Steinbrenner made remarks also foreshadowing trouble with Winfield, who had gone hitless in the White Sox series.

"David knows that if he doesn't do what he's supposed to do, the comparisons between him and Reggie [Jackson] will be made." In a few weeks, that comment turned into self-fulfilling prophecy.[65]

One of the reasons Martin had cancelled the workout was to honor Pete Sheehy. Sheehy, the clubhouse attendant who had been with the team dating back to 1927, had died during the Chicago series after a short illness. A mainstay in the clubhouse, which was named in his honor while he was still with the team, Sheehy's time with the Yankees spanned from Babe Ruth and Lou Gehrig to DiMaggio, Mantle, Reggie, Winfield, and Mattingly. Few people in organized baseball had seen and been as close to some of the most iconic names in the game as Sheehy. Martin, who had known him for over thirty years, was too distraught to talk to reporters when he was informed of the news. The Yankees wore black armbands in his memory the rest of the season.

PRESSING ON, THE TEAM hosted Boston for a four-game series. It would be one of the most exciting Yankee Stadium had seen in years. In the first game, a Friday night matchup, Rickey Henderson thrilled the crowd with a leaping catch at the 385-foot mark in right-center field, robbing Bill Buckner of a home run. Then the Yankees tied the score in the bottom of the ninth on a one-out single by Pagliarulo, whose average was now up to .239. In the tenth, a Winfield double followed by three walks forced in the winning run. A Toronto loss that night put them just six back.

The following day, the Yankees scored 3 runs early and won 3–1, picking up another game in the standings. Their rise was not going unnoticed. In the bottom of the eighth inning, the fans looked over at the out-of-town scoreboard and saw that the Royals had taken a

4–2 lead over the Blue Jays late in the game. In unison, the crowd stood up and began cheering.

"I think the people are kind of feeling it around here. The last two games, they're getting up and getting crazy in the first couple of innings. I can feel it, I know that," said Mattingly.[66]

"Mark down Aug. 17 as the first time this season the fans at Yankee Stadium reacted to a score affecting the A.L. East race," wrote Moss Klein of the *Star-Ledger*. "And mark down Aug. 17 as the day the Yankees decided that The Chase had become The Hunt."[67]

On Sunday, August 18, Billy Sample, who had appeared in only forty games so far, played hero. With the bases loaded and one out in the seventh inning and clinging to a 1-run lead, Sample, playing left field, made a diving one-handed catch in short left to prevent the runners from advancing. The next batter, Wade Boggs, singled to left field. While the tying run scored, Sample threw out the go-ahead run at the plate. Fans gave him a standing ovation as he headed back to the dugout.

"That's more impact for me than I've had in a whole year," said Sample, who refers to it as his "Yankee inning."[68] The Yankees scored 2 in the bottom of the seventh and hung on to win, 4–2. The next day, a Monday-afternoon affair, the team battled back from a 5–3 deficit, scoring 3 runs in the seventh inning to take a 6–5 lead. In the top of the ninth inning, with Bob Shirley on the mound, Red Sox second baseman Marty Barrett sent a high drive deep down the left-field line. It looked like a certain game-tying home run. But Griffey, having entered the game the inning before, raced over toward the wall, his eye keeping track of Barrett's deep drive. Timing it perfectly, Griffey dug his right foot into the padding and used it to catapult himself above the left-field wall. Reaching up with his glove nearly two feet over the fence, Griffey snagged the ball, which first hit the palm of his glove and then started heading up and out, before he closed the webbing around it. His momentum nearly sent the upper half of his body, along with the ball, into the first row of seats. But bounding into the wall, Griffey immediately tumbled back onto the warning track, where he proceeded to somersault backward before standing up, fixing his cap, and tossing the ball back to the infield. The fans gave Griffey a three-minute standing ovation. Rich Bordi came in to record the last out, and the Yankees had a four-game sweep of the Red Sox, while moving within four games of first place.

After the game, the buzz was all about Griffey's catch.

"He might have just killed an entire team with that one [catch]," said Barrett, as the Red Sox faded further out contention.

"I practically screamed," said Steinbrenner, who was watching the game from Tampa. "I wanted to get on a plane and congratulate Griffey myself."[69]

The Yankees flew out to the West Coast, starting with a three-game series against the Angels. In the first game, they hit 5 home runs for an 8–5 win. Two of them belonged to Mattingly, who now stood at 22 home runs with 100 RBIs. It was the earliest in a season any Yankee had reached 100 RBIs since 1961. Also hitting .331 and playing spectacular defense, Mattingly was not letting down anyone who had high expectations following his batting title season. Now he was being talked about as the American League Most Valuable Player.

"If this guy's not, with the arguable exception of [George] Brett, the best all-around hitter in baseball, then Malcom Forbes is a party-pooping peasant," wrote the Bergen Record's Mike Celizic.[70]

"With Mattingly, you don't even bother to use the 'awesomes' and 'outstandings.' You just can't describe him to people who don't see him on a regular basis. And the most amazing thing is that this is just his second full season," said Niekro.[71]

More than that though, Mattingly was already exhibiting the qualities that would eventually see him named team captain in the early '90s. Sample recalls Mattingly having a fierce at bat against Mariners reliever Ed Nunez. After fouling off several pitches, Nunez finally struck him out with a fastball.

"And Donnie is coming back to the dugout and I am near the bat rack and Donnie says, 'I love it. He challenged me,'" said Sample. "After the game he had a clubhouse attendant take a glove with three beers and a note to Nunez that read, 'Now that's baseball.'"[72]

Mattingly was named American League Player of the Month for

hitting .390 with 11 home runs and 23 RBIs in August. His team-mate, Righetti, won Pitcher of the Month, going 4-0 with 5 saves and a 1.17 ERA in the month.[73]

A 13–10 win in Anaheim the next night put them three games out of first, the closest they had been in a month.

"There's almost nothin' that New Yorkers love more than base-ball. And there's nothin' that excites them more than the possibil-ity of a subway series between us and the Mets, which is startin' to look like a real possibility, with the way we're both playin'," noted Niekro in his book journal.[74]

After losing the final game against the Angels, the Yankees moved on to Seattle and swept a three-game series with the Mar-iners. Niekro recorded victory number 296, and Baylor tied the American League all-time record for being hit by a pitch. Outside of Henderson being evicted from his New Jersey apartment for failure to pay rent, the wins were not matched by much contro-versy or back-page stories.[75] After losing both games in a short two-game series in Oakland, they came back home for one of the greatest home stands in team history. It started with a 4–0 win by Niekro against the Angels, career victory number 297. In twenty-two and two-thirds innings against the Angels that year, Niekro had given up only eight hits and no runs. The next day, Friday, August 30, they lost, 4–1. They would not lose again until September 11.

After the 4–1 loss, they took the final two from the Angels. They then swept the Mariners in three games, with Niekro getting win number 298 in the process. After the final game against Seattle, Steinbrenner walked into Martin's office and, in front of the press, proceeded to "shower" him with a bucket full of confetti, mimick-ing the Harlem Globetrotters. Winning apparently put everyone in a good mood. It also put the Yankees just two and a half games behind the Blue Jays. Oakland came to town and the Yankees took all three from them as well. Willie Randolph had the first 2–home run game of his career, earning him a reluctant curtain call.

"I feel in a way that it's showing up the opposition and I don't want to do that," he said. "But I don't want to ignore the fans, either."[76]

Niekro won game number 299. Fans began chanting, "MVP! MVP!" after Mattingly hit his twenty-seventh home run.

The serenity of the clubhouse was temporarily broken when, during the first game against Oakland, Steinbrenner demanded that the control room at Yankee Stadium replay a controversial call that went against the Yankees. The decision went against league directives that recommended against "showing-up" umpires. Even his own players called out Steinbrenner.

"They shouldn't be showing the replay after a play like that. It can cause trouble," said Ed Whitson.[77]

While Steinbrenner admitted he may have been wrong to show the replay, he brushed it off by saying the Yankees needed only the best umpiring while fighting for first place.

Winning, however, allowed the team to move on with little impact. After their 10-1 home stand, they flew out to Milwaukee for a quick three-game series against the Brewers. They were just a game and a half out of first place. They took the first two games after scoring 22 combined runs. Mattingly contributed five more hits, and Ron Hassey, Griffey, and Pagliarulo drove in 3 runs apiece.

There was, however, a warning sign. Whitson was getting lit up every time he stepped foot on the mound. Over seven previous starts, he was pitching to a 7.71 ERA. But the offense had bailed him out, and somehow he was 3-0 during that span. But his difficulty in recording outs was starting to grate on some people.

By taking the first two games in Milwaukee, the Yankees had won eleven in a row, the longest streak in the Majors that year and the longest by the team since 1964. The Blue Jays were keeping pace, however, winning four in a row and preventing New York from gaining further ground. With one game left in Milwaukee, the Yankees tried to bolster their starting pitching by putting in a waiver claim for Tom Seaver.

"We're trying, believe me, we're trying," said Steinbrenner regarding a possible trade with Chicago to acquire the legendary Met. But the White Sox wanted outfielder Dan Pasqua, an up-and-coming slugger who'd made significant contributions that year, or two Minor League prospects, one of which was Jay Buhner. The Yankees rejected the offer, Seaver stayed with Chicago, and Buhner remained with the Yankees to be traded away three years later in another infamous deal.

The Yankees lost the final game in Milwaukee, ending their winning streak at eleven. It dropped them two and a half games out of first as they headed home for a critical four-game series against the Blue Jays.

IF THE FIRST THREE games in San Francisco were any indication, it looked like the Mets trip to the Golden State could end in disaster. Despite a ninth-inning comeback in the first game, the Mets lost in extra innings when Chili Davis crushed a 3-run home run off Leach. Then, despite giving up only 2 runs, Gooden's consecutive-win streak came to an end when the offense failed to hit off the 5-10 Jim Gott. The good news was that, despite losing two of the first three games, the Mets still managed to pick up a game in the standings. A win in the final game in San Francisco kept them two back as they headed to San Diego.

The Padres, defending National League champions, were desperately clinging to a last-ditch hope of catching the Dodgers in the National West. But as they had done with the Expos and Cubs, the Mets came in and effectively ended their season. Hernandez led the charge with five hits in the first game, becoming the first Met ever to have multiple five-hit games in one season. Fernandez, now over his composure issues, went the distance. For the first time all season, the Mets' offense gave him more than 5 runs of support, knocking in a dozen runs in a 12–4 win.

Then, over the next two days, it became the Gary Carter Show. First, Carter hit 3 home runs and drove in 6 in an 8–3 win. It was Carter's second career 3–home run game and gave him the team lead in home runs. It was also rather ironic. The Mets' offense, which for a month had been among the worst in the league and in franchise history, now had the only two players in the National League to hit 3 home runs in a game that season.

The next day, in the series finale, Carter hit 2 more home runs, becoming the thirteenth player in history to hit 5 in consecutive games. The Mets completed the sweep, their first in San Diego since 1977. Still, the three wins only brought them one game closer to first, as the Cardinals kept winning. Moreover, for the first time all season, the Mets were finally the focus of an off-the-field controversy.

As Carter was hitting the last of his 2 home runs in San Diego, his first baseman was headed out to Pittsburgh for the drug trial of Curtis Strong. Hernandez's time to testify had come.

THE NEWS BROKE WHILE the Mets were in San Diego. Hernandez was one of nearly a dozen players being called to testify in Curtis Strong's trial. Before Keith could even get there, former teammate Lonnie Smith had already implicated him on the stand. He told of a night in 1982 when he bought $300 worth of cocaine from Strong, which he then shared with Hernandez and teammate Joaquin Andujar in Smith's hotel room.

The next day, Friday, September 8, Hernandez checked out of his Pittsburgh hotel—which he had stayed in under an assumed name—and walked to the federal courthouse. A throng of reporters and photographers greeted him there. He did not say a word, instead walking past everyone and preparing himself for what would be one of the hardest days of his life. Taking the stand, Hernandez publicly admitted for the first time he used cocaine.

"There was a time in my life when I did this thing," he told the jurors during his three hours' worth of testimony. Explaining the problems he encountered after just separating from his wife, he described how the drug had taken a hold of him.

"It wasn't everyday use, but it got to a point where I realized I had to get away from it. I felt the more you do it, the more it starts getting control of you. It gives you an insatiable desire for more."[78]

Hernandez said he had given up the drug when he saw how it was controlling Smith's life. He had stopped years before and had never done it as a Met. Still, he was sorry for any embarrassment he may have caused his current and former teams.

The revelation was just one of many details to emerge from the trial that shook the baseball world. Tim Raines admitted that he used to keep a vial of cocaine in his back pocket during games. He slid headfirst to avoid breaking it. Dave Parker, one of the game's biggest stars, was among many outed as a user.

Hernandez, like all others who testified, received immunity for his testimony. Eventually, Strong was convicted of selling cocaine and served four years in prison. In 1986 Hernandez was one of a handful of players who, in place of a yearlong suspension, donated a percentage of their salary to substance-abuse-awareness programs, submitted to drug testing, and did community service.

In the long-term, Hernandez's reputation would suffer little from this episode. The drug trials rocked the baseball world at the time but would be lost in the confluence of labor strife and performance-enhancing-drug scandals that followed in the '90s and '00s. In the short-term, Hernandez had to worry about the reaction of his teammates, Mets fans, and baseball fans at large.

HERNANDEZ MADE IT BACK just in time for the start of the last series of the trip, a three-game set with the Dodgers. He did not have to worry about his teammates. One by one, they lined up to tell reporters that it was all in the past. They supported Keith. Did not think any less of him because of what happened. And they could not wait to have him back.

What Mets fans thought would have to wait a few more days. What opposing fans thought, however, would be tested that night. Late in the game, Hernandez was called on to pinch-hit.

"Think I'll get booed?" he asked pitching coach Mel Stottlemyre as he made his way out of the dugout.

"Fuck those people!" replied Stottlemyre.

At least Keith knew where he stood with his team.[79]

Some fans booed. Some cheered. Most did not react. It was hard to tell if this was what he could expect elsewhere. After all, this was laid-back Dodger Stadium. But at least the fact that there were not overwhelming boos left some hope for the rest of the season.

Meanwhile, outside of Hernandez's ordeal, Gooden and Fernando Valenzuela faced off again in another much-hyped matchup. While the first two encounters were good, the third was beyond anyone's expectations. The two traded zeros for nine innings, with Gooden tapping out in the tenth and Valenzuela in the twelfth. The two gave up only eleven total hits and struck out a combined fifteen. In the top of the thirteenth with two out, Strawberry delivered the biggest hit of his young career when he doubled in 2 runs. Orosco worked out of a bases-loaded jam in the bottom of the inning to preserve the win.

A heartbreaking loss in the Saturday game prevented them from gaining on the Cardinals. The game was noteworthy for the simmering tensions between the two teams. Dodgers shortstop Mariano Duncan was not pleased with the pitch selection from Ed Lynch. Rather than challenge him with fastballs, Lynch kept throwing off-speed pitches, and Duncan could not make solid contact. In the sixth inning, when Duncan struck out, he walked back to the dugout and yelled at Lynch for pitching, as Dodger Pedro Guerrero would say, like "a sissy."[80] Lynch, like just about every other member of the Mets, was not about to take shit from a Dodger, especially not one who had just struck out. When Lynch hollered back, telling him to go sit on the bench, Duncan charged the mound. He was immediately stopped by Knight, the Gold Glove third baseman with whom few Major Leaguers wanted to tangle.

"Lynch was truly angry with Duncan, who was bush all the way," said Hernandez. "It was no secret; Eddie was sensitive to the charge that, for being such a big guy, he didn't throw very hard. He would have fought Duncan, gladly, if Knight hadn't intervened."[81]

Order was quickly restored, but when the Dodgers pulled the game out in the bottom of the ninth, it hurt all the more.

A measure of redemption came the next day. Tied at 3 in the fourteenth, Mookie Wilson stepped into the box to lead off the inning. Nineteen-eighty-five had been hard for Mookie. His shoulder injury was the first in a series of injuries that hampered parts of the next several seasons. The outfielder had missed two months of the year, having only just returned on this road trip. When he got back, he found a crowded outfield. Strawberry was unstoppable. Foster was providing pop in the lineup. The dirty, gritty play of Dykstra was making him a key component, even if his average had tailed off a bit.

There was not a person in the world who had a negative thing to say about Mookie. Years later, when those who knew the team well described the Mets of the mid- and late '80s, almost every player was deemed an asshole for one reason or another. Not Mookie. Wilson was forever smiling. Loved to laugh. Always had a good word to say about anybody. The guy just seemed to have an innate joy in being alive.

He was not that bad a ballplayer either. Mookie had played through the lean years. Persevered through horrible play and sparse crowds to now be on one of the best teams in baseball. But his zest for living was not going to be enough to keep him in the lineup. He had to earn it.

So when Mookie stepped up to box in the top of the fourteenth at Dodger Stadium, he needed a big hit. Batting righty, he drilled a curve ball just over the 370-foot sign in left field. It was just his fourth home run of the year and only the twenty-ninth of his career, but it was the biggest one he ever hit. The Mets won the game 4–3 and pulled to within a half game of the Cardinals, with St. Louis headed to Shea that Tuesday. The Mets had gone 7-3 on their West Coast trip, picking up two and a half games in the standings and putting themselves in a position to knock St. Louis out of first with just twenty-three games left in the year. As for whether that home run earned Mookie a spot back in the lineup, he started twenty-one of those twenty-three games.

TUESDAY, SEPTEMBER 10, 1985. The Cardinals came into Shea having lost the day before, an off day for the Mets, meaning the teams were now tied atop the standings, both 82-53. The atmosphere at Shea Stadium was electric. It was unlike anything Flushing had seen since the '73 World Series. Fifty thousand–plus people, a sellout crowd, had come to see their beloved Amazin's take back first place and then march to the postseason.

Sure, the Yankees were also making a run for it. But the Yankees were corporate. They were a daily soap opera with villains straight out of a black-and-white silent movie. Steinbrenner may as well have had a handlebar mustache to twirl as he tied Billy Martin up to the railroad tracks. Meanwhile, the Mets were winning *and* they were fun. They were gritty. They did not take shit from opposing teams. They partied hard. And they were cocky as the day is long. In short, the Mets were New York City in the 1980s. And New Yorkers responded in kind.

Now here they sat, awaiting perhaps the biggest regular-season series their team had ever played in. The stadium was rocking. Even when the Mets quickly fell behind 1–0 in the first inning, they did not give up. In years past, a moment like this would have brought on the inevitable thoughts of "well, this game is over." But not now. Not with this team. And they were right.

First, Mookie singled to lead off the bottom of the first. Then, with one out, Hernandez came to the plate. It was his first at bat at Shea since admitting in court that he had used cocaine. No one was certain before the game how fans might react. But when Hernandez stepped in the box, the fans made their feelings clear. They gave him a thirty-second standing ovation.

"That ovation meant more to me tha[n] the one in St. Louis in '83, when I went back there for the first time after being traded to the Mets," said Hernandez.[82]

It was the kind of moment that made him want to finish his career in New York.

Hernandez singled to left-center, tying the game, then moved to second on an out by Carter. Danny Cox, the Cardinals' starting pitcher, intentionally walked Strawberry to put runners on second and first. And then the fireworks began, as Foster strolled—in every sense of the word—up to the plate.

Foster was in no rush when he went up to bat, ever. He took his time. Stepped in. Stepped out. Stepped in again. Called time. Took in the view of the field. Maybe had a quick moment of prayer. Maybe just needed to gather his thoughts. Ah, now he was ready.

It was a routine that drove pitchers crazy. And when Foster pulled his routine this time, Cox was not having it. Even though catcher Darrell Porter was setting up outside, Cox's first pitch fastball drilled Foster right in the ass. It was as clear an intentional hit as there had ever been in baseball.

"I was just pitching in, and it hit him," said Cox unconvincingly after the game. "That's just part of my game. Delaying is part of his."[83]

Foster then did something odd: he almost started a fight. The normally quiet, deeply religious Foster, bat still in hand, began walking toward first but not before pointing his bat at Cox and exchanging a few unfriendly words.

"I guess I just forgot where the baseline was," said Foster.[84] And then, quickly, the two approached each other. Before they could get close enough to actually do anything, both benches emptied onto the field, with Strawberry leading the charge for the Mets from first base. It was the third bench-clearing incident for the Mets in six weeks.

The incredible irony of the moment would not be realized for another year when, during a brawl in Cincinnati, Foster sat on the bench, refusing to come to the aid of his teammates. It effectively ended his career in New York. But that was still a year away. Here and now, the exchange of unpleasantries only further energized the team and the crowd.

After the umpires restored order and issued warnings to both teams, HoJo came up with the bases loaded. When Cox tried to sneak a fastball past him, Johnson turned on it, sending the ball off the scoreboard in right-center field. Shea Stadium erupted. It felt like the building might actually fall down. The Mets launched themselves out of the dugout, following the flight of the ball, then jumping up and down as it crashed down against the scoreboard.

Here, the Mets had been challenged and answered the best possible way you could: with a grand slam.

"In a way," said Johnson, "it was an insult to me. He hits George and loads the bases, but he's probably figuring I'm an easy out."[85]

The Mets needed every single one of those runs, because after the grand slam, they got only two more base hits the entire game. Meanwhile, the Cardinals chipped and chipped away until it was a 5–4 game in the ninth. But McDowell closed it out, and the Mets took the first game and with it, a one-game lead in the division.

Talk after was, of course, about the Cox-Foster altercation, but also about the intensity of the game and of the fans. Hell, the crowd was so excited they even cheered when the scoreboard showed the Yankees had taken a lead against Milwaukee. Yeah, the Yankees were corporate, but meeting and then beating them in the World Series sure would be nice.[86]

That energy carried over into the next game, where a matchup of Gooden and John Tudor provided a pitching performance for the ages. Tudor, the lanky left-hander, had been a decent pitcher for Boston and then Pittsburgh before landing in St. Louis in '85. There, in Gateway City he had the season of his life. On May 29, he was 1-7 with a 3.74 ERA. Going into this start on September 11, Tudor was 17-8 with a 1.95 ERA. His eight shutouts led the league. From June 3 to August 12, Tudor made fifteen starts. He was 14-1 over that time, with six shutouts. He was not the only reason the Cardinals had surged ahead in the division, but he certainly was among the main ones. And the only reason Tudor was not running away with the Cy Young Award in a landslide was because of the twenty-year-old opposing him on the mound that night.

In front of the largest Shea Stadium crowd in eight years, both Tudor and Gooden put on a display. In some ways, it was boring beyond all belief, because little happened. But for baseball purists, it was as good a game as could possibly be played. Both faced the minimum nine batters through the first three innings. Tudor did not allow a hit until the sixth. Gooden did not allow more than one runner on base until the seventh. When the game reached the tenth inning, scoreless, Tudor had faced only two over the minimum. Gooden, meanwhile, had pitched nine shutout innings without a win for the second time that season. The Mets had failed to score for him in twenty-four innings.

Jesse Orosco took the mound in the tenth and, with two strikes on César Cedeño, gave up a long home run to left. It was just 1 run, but against Tudor, it might as well have been 20. In the bottom of the inning a Backman single was erased on a line-drive double play. Carter then walked, but Strawberry was no match for St. Louis's left-handed Cinderella story. He struck out to end the game.

The Mets were disappointed but not down on themselves. Tudor had pitched a phenomenal game, and not just against them. It was what he had been doing for months now. His ten-inning performance gave him three consecutive shutouts. But more important for the Cardinals, it brought them back into a tie for first place with one more game to go in New York. Meanwhile, as the two teams got back to their hotels to rest up for the next day's matinee affair, the Yankees were flying back to the city for their matchup with the Blue Jays. New York was about to get a baseball experience it had not felt since Eisenhower was president.

# 8

# "I'm Going to Kill You"

IT WAS BEING DUBBED "Baseball Thursday." With three weeks left in the season, both New York teams were home to play the team they were fighting with for first place.

"Never have the two teams played home games on the same day that were so meaningful," said Bob Mandt, vice president of stadium operations at Shea.[1] In fact, never had the two teams played meaningful games anywhere on the same day so late in the season. The two had traded subpar and championship seasons over the years. Now, a subway series was in the air.

"Baseball was the talk of town yesterday," wrote the *New York Times'* Bill Geist. "[It was] described by many fans as the greatest day for New York baseball since Oct. 10, 1956, when the last game of the last Subway Series was played."[2]

George Steinbrenner, giddy over meaningful September baseball in the Bronx for the first time in four years, even got limos for each of the players as they arrived back in New York in the early morning hours after getting back from Milwaukee. The Boss was treating this like a playoff series, as was the Yankees' brass. A thick scouting report, the "most extensive report" Billy Martin had ever seen for a regular-season series, was put together by general manager Clyde King and scouts Al Cuccinello and Doug Holmquist.[3]

"BASEBALL THURSDAY" STARTED IN Flushing. Despite being an afternoon game with school back in session, over forty-six thousand were on hand. The Mets, stifled by John Tudor just fifteen hours earlier, came out swinging against twenty-game winner Joaquín Andújar. After a first-inning walk and a single, the Cardinals starter got Keith

Hernandez to ground into a double play. It scored a run, but looked to kill a potentially huge inning. But then the Mets attacked. Gary Carter singled. Then Darryl Strawberry, Danny Heep and Howard Johnson doubled. Before it was over, the Mets were up 4–0, and Shea was delirious thinking about first place.

In the second inning, the Mets did not let up. Wally Backman doubled—the team's fourth in eleven at bats—plating another run. A based-loaded hit-by pitch scored one more. It was 6–0 after two innings, and with Lynch on the mound, the Mets could smell first place just seven innings away.

But the Cardinals would not die. They scored 3 in the third. Then 2 more in the fourth. It was now a 6–5 game and the momentum had swung completely toward St. Louis. As it had done in the first game after HoJo's grand slam, the Mets' offense went quiet. They mustered just two hits between the third and eighth innings. Then, in the top of the ninth, Willie McGee, on his way to a batting title and the National League Most Valuable Player Award, touched up Jesse Orosco for a home run with one out, tying the game.

The air went out of Shea Stadium when McGee's ball landed beyond the left-center-field fence. These Cardinals just did not stop. Hours earlier, the ballpark was giddy with the thought of first place. Now, fans were wondering if maybe this was just St. Louis's year.

The Mets, however, were still in it. All they needed was 1 run. Just 1 run, and first place was theirs. In the bottom of the ninth, Mookie Wilson led off with a bloop shot to short. Ozzie Smith fielded and fired to first, but Wilson beat out a bad throw. Backman bunted him over to second. The heart of the order was coming up. Now the crowd was back into the game. Just need a big hit here, and we are in first.

And who better to deliver that big hit than Hernandez. Bare hands clutching his bat, arms extended back, Hernandez stayed inside a low pitch, driving the ball to left field for a hit. Mookie came racing around third. There was going to be a play at the plate. But left fielder Vince Coleman could not come up with the ball, watching it scoot right under his glove and continue into the outfield. Wilson scored easily, and the Mets took the game and the series.

Anyone at Shea, at that moment, would have thought the seventh game of the World Series had just been decided on that single. The Mets spilled out of the dugout, splitting into two groups. One headed toward Wilson at the plate, the other went to meet Hernandez at first. Both were mobbed. Hernandez, though intense, rarely displayed more emotion on the field than was necessary. A fist pump every now and then and that was about it. But here, the excitement of the moment exploded out of him. He high-fived (with both hands), he embraced teammates, and he even came out of the dugout for a curtain call and pumped his fist in the air.

The win was exhilarating, and not just because a loss after leading 6–0 would have been devastating. The Mets had gone up against the best team in the division (or second-best team as far as they were concerned), played three incredibly intense, 1-run games, and come away winning two. The news was great even off the field. Before the final game, a coin flip determined that if the two teams were tied at season's end, the one-game playoff tie breaker would be played at Shea. It was great news that the Mets hoped they would not need. Because they now stood one game ahead in the division race with just twenty-four left to play.

ABOUT THREE HOURS AFTER Hernandez singled in Wilson, the Yankees began the most important four-game series they had played in years. It would not be easy. After all, the Blue Jays were in first place for good reason. They had one of best outfields in baseball, featuring the power and speed of George Bell, Lloyd Moseby, and Jesse Barfield. Combined they hit 73 home runs and stole eighty bases in 1985. Their pitching staff boasted Cy Young contender Dave Stieb, who had possibly the league's most devastating slider behind only Ron Guidry. Stieb was supported by former Yankee Doyle Alexander and future Yankee Jimmy Key. Most devastating, however, was the Toronto bullpen. Featuring Bill Caudill, Dennis Lamp, and Tom Henke, a late-inning lead for the Blue Jays was about as safe a bet as you could make. Taken together, the Jays were possibly the best overall team in baseball. It was certainly the best squad Toronto had assembled since joining the Majors as an expansion team in 1977. A dominating performance in this series could effectively end the race for first.

Early on, it looked like that was exactly what would happen. In a duel between Guidry and Stieb, Stieb kept the Yankees hitless until the fifth inning. Guidry gave up an early 2-run home run to Ernie Whitt and allowed 2 more runs, putting the Yankees in a 4–1 hole going into the bottom of the seventh inning. Walks and an error knocked Stieb out, forcing the Yankees to try and rally against one of the league's best bullpens. But through a combination of seeing-eye singles and outs, they scraped together 3 runs to tie the game. With two on and two out, Ron Hassey came up in the biggest spot of the year. The big burly catcher, acquired by the Yankees that offseason as a backup to Butch Wynegar, was a favorite of teammates for his work ethic and easygoing manner.

"He gets hit with more foul balls than anybody. But he keeps smiling," said Winfield.[4]

Hassey had become a favorite of Martin's too and was seeing increasingly more time behind the plate. That was in part because he was hitting .370 with 6 home runs over his last sixteen games. Ron, despite or perhaps because of his performance, was rumored to have been a possible part of the Seaver trade just a few days earlier. Now, here he was, with the Yankees' entire season seemingly resting on his enormous shoulders.

Blue Jays reliever Lamp threw two balls, then grooved a fastball down the middle. Hassey, a left-handed batter who crouched down, holding the bat nearly perpendicular to the ground, swung about as hard as a player could and sent the ball ten rows deep into the upper deck in right field. The 3-run shot gave the team a 7–4 lead, and sent the crowd into a frenzy.

"Hassey's homer spawned a wild celebration in the stands, the loudest and most energetic in the Stadium since the 1981 World Series," said the *Bergen Record*.[5]

Guidry went eight innings before yielding to Brian Fisher, who closed out the game for the Yankees. They were now a game and a half out of first, with three more games at home against the team they were chasing. It was, without question, the high-water mark for the team so far.

BETWEEN THE METS AND the Yankees, Thursday, September 12, 1985, was the most exciting day of baseball played in the city in over a quarter century. Over one hundred thousand fans had gone to Shea and the Stadium to witness it. They had not been disappointed. The Mets left town with a one-game lead in the division, and the Yankees were just a game and a half out, winners of twelve of their last thirteen and having just delivered what appeared to be a serious emotional blow to their foes. Fans from both sides were now openly debating which team would win if and when they met in October. It was an incredible moment in the history of New York baseball, the first to occur between the Mets and Yankees.

Little did the two teams know that by the following weekend, both of them would appear out of the race for good. For the Mets, it was a series of ill-timed losses. For the Yankees, it was a result of the strangest eight-game stretch in the team's history.

IT WAS ALL GOING to be so perfect. A Friday night in the Bronx. Yankee Stadium filled with fifty-three thousand fans bursting with excitement over a playoff race and the chance to see history. A team looking to pull within just a half game of first place after a season of so many ups and downs. It was almost the exact way Phil Niekro would have wanted to win his three hundredth game. Almost.

"I suppose if you could write your own script it would be the last game of the season. I would pitch a no-hitter, and we would win the pennant, but this isn't such a bad way," Niekro said before the game.[6]

It was all going to be so perfect . . . and then, it wasn't. It started before the first pitch. Going back to the first game against Toronto, as the Canadian national anthem began playing, fans started to boo. Embarrassed, Yankees officials were certain to note before the singing of the anthem before the second game that Canada had played a key role in the Iran hostage crisis. People in the crowd booed the anthem anyway. Then, after taking an early 1–0 lead, the Yankees fell behind 3–1, never to recover. Niekro went the distance, but the Yankees failed to record a hit over three and two-thirds innings against the Blue Jays' bullpen. Niekro and the fans missed out on history. More importantly, the Yankees fell two and a half games out of first.

The next night, more embarrassment. Mary O'Dowd, a New York singer, began the Canadian national anthem, "O Canada," off key. Then she forgot the words.

Rickey Henderson, standing next to teammate Rex Hudler, couldn't stop laughing.

"Oh man oh man, she messed up," said Henderson, slapping his glove to his knee. "Oh Hud, that is terrible."

Toronto and its people were not as amused. The mayor said the three days' worth of insults to the anthem left him "somewhat disgusted." The U.S. ambassador to Canada actually felt the need to offer an apology to the entire country.[7]

Things only got worse from there. Staked to an early 2–1 lead, Bob Shirley could not get out of the fifth inning. Martin visibly showed his disgust as he removed the pitcher from the game. Tied at 2 in the sixth, Martin brought Dave Righetti into the game to keep the score tied. Rags gave up a walk, two singles, and a double. Before the inning was over, the Yankees were down 7–2. Righetti, after being removed from the game, was booed by the crowd. Two runs in the eighth brought them within 3 with one out. But Mattingly struck out, and Winfield grounded out, moving the game into the ninth.

As the Yankees' beat writers began putting what they assumed would be the finishing touches on another Toronto win, a familiar face made his way into the press box and took an empty seat next to Murray Chass of the *New York Times*. The fifty-five-year-old owner of the New York Yankees was flabbergasted over his team's performance. All though the game had yet to end, Steinbrenner came to put on a show for the writers.

"Where is Reggie Jackson? We need a Mr. October or a Mr. September," said The Boss, overlooking that it was he who decided to let Jackson go three years earlier. Then came the words that would, unfortunately, immortalize a future Hall of Famer.

"Winfield is Mr. May."

It was a moniker that attached itself to Dave Winfield for the rest of his career. Never mind that that very night, Winfield had driven in his one hundredth run, the fourth consecutive year he had reached that milestone.

To drive his point home, Steinbrenner held in his hand a stat sheet showing that, for the series, Ken Griffey was 0 for 8, Don Baylor 0 for 7, and Winfield 3 for 11 with "only" 2 runs batted in. It did not go unnoticed by some that Steinbrenner had named three black players. Steinbrenner then continued his harangue.

"My big guys aren't coming through—Winfield, Baylor, Griffey. That's a fact."

As the Yankees went down in order in the ninth, he let fly with an all-encompassing jab at his team.

"We've been out-played, out–front officed, out-managed, and out-owned. I blame myself as much as anybody."[8]

Steinbrenner's comments got back to the locker room in a hurry. Resentful players kept their feelings to themselves, at least for one day. But the next day, the verbal tirades got worse. They fell behind 6–0 early, with Ed Whitson not making it out of the top of the third inning. The Yankees were held to one hit until the seventh, and eventually lost the fourth game, 8–5. The loss dropped them four and a half games out of first, their largest deficit since the end of August. An irate Steinbrenner let loose outside the clubhouse after the game.

"They've got to be embarrassed. I'm embarrassed, but not for them. For myself. What good would it do to be critical of them," said Steinbrenner. But with another sheet of paper in his hands showing his team's stats for the series, he proceeded to do just that, with the usual shots at those with big salaries.[9]

"We need the big performance out of Winfield, Griffey and Baylor, the guys who are making the big money. Mattingly's doing ok, but if we're going to win, we've got to get the big numbers against the tough pitchers. My big-money players aren't playing like money players."[10]

Then he went even harder at Griffey, the man who just a few

weeks early he was willing to fly one thousand miles just to say thank you for a game-saving catch.

"Some guys just quit on me today. Griffey [who made an error in left field but homered in the ninth] for one. He wants to be traded? I offered him to everybody in both leagues. Nobody wants a 36-year-old outfielder with a million dollar contract. And Winfield . . ." Steinbrenner's voice trailed off before he could finish his thought.[11]

Steinbrenner always felt these kinds of in-your-face quotes would challenge his players to rise to the occasion. More often than not, it did just the opposite.

"You wonder why no one wants to talk to you," said Winfield to the press after hearing The Boss's comments. "The man upstairs doesn't get involved for the first 130 games. Now he gets involved and he gets the press and the fans involved. Guys get tentative. They don't feel comfortable. It's like rattling a stick across a cage with some animals in it. Guys are getting upset."[12]

"We've got an owner who feels he has to say things about the players," said Mattingly. "To belittle him [Griffey], to me, is out of control."[13]

The Bergen Record's Mike Celizic summed up the situation succinctly, writing, "The Boss is embarrassed [not mad, mind you], the players are upset, the manager can barely talk because some sawbones stabbed him in the lung more than a month ago, and the Yankees are 4 1/2 games out of first place with 20 games to play. Yes, this must be the Bronx."[14]

The losing, the comments, the discord, it all spelled trouble for Billy Martin. He had been through this too many times, and those who had been around the club long enough knew where this storyline always led to. The pressure was going to come crashing down on Billy, meaning either more drinking, more erratic behavior, or both. In this case, it would be both.

FOR WHAT MUST HAVE felt like the fiftieth time that season, the Mets gathered their passports and boarded a plane for Montreal. The euphoria of Baseball Thursday hung strong in the air, and the adrenaline rush from Hernandez's big hit would be enough to get them through one more flight north of the border. The Mets could have left New York all but eliminated from the race. Instead, as they took off that Thursday, they were in first place by one game. Yes, they had to keep winning. But so did the Cardinals. And now St. Louis had just a little bit more pressure on them with three weeks to go in the season.

The Mets were not taking anything for granted though. Their opponents in those three weeks would love nothing more than to play spoiler for the cocky bunch from New York. These guys hadn't won anything yet, many opposing teams were starting to feel, but they walk around like their shit don't stink. Certainly the Expos fell into that category. Hubie Brooks may not have wanted to admit it, but he would have been happy to hurt the chances of the team that seemingly gave up on him. And how nice would it be, some of his former teammates must have thought, to keep Camera Carter from flashing that smile in the postseason.

Now, the strike also came back into play. Having missed two games because of the stoppage, the team had to get to the ballpark early as part of a doubleheader. By now, the rush of the previous day's win was starting to wear off. The Mets looked tired in the first game, and played that way too. The offense couldn't break through. The defense was wobbly. A late cover on a double steal resulted in an errant throw and a run. The Expos won 5–1, and Davey Johnson was not pleased.

"I guess you're supposed to have those games once in a while," said Johnson to reporters in between games of the twin bill. "But I don't accept them. We're in a pennant race."[15]

Johnson said it was more than just the botched coverage. Several players—he would not say who—had screwed up. He made sure to note that he had addressed it directly with each of the offenders.

"It's never understandable to me to make a mental mistake," added Johnson. "I can't stand losing. But I can't stand losing even more when mental mistakes are part of the loss."[16]

This was hardly a Billy Martin–like outburst. But it did not need to be. Johnson had earned the respect and admiration of his players, many of whom he'd managed for almost their entire professional careers. They trusted him. Looked up to him. Did not want to let him down. Johnson's comments were more in line with a parent who says they are not mad, just disappointed. It was not the ramblings of some sideshow fueled by alcohol or an overbearing cruel owner. Comments in those situations were a dime a dozen. All just part of the scenery.

Not with the Mets. Not with this team or this manager. Johnson was not playing some strategic mind game of chess with his boss. He was just trying to get his team into the playoffs.

"I'm intense," said Johnson. "I was intense as a player, too. But I try not to show it. I guess I've learned you can run only so fast."

So how did he see himself as compared to the thrice fired Yankees manager?

"Am I different from Billy? I hope so. I admire him as a manager. But he's more volatile than I am."[17]

Maybe that is why the Mets made no mental mistakes and came out swinging in the second game of the day. George Foster, homerless in a month, hit a 2-run shot. Carter added another one in the ninth for good measure, and the Mets took it, 7–2. The win kept them in first place, but by just a half game. Out in Chicago, the Cardinals beat up the Cubs 9–3. St. Louis walked ten times and stole eight bases in the game, showing they were not going to lay down and die. The last loss in New York had been tough, but they were not dwelling on it.

DAVEY JOHNSON HATED MENTAL mistakes. He may have been more lenient on fielding errors. But no matter how lenient he was, the next day's game must have driven him crazy. He watched his team make four errors, one almost a facsimile of the messed-up caught-stealing attempt from the day before. It was, by some accounts, their worst performance of the year. In some ways, even worse than the beat down in Philadelphia. At least that had been bad pitching. This? This was far worse. Sid Fernandez was again a hard-luck loser, receiving no run support in a 5–1 loss. The Cardinals came back from a 2-run deficit to beat the Cubs. The Mets were now on the outside looking in, a half game out of first. Afterward, the club-house was glum. Players looked as if they were attending a funeral.

In the final game in Montreal, old controversies returned. Strawberry, complaining of soreness in his injured thumb, asked for a day out of the lineup. It did not sit well with his teammates or his manager. They were having flashbacks to the '84 pennant race when their right fielder seemingly quit on them. Only this time, things were much more intense and they were far closer to taking the division.

"When you see Gary Carter taping up his knee the way he did and Ray Knight taking cortisone shots in his hands so he could play, and you see these guys doing everything they could do to get themselves onto the field at almost any cost, and one guy doesn't, you tend to get a little upset," said Backman.[18]

But Davey Johnson could not force him to play, so Heep ended up in right. In what many hoped was a sign of destiny, Heep hit a 3-run home run in the first inning, which accounted for the winning runs. The win allowed them to keep pace with St. Louis, because the Cardinals completed the sweep of the hapless Cubs to stay in first.

After the game, the talk was of Heep's performance and how he came to be in the lineup.

"It's a little disappointing," said Davey Johnson. "I know it probably hurts but not enough that he couldn't take a couple of aspirin and go out and play. But I didn't want to send him out there hurting. Actually, he turned out to be our MVP because it was [M]r. Heep who got us going."[19]

The Mets came back to New York for their last extended home stand of the year. It was seven games against the last three teams in the division: Philadelphia, Chicago, and Pittsburgh. This was a golden opportunity to beat up on the bottom dwellers of the National League in the Phillies and Pirates, and the continuously collapsing Cubs.

IT ALL STARTED OUT great on Monday, September 16 when Dwight Gooden dominated the Phillies. Doc extended his scoreless innings streak to thirty-one, striking out eleven and giving up only two hits in yet another complete-game shutout victory. Gooden himself had as many hits as the Phillies entire team, and drove in 2 runs. For his career, Doc was now averaging at least ten strikeouts a game per every two and a half starts.

"If you searched the world over," said Phillies manager John Felske, "I don't know how many millions of people, but I don't think you'd find another Dwight Gooden. He's already a great pitcher. He dominates the game."[20]

"We've got to be careful. We don't want the Department of Interior to get after us," said Frank Cashen to Davey Johnson after the game.

"Why," asked Johnson.

"Dwight Gooden is one of America's great natural resources," responded Cashen.[21]

While the Mets and their opponents were praising the greatest pitcher in the game, the Cardinals kept winning. They swept a doubleheader against the Pirates, even with Tudor finally getting roughed up.

Gooden may have dominated. Carter may have hit yet another home run and done another curtain call. Everything may have looked great at the start of the home stand. But the Cardinals had still picked up a half game in the standings. The Mets were now one game out of first.

The next night, the Phillies knocked around Ed Lynch and took the game 5–1. The fans, who just a week earlier had been dreaming about a subway series and cheering in ecstasy for the hometown heroes, now booed everyone in sight.

Lynch gets taken out of the game in fourth after giving up 5 runs.
Boo!

Ray Knight makes an error at the start of the sixth.
Boo!

Ron Gardenhire fails to make a play at second.
Boo!

The Mets get only five hits off Shane Rawley.
Boo!

Meanwhile, the Cardinals bashed the Pirates 10–4 and swept Pittsburgh. Now the Mets were two games back.

"Yeah, the fans probably make too much out of one game," said Hernandez, addressing the boos and attempting to show the team was not panicking. "St. Louis isn't going to win every game."[22]

Maybe they were not going to win every game. But the Cardinals had now won six in a row since Mookie crossed home plate on Baseball Thursday. They had made up three games in the process. Worse, the Mets found out they were now losing Doug Sisk for the final two weeks of the year. While some fans probably rejoiced at the news, it was a key loss. Sisk had given up only 1 run over eleven innings in his last seven appearances, winning two games in the process. But bone chips were found in his pitching elbow, and Sisk would not pitch again until the end of May 1986.

Away went the Phillies and in came the Cubs for two games. With the Mets down 2–0 in the first game, Knight came up with bases loaded in the fourth. If there was any human being on the planet who needed a base hit it was Knight. Ray had been mercilessly booed by fans for weeks now. His average hovered around .200, and he was not producing much power at the plate. Years later it would be hard to imagine that a future World Series MVP would be so despised by the hometown faithful. But outside of Sisk, there was no player on the '85 Mets that the fans disliked more than Knight. Moreover, Knight was one ground ball away from tying a Major League record he wanted no part of: most consecutive games grounding into a double play. He had done it four in a row, and if he did it in this game, he would tie the record. And if he did it in this at bat, he might be booed out of the stadium.

But Knight came through with a huge double off the right-field wall, giving the Mets the lead. Roger McDowell preserved the win to keep them two games out because the Cardinals won, again. The Mets won again the next night, pounding the Cubs for 3 home runs, including one from Strawberry, now playing through his thumb pain. All three Mets players who homered—Carter, Strawberry, and Foster—took curtain calls from the crowd. The routine was getting so irksome to opposing players that when Cubs pitcher Ray Fontenot—who had given up all 3 home runs—was removed from the game, he gave the Shea crowd a mock curtain call tip of the cap, before flipping them off.

Taking all nine games at home against Chicago that year, it was only the third time in team history they had swept a season series at Shea. And finally—finally!—the Cardinals lost a game. The Mets knew it for certain because they had the Cardinals-Phillies game on the television in the manager's office while they finished off the Cubs.

"I checked four times," said Hernandez, who served as the provider of updates for his teammates. "It's the way it has to be," he added, referencing the inevitable scoreboard watching that would take place the rest of the year.[23]

The Mets were back to just a game out of first, with the 50-94 Pirates coming to town. St. Louis was headed to Montreal, and while the Expos were out of the race, they were still a difficult team to beat. The next three games looked like a clear break for the Mets.

The Pirates, however, had other ideas. They took the Mets to extra innings in the first game, where New York left three runners on base over the tenth and eleventh innings. Meanwhile, Bill Latham, filling in for the injured Sisk, gave up 2 runs in the top of the eleventh. The Mets came up empty in the bottom of the inning. The fickle hometown crowd sprinkled in boos throughout the night, with Foster receiving the worst vitriol after misplaying a fly ball into a run. The Cardinals, starting a seven-game home stand on the way to playing thirteen of their final sixteen games at home, recovered from their loss the day before and beat the Expos. The Mets were two games back.

A Gooden home run—the first of his career—was part of a 12–1 drubbing of the Pirates the next day. It was no secret that Gooden thought of himself as a good hitter, not just for a pitcher, but in general. He had even talked about preferring to hit a home run over pitching a no-hitter.

"I knew there would be no living with him from now on," said Strawberry of Doc's homer.[24]

"He has been talking about it for two years, so I'm glad he finally did it. Of course, now we'll never hear the end of it," said Hernandez.[25]

It was the first time in eight years a Mets pitcher hit a home run at Shea. Gooden also set the team's single-season record for hits by a pitcher. His record improved to 22-4 and though an unearned run prevented yet another shutout, he had not given up an earned run in thirty-nine innings.

The home run was a great moment in a season of great moments for the young pitcher. But for the team, the win merely kept them from falling further behind in the standings. And in the final game of the series, the team suffered perhaps its most embarrassing loss of the year. Bob Kipper, a rookie pitcher who in eight-plus innings over three appearances had given up 14 runs, stifled the Mets for two hits over eight innings. The Pirates, meanwhile, got to Terry Leach early and often. A ninth-inning rally was too little, too late. The Pirates, the worst team in baseball, took two out of three. The Mets walked back into the clubhouse just in time to find out that Tommy Herr had hit a 2-run home run with two out in the bottom of the ninth inning to beat the Expos. The breaks all seemed to be going St. Louis's way, a reality not lost as the players took on a sullen appearance in postgame interviews.

"At this time of the season," said Backman, "a team 40 games out should not beat us two out of three. The Pirates did. There's no question about it, we've hurt ourselves this weekend."[26]

The Mets hit the road. Ten games over eleven days that would culminate in a three-game set in St. Louis. New York, now three games out, was trying to be realistic. The odds were slim that they would be in first place when that series started. At the very least, they wanted to be within three games or fewer. That would put their fate in their own hands. But they had seven games to take care of before then. And while their opponents—the Phillies, Cubs, and Pirates—might appear to be pushovers, the Mets had just learned that no win would come easy.

Sensing the tension and concern within his teammates, Foster felt the need to step up. He had been around for years. Played for the dominating teams of the Big Red Machine and the horrible Mets teams of the early '8os. He knew the pressures of a pennant race. He also knew this was a young team. He'd been in this spot before. So had Carter, Hernandez, and Rusty Staub. But for almost every other player, this kind of pressure was brand new. Even 1984, which had been exciting, did not match this.

Foster was not the most outgoing guy. Of the entire team, few would have picked him as the one to grab the bullhorn and rally a crowd. But now, with the Mets' season teetering on the brink, he felt the need to step in. So, as the Mets gathered in the clubhouse of Veterans Stadium before their first game of the road trip, Foster called a team meeting. There was no yelling. There was no in-your-face talk of stepping up your game or to stop dogging it. It was not a movie moment, filled with inspirational words and tired sports phrases. Instead, it was a plea to just stay focused.

Don't give up.

Don't think the St. Louis Cardinals can "walk on water."

Stay focused on winning each game because that was what you can control.

"The main idea of the meeting was to tell them not to keep looking at the scoreboard," said Foster. "Don't worry about the Cardinals. Play your own game, don't try to hit a five-run home run. We've got to tie them by Oct. 6, that's the message."[27]

His teammates appeared to take Foster's message to heart. They looked sharper, more focused in Philadelphia. The results showed on the field. The Mets won both games against the Phillies by a combined score of 11–2. Carter hit his thirtieth home run. Fernandez threw a two-hitter. The Mets stole bases. They moved runners over. They beat up a team they should have beat up. In the process, the team record went to 92-59, already making 1985 the second most successful regular season in team history.

Foster's message about the team just focusing on their games was true, to a point. The Mets losing games certainly did the team no favors. But facts were facts: they were three games behind with less than two weeks to play. They had to pay attention to what the Cardinals were doing. Case in point: while the Mets were beating up the Phillies, the Cardinals were beating up the Pirates. The same Pirates who had played like contenders in New York had wilted in St. Louis. A dropped routine fly ball had given the Cardinals one of the games. New York remained three games out.

THE METS BLINKED IN Chicago and badly. In the first game, they built a 4–1 lead going into the bottom of the sixth. The Cubs chipped away against Ron Darling and McDowell, tying the game going into the bottom of the ninth. There, with two out and no one on, Orosco gave up a walk to Davey Lopes. He then had him picked off first base after Lopes broke too early on an attempted steal, but Hernandez got the ball stuck in his glove trying to throw to second, and Lopes made it in time. That was followed by a walk, and then a single.

Game over.

Orosco sat on the bench after, his head buried in his hand. Later that day, the Cardinals won again. Four games back.

"It hurts," said Davey Johnson after the game, a shell-shocked look on his face. "Darling's got a 4–1 lead, and that should be enough. Then I had my best relief pitcher out there, and my other stopper ready. But it didn't work out that way."[28]

Gooden staunched the bleeding somewhat the next day, tossing his eighth shutout of the year. It broke the team's all-time record, and extended his streak of not allowing an earned run to forty-eight innings. But the Cardinals won again. Still four games out.

BILLY MARTIN'S ERRATIC BEHAVIOR started the day after the Blue Jays left town. The Indians came to New York for a makeup game, and with Toronto off, the Yankees had a chance to pick up a free half game for first. Before the game began, reporters gathered in Martin's office for the usual pregame questions and quote-grabbing opportunities. As Billy walked in, his office phone began ringing.

"Who is this," he quickly snapped at the caller, before saying he couldn't talk as he was about to begin a press conference. A short time later, the phone rang again.

"I told you before," Martin yelled at the Yankees' switchboard operator, "I'm in the middle of a press conference."[29]

Though Billy did not say, most of the reporters assumed the incessant caller was Steinbrenner.

Once the game began, the Yankees looked like they might be righting the ship. Joe Cowley pitched into the eighth, leaving the game with a 4–3 lead that the Yankees pushed to 5–3 heading into the top of the ninth. On the mound stood Brian Fisher, the rookie whose fastball and slider had captivated Martin earlier in the year. Fisher, of San Antonio, Texas, and Aurora, Colorado, had started playing baseball as a shortstop and then catcher. Toward the end of high school, the six-foot-four Fisher starting pitching and found he had a blazing fastball. He was drafted by the Braves in 1980 and spent four years in the Minor Leagues. Brian was playing winter ball in Puerto Rico in December of 1984 when his father called to tell him he had been traded to the Yankees.

"I was like, 'Who did I get traded for?' He said, 'I don't know.' I said, 'Well Dad it kind of makes a difference if I got traded for a Major League player or for a Minor League one.'"[30]

Fisher was traded for Major Leaguer catcher Rick Cerone and that spring immediately impressed the team. But there was no place for him on the roster, and he spent the first month of the year in Triple-A Columbus. One week after Martin became manager, Fisher, a starter his whole career, was called up to give the Yankees help in the bullpen. He was an immediate hit, becoming a right-handed option to help supplement the lefty Righetti to close games. Rather than pout about sharing closing duties with a rookie, Rags took Fisher under his wing.

"He was the best individual I have ever played with in terms of how he treated people," said Fisher of Righetti. "He was the definite glue and the power of that pen. He was unselfish. He was awesome."[31]

Starting that ninth inning against Cleveland, Fisher was in the running for Rookie of the Year honors. His ERA stood at 2.00, he was 4-3, and he had converted 12 of 14 save opportunities.

But he began that ninth inning by giving up three straight singles to load the bases.

The Yankees desperately needed to hang on to this 2-run lead. So most people wondered why Martin, in this critical moment, was not bringing Righetti in to face the left-handed Brett Butler. Instead, Martin allowed Fisher to stay in the game while Righetti stood on the mound in the left-center-field bullpen, helplessly watching what happened next. Butler grounded out to knock in a run. The next batter also grounded out without causing any trouble. With runners on second and third and two out, Fisher then allowed a triple to Julio Franco, followed by an even more devastating 2-run home run to Andre Thornton. A walk, a stolen base and a Joe Carter single later, and the Indians had taken a 9–5 lead. Throughout the entire rally, Righetti remained in the bullpen. Fisher saw his ERA rise from 2.00 to 2.56. The Yankees fell five games behind the Blue Jays.

After the game, everyone was left scratching their heads. Why had Billy left a rookie pitcher in the game so long when the situation seemed to obviously call for Righetti? Everyone else may have seen it, but Martin did not, and he was irate at anyone who disagreed.

"I went with him [Fisher] because that's what I thought was best for the team, not what you guys [the media] or the fans want," said a clearly annoyed and angry Martin. "Do I have to repeat myself again? I did not want to want to waste two pitchers in a losing game. I had Righetti warming up but when they popped him [Fisher] quick with that home run, I had him [Righetti] stop throwing."[32]

"To be honest, I have no idea—and neither does Dave [Righetti]—why I was out there that long," said Fisher. "Billy never said anything to me about it. But I did give up 6 runs and that was devastating at the time."[33]

Most likely, Martin was reacting to something Steinbrenner had said a few days prior. Martin had brought Righetti into a game in the fifth inning, prompting The Boss to ask the *Washington Post's* Tom Boswell to ask Martin why he used his closer so early.

"Ask Billy, but don't tell him who told you to do so," Steinbrenner told Boswell.[34]

But Martin knew damn well where the question came from. Combined with the criticism of his players, not to mention losing games in the standings every day, Martin began to fray. So in response to the question of why he would use his closer so early, he decided at the next opportunity to just not use his closer at all. It cost the Yankees a game.

The Yankees flew out to Detroit for a three-game series with the

Tigers, and things only deteriorated further. In fact, with each passing day, things seemed to get progressively worse in every possible way. Before the start of the first game, Martin got a less than inspiring phone call from Steinbrenner.

"If we're not going to win," The Boss told him, "let's go down fighting. Let's not lie down like dogs.[35]

Steinbrenner could not have been pleased when Guidry proceeded to give up a career-high 5 home runs and the team managed only four hits, falling 9–1.

The following night, the Yankees hoped history would be on their side when Phil Niekro tried again for win number three hundred. The moment now had even greater Hollywood-magic-type possibilities, as Phil's brother, Joe, a successful pitcher in his own right for over a dozen years in the National League, had been traded to the Yankees days earlier. Joe had the pleasure of calling their ailing father, whom neither was sure might live long enough to see Phil hit the milestone, and letting him know that Joe would be seeing the game in-person, as a teammate of his brother's.

There was, however, no magic moment that night, outside of one of the most bizarre episodes in team history. The score was tied at 2 in the top of the sixth inning when, with two runners on, Mike Pagliarulo came to the plate against Tigers pitcher Mickey Mahler. A journeyman spot-starter and reliever, now on his fifth team in eight seasons, the left-handed Mahler was known for a decent curveball that could be hell on lefties. With their season slowly fading away and in need of a big moment, Martin had an idea.

"He's [Pagliarulo] a natural right-handed hitter. He hits right-handed in intrasquad games and hits the hell out of the ball," Martin explained to reporters after the game.

Martin was not totally incorrect. Pagliarulo had been a switch hitter in high school and had batted right-handed in college. Just two weeks before the Detroit game, Pagliarulo had volunteered to bat righty in a simulated game for pitcher Marty Bystrom.

"I hit a ground ball one at bat. Then I get a base hit. Then I hit a ball off the wall to the opposite field," recalled Pagliarulo.

So Martin, with a nod from Lou Piniella and not wanting to

sacrifice defense for a pinch hitter, sent Pagliarulo up to bat from the right side of the plate. The problem was that Pagliarulo had never hit righty against Major League pitching and had not even attempted to do it during an actual game since playing at the University of Miami in 1981.

"Then," when actually facing Major League pitching noted Pagliarulo, "all the sudden, hitting right-handed is not easy. But in Billy's mind it's, 'I just saw you hitting right-handed off Marty Bystrom, a right-handed pitcher."[36]

As he strode up to the plate, setting his feet in the right-hand batter's box, Tigers catcher Bob Melvin could not help but ask, "What are you doing?"

"I'm trying to get a base hit," Pagliarulo responded, "what do you think?"[37]

Years earlier, this may have been the exact kind of kooky stunt that would have had people lauding Martin as a genius, willing to try anything to win a game. But when Pagliarulo ended up striking out looking, it merely called into question if Martin was losing his grip on both the team and reality.

"Pags hitting right-handed? He had no chance hitting right-handed. It was like sending me up there hitting left-handed," said Baylor.[38]

The Yankees ended up losing 5–2. Mahler, giving up only one hit in seven and two-thirds innings of relief, picked up the last win of his Major League career.

The Yankees had now lost six in a row, their longest losing streak in three years. Only a two-game losing streak by the Blue Jays prevented them from dropping further in the standings. Niekro had missed out on history, yet again. Moreover, Martin's actions with Fisher and Pagliarulo had people talking, one person in particular.

"Publicly, Steinbrenner has even had some good things to say about Martin," wrote Moss Klein the day after the 5–2 loss, someone whom The Boss frequently leaked to over the years and often tried to use to plant negative stories or to play against a competing newspaper (which Klein grew tired of quickly). "But privately, he's making the tiresome old charges about Martin losing control, wearing down physically, all the usual charges that the owner has used so many times in his affairs with Martin throughout the years."[39]

It got to a point where Steinbrenner was so concerned about Martin's mental state, he asked Billy's friend and agent Eddie Sapir to fly to Detroit and make sure he was okay.[40]

Even the players were having a hard time understanding their manager's line of thinking.

"On the bench, he [Martin] had guys with something like 4,000 at-bats [combined] right-handed," said one unidentified player about the Pagliarulo incident. "And he goes with a guy who has never swung a bat right-handed. How do you do that? Explain that to me."[41]

The next day, in desperate need of a win, Joe Niekro failed to make it out of the second inning in his team debut. The Yankees lost 10–3, the first time they had been swept by the Tigers since 1970. Martin, searching for answers, seemed almost ready to give up.

"All of a sudden, the pitching has stopped and the hitting has stopped. You can't even manage. What can you do?"[42]

They fell five and a half games back of first.

"The Yankees, who just one week ago looked like a team headed for the World Series, once again bore more resemblance to a team that had lost interest in itself and the season," wrote Klein.[43]

"They're out of it," wrote Keith Hernandez upon hearing of the Yankees' loss. He blamed their lack of pitching and their owner.

In the week since Hassey's stadium-shaking home run, the Yankees had lost seven straight games, four games in the standings, their owner was bickering with everyone, and their manager seemed to be losing his mind. Someway, somehow, it all got worse when the team got to Baltimore on Friday September 20 for a three-game weekend series against the Orioles.

It started in the seventh inning of the first game. The score was tied at 2, and Baltimore had a runner on first with two out. With Bordi on the mound and a 2-0 count on Lee Lacy, Wynegar looked over to the Yankees' dugout for a sign from his manager. At just that moment, Martin scratched his nose.

"Billy's pitchout sign is when he puts his hand to his nose," explained Wynegar after the game. "I looked over and saw him rubbing his nose. I just happened to look over at that moment."[44]

With a 2-0 count, it seemed odd that Martin would call for a pitchout. But the baserunner, Alan Wiggins, had already stolen two bases in the game, and Wynegar was given what he thought were his marching orders. There was only one problem: Martin was not calling for a pitchout. He simply had an itchy nose.

Wiggins did not steal and the count went to 3-0, with Lacy eventually walking. Cal Ripken and Eddie Murray followed with back-to-back singles, scoring 2 runs and giving the Orioles the game. The Yankees fell six and a half back. Afterward, Martin tried to shrug it off as a "what can you do" moment. But for many, it simply bolstered the idea that Billy was losing it and bringing the team down with him. Then, approximately three hours after the game ended, the seemingly inevitable happened: Martin got into an altercation.

THE YANKEES STAYED AT the Cross Keys Inn for a reason: situated several miles northwest of downtown Baltimore, its seclusion robbed players of a chance to get into trouble. The hotel bar was the place to grab a drink and reflect on the game without doing much damage to themselves, others, or anyone's property. Following the loss to the Orioles, Martin and several players headed there. Despite the losing streak and the bizarre mishaps, by all accounts, Martin was in good spirits throughout the night. As often happened, Billy engaged with fans who recognized him. He sent over a bottle of champagne to a couple who'd been married only hours earlier. All was civil.

Then, around 1:30 in the morning, the man whom Martin had so recently charmed by buying him champagne approached Billy, clearly agitated. He had just stepped away to use the bathroom and while gone, Martin had talked to his new bride. After returning, the man and his wife went back to their table. But almost immediately, the man got up and approached Martin.

"We've got to talk," said the man, starting a conversation that was witnessed by several reporters sitting with or near Martin. "You said something to my wife."

"Get lost, pal," Martin replied.

"You told my wife she has a pot belly. I just married her this afternoon."

"I didn't say she had a pot belly," said Martin, seeking to correct the record. "I said this woman here," as he pointed to another woman seated at the bar, "has a fat ass."

Pushing and shoving ensued. Several players came to stop Martin from getting into yet another fight. The man was asked to leave by the bar manager, but that was not good enough for Martin. He tried to follow the groom out of the bar but by the time he got to the lobby, the man had disappeared.

"He [Martin] thought that Steinbrenner had sent the guy, that it was a set up," said Klein. "That Steinbrenner had sent him in to provoke him so he could get into a fight and he could fire him."[45]

There was no evidence that that was the case, and by Martin standards, this was a pretty mild incident. No punches were thrown, no one was knocked out, and no one received any serious injuries. That would have to wait about another twenty-four hours.

The Yankees got back to business that Saturday. With Cowley on the mound, they ended their eight-game losing streak, taking the second game against the Orioles 5–2. While they failed to pick up a game on Toronto, the win seemed to immediately ease some of the pressure on everyone. The good feelings continued as everyone got to the bar at the Cross Keys Inn.

Just like the night before, several players went to the bar. Martin was there too, seated at the bar. Just like the night before, by all accounts, Martin was calm and in good spirits. Then, someone came over to warn him: Whitson, sitting at one of the tables opposite the bar, was getting into it with a fan, and it looked like Whitson was going to seriously hurt the guy. No one disputes that Martin approached the table looking to prevent his pitcher from getting into trouble. There was no reason for Billy to be looking for a fight. But in a moment's time, he suddenly had one.

BORN IN TENNESSEE, EDDIE Lee Whitson liked country music, a good beer, and his views had a conservative bent to them. Whitson was the definition of a good ole country boy. He was from a small town and, for most of his early career, had played for small-market teams. Whitson was never one of the league's premier pitchers, but after going 14-8 for the National League champion Padres in 1984, Steinbrenner offered him a five-year, $4.4 million contract. Whitson at first declined the offer, but reconsidered after The Boss added an option for a sixth year and Whitson's choice of teams to be traded to should things not work out. It was a fairly large amount of money for a pitcher who had been mostly average his entire career, but it was not necessarily anything new for Steinbrenner.

Whitson's time in New York was hell from the beginning. He injured himself pulling up his socks just before his first start in Boston. He was 1-6 in his first seven decisions with a 6.23 ERA. There was no explanation for it. He and his teammates felt his stuff was just as good as it had been in San Diego the year before, yet he was not fooling any hitters. In fact, he was getting crushed in outing after outing.

Yankees fans had been looking for any sign to cheer the big free-agent acquisition. When it looked like no sign was coming, they began to unmercifully taunt Whitson. But it went beyond booing whenever Whitson took the mound or left a game early. Whitson claimed fans began following him home from Yankee Stadium. They left tacks underneath the tires of his car. Hate mail began pouring in, some of it incredibly threatening. Whitson would show stacks of it to reporters, many of whom began to empathize with a man they could see was just not meant to pitch in an environment like this.

"It's like working in an office and your boss comes in and says, 'You suck,' after you've tried your best," Whitson said twenty-five years later. "Now multiply that by 50,000 bosses, all of them telling you that you suck, and imagine what that feels like."[46]

In addition to the fans, Whitson had to contend with a manager that simply did not like him. Billy's habit of looking upon certain players more favorably than others rankled Whitson, as did Martin's incessant screaming and second-guessing of any pitcher who made what he thought was a mistake on the mound. Martin, in turn, could not stomach Whitson's makeup as a player, his inability to shake off the fans taunting and just pitch. John Montefusco, an oft-injured starting pitcher on the team, had predicted trouble between Whitson and Martin from the start.

"Watch out for Martin and Whitson," he had told Moss Klein after Billy became manager. "I know Whitson. I've been on teams with him before, with the Giants and Padres. There's no way—no way in hell—that Whitson will be able to deal with Billy. There's gonna be bloodshed, believe me."[47]

Despite all of it, Whitson managed to turn things around starting in mid-June, going 5-1 over nine starts and lowering his era below 4. But in August, it came apart again. Some felt it was the firing of Mark Connor that had started Whitson's decline. He'd been close to the Yankees' pitching coach, who acted as a buffer between him and the manager that could not stand him. Though he was 2-0 in August, Whitson failed to get past the fifth inning in four of his six starts, and never gave up fewer than 4 earned runs in a game. After his start against the Angels on August 31, Martin claimed Whitson had injured his back just before giving up a home run to Ruppert Jones, but had not told anyone. When asked about his injury, Whitson told reporters, "Go ask Billy, he has all the answers."[48]

Trouble was already brewing.

Heading into Baltimore, Whitson had given up 13 runs in his last fifteen innings (though he had still managed to win two games). He was slated to start that Friday night but was scratched right before the game and replaced with Rich Bordi. Asked afterward what happened, Martin told reporters, "Whatchamacallit's arm isn't ready."

Whitson—the whatchamacallit in question—denied anything was wrong with his arm.

"I feel fine. Talk to the man. He has all the answers."[49]

Whitson, always a bit high-strung, proceeded to laugh as he showed reporters his "fine" arm. Then, seeing a *Playboy Magazine* lying around with a "Miss May" centerfold, he laughed even harder.

"Do you think Winfield is a friend of hers," he asked. Whitson then walked across the clubhouse to find Winfield, who was talking to several of the beat writers.

"Look, you're Mr. May and this is Ms. May. Do you know her?" he asked his teammate.[50]

The pitcher seemed to be falling apart under the pressure.

Informed of Whitson's retort about his arm being fine, Martin grew agitated, saying Whitson had told him before that his arm was sore, and he was not ready to pitch. By this point, things were coming to a head and a confrontation was almost inevitable.

Enter Albert Millus, then a twenty-nine-year-old attorney from Binghamton, New York. Millus, a Yankees fan, had come to Baltimore to meet some friends and watch the series. He had decided to stay at the Cross Keys Inn based on a friend's recommendation, specifically because that was where the Yankees stayed. He roomed across the hall from Winfield and saw several players that weekend. On Saturday night, he was sitting at a table in the Cross Keys Inn bar with a friend. At the table next to them sat Whitson. In the bar at that moment were several Yankees players, team personnel, and team beat writers.

Millus knew Whitson played for the team, but did not know exactly which player he was. Suddenly, he saw Whitson become visibly agitated, point toward Martin at the bar and say, "There's the son of a bitch who's causing my problems."

Then, noticing Millus and his friend staring at him, Whitson swung around in their direction, pointed his finger in Millus's face and asked him what business was it of his. Millus, thinking he was talking to a rookie making the league minimum, told Whitson if he were making $90,000 a year, he would not be "acting like a little kid."

"All of the sudden, he jumped up, and I think he let out a roar and he grabbed me by the throat. Completely took me by surprise," recalled Millus. Whitson's grip was strong enough to leave a mark that was still visible days later.[51]

At this point, someone warned Martin, who rushed over to stop Whitson from causing any further harm. At that moment, there was no worse person in the world for Ed Whitson to see than Martin.

"Eddie, you're drunk, you don't need this," said Martin, trying to restrain his pitcher.

Whitson was having no part of it. He began cursing at Martin. In response, Martin called Whitson crazy.

"What's the matter with him," Billy asked as several players joined in to break up the scuffle. Whitson, more livid now at being called crazy, called Martin a "motherfucker." That was good enough for Billy, who responded by punching Whitson in the face, splitting his lip. At that point, Ron Hassey grabbed a still seething Whitson and pulled him into the hotel lobby.

Martin immediately set out to continue the fight and pursued Whitson into the lobby. Whitson, his arms pinned to his sides by teammates trying to end the scuffle, was trained in martial arts. He knew how to defend himself in a situation just like this. As Martin approached, Whitson let rip with the kick of a man unleashing months of pent up anger and frustration. He got Martin square in the groin, sending Billy to the ground screaming in pain.

"Now you did it. I'm going to kill you. I have to do it. I have to do it," said a still writhing Martin.

As Martin lay on the ground, Whitson was dragged outside the hotel and into the parking lot. Instead of ending the fight, Martin broke loose from those trying to restrain him and headed straight outside. Once Whitson saw him, he charged straight ahead, like a bull heading toward a matador. He tackled Martin hard, sending him into the lot's concrete pavement. By this time, Martin had a broken arm, broken ribs, and a bloody nose. The two were screaming at each other as they fought: Martin about how Whitson was finished with the Yankees, Whitson about how Martin had tried to ruin him. This all happened in full view of many of the Yankees' beat writers, most of whom had tired of the antics of Billy and the Yankees, even if it made for good copy. As the police showed up and the fight seemed to end, many of the writers went back to their rooms to try and file this new story, though it was so late in the night that it was past deadline.

Whitson was escorted by several teammates around the back of the hotel to a service elevator, where they proceeded to bring him up to his third-floor room. Martin went back into the bar to cool down and recover from his injuries, which were many. But

Billy could never back away from a fight until it was truly over . . . until he won.

He went looking for Whitson, first asking the hotel clerk where his room was and then, when not getting the information, getting into the elevator and heading to the third floor. In a case of incredibly bad timing, Whitson just happened to be walking past Martin's elevator when the doors opened. Seeing each other again, they both began shouting and tussling a fourth time. Several of the beat writers were already on the third floor, having gone there to wake up a colleague who had missed the whole thing, and saw the final act of the fight. The noise was so loud that the *Daily News*'s Bill Madden, sitting inside his third-floor room on the phone with his New York office trying to get the story in, could hear everything and continued dictating the story in real time.

Martin and Whitson were quickly escorted back to their rooms and the fight, which took place in four separate parts in or around the hotel, was finally over. Piniella, having been out to dinner, missed the whole thing. He got back to the hotel to find several police cars in the parking lot. Willie Horton told him what happened, and he immediately went up to Martin's room.

"He was standing there in his underwear, his arm in a sling, with scratches and cuts all over his face," Piniella recalled.[52]

Everyone who saw him that night and over the next few days agreed that Martin, by far, got the worst of the fight.

It did not take long for word to get back to Steinbrenner about the altercation. Before issuing any kind of verdict, The Boss wanted to know exactly what had happened. He was already wondering if Martin was cracking. If Billy deliberately set out to attack one of his own players, The Boss would be left with little choice but to fire him. In an odd way, the Martin-Whitson encounter helped Steinbrenner avert what surely would have been an abundance of negative press. The day after the Martin-Whitson incident, the *New York Times*' Murray Chass broke that Steinbrenner has been responsible for killing two trades that could have paid immense dividends for the team. The first would have sent Mike Armstrong to the Tigers for Darrell Evans, who was leading the American League in home runs. The second would have sent Ken Griffey—whom Steinbrenner had repeatedly been claiming no team wanted—to the Pittsburgh Pirates for pitcher John Candelaria. The brawl at the Cross Keys took away any attention this story would have otherwise gotten.

In the end, Steinbrenner did not take disciplinary action against either Martin or Whitson. But the incident almost certainly sealed Billy's fate once the season was over. Moreover, the beat writers following the team, who had hoped to get through just one season without Billy self-destructing, expressed how fed up they were with the whole stage play now coming to the end of its fourth act.

"Billy did well to get the Yankees as far as that series with Toronto at Yankee Stadium," wrote *Newsday*'s Steve Jacobson. "Then, under the mounting pressure of failure, he appears to have lost his grip. The items of the past two weeks are something from a psychiatrist's notebook."[53]

Others lamented on the tired refrain from Martin that it was never his fault when a fight broke out.

"You can argue all you want about whether Billy Martin has a drinking problem," wrote the *Bergen Record*'s Celizic. "The fact remains that he has a history of airing out his fists in barroom brawls. In Martin's ethos, that's not a drinking problem. He is never at fault. It's always the other guy."[54]

The Martin-Whitson brawl was the last in a series of events over eight days that rivaled anything ever experienced in the franchise's history. Not even the chaotic Bronx Zoo years could top the bizarre-on-top-of-bizarre episodes that occurred between the time Hassey hit his go-ahead home run against the Blue Jays and Whitson and Martin had one last go of it outside the third-floor elevator of the Cross Keys Inn.

Regardless of the insanity, the Yankees still had a season to fight for. The next day, Martin arrived at Memorial Stadium with his right arm in a sling, joking about the previous night's incident.

"This guy [Whitson] flights like a sissy, with his feet," said Martin. But "if he can pitch, he'll pitch. I never said I had to like my players. And if I have to yank him out, I'll do it. But I'll watch his feet."[55]

Whitson, on the advice of his lawyer, offered no immediate comment. Eventually he issued a statement expressing his regret for the incident and that he was now focused on winning the pennant race. Martin said that Whitson's next start would be held back until the team's next road trip. He did not want him getting booed at home. On the field that day, Guidry won his twentieth game, the third time in his career he reached that mark, and the Yankees picked up one game on the Blue Jays.

After an off day—noteworthy only for Martin stopping into the Copacabana night club, site of his ultimate demise as a Yankees player, for a beer—the team returned to New York, where Niekro tried one more time for win number three hundred. Martin was late to the stadium after having to go to the doctor's for further evaluation after the fight. It was discovered that in addition to the broken arm, he had a few cracked ribs. The clubhouse atmosphere was funeral like, with one player yelling at the press if anyone actually wanted to talk about baseball.[56] The funereal atmosphere was broken by an unwelcome visit from Steinbrenner.

The day before, Peter Ueberroth had issued a letter asking all players to individually participate in a drug-testing program. The letter was not sent directly to the players but given to ownership to distribute. Owners rushed to get their players to agree to the program. At least that is what Steinbrenner wanted his players to think. Brandishing copies of the letter, Steinbrenner walked into the clubhouse, informed the team that the Mets had all already agreed to take part (which was not true) and that he wanted all of them to do the same. Winfield, the team's player rep, walked into this impromptu meeting late. He saw an attempt by the owners to go around the union, and he was not having it.

LIFE WITH THE YANKEES had been rough for Dave Winfield. The St. Paul, Minnesota, native had been drafted in baseball, football, and basketball. It was an amazing accomplishment, a testament to the incredible athletic ability of this six-foot-six, 230-pound giant of a man. Winfield chose baseball, signing with the Padres and skipping over the Minor Leagues to head straight to the Majors. He quickly showed power, speed, fielding prowess, and a rocket of an arm in the outfield. With the Padres in the late '70s, Winfield made a name for himself, making the All-Star team four times, winning two Gold Gloves, and hitting mammoth home runs that seemed to leave his bat and just continue going straight up.

Winfield became the prized free agent of the 1980 off-season, and Steinbrenner swooped right in with his charm and big city appeal. Winfield was hooked, and signed a ten-year, $23 million contract. It was the largest contract, by far, anyone had ever signed to that point. But the deal was not supposed to be that large, at least not in Steinbrenner's mind. The Boss had failed to grasp what a cost-of-living adjustment in the contract truly meant in terms of salary and compensation. He thought the deal was for $16 million, not $23 million. After Winfield signed, the Yankees' beat writers figured out what Steinbrenner had not, and posted the $23 million figure. Steinbrenner was livid, most likely embarrassed that a player had gotten one over on him. According to Winfield, he felt bad about the situation and offered to renegotiate the cost-of-living adjustment to defer some of the payments. A new deal was struck, but many believed Steinbrenner never truly forgave Winfield for besting him in negotiations.

In Winfield's first year, the Yankees made it all the way to the World Series. But his 1-22 performance in the Fall Classic left a bad taste in The Boss's mouth. This was not what he was paying him all this money to do. Then in 1983, while warming up between innings in Toronto, Winfield threw a baseball toward a seagull sitting in the outfield. He thought it would move: it did not. The ball nailed the bird straight on, killing it. Animal lovers were outraged, and Toronto police came into the clubhouse afterward to arrest him on charges of animal cruelty. The charges were eventually dropped. The following year, Winfield lost out to Mattingly for the batting title, and the fact that most fans had been rooting for Mattingly hurt him deeply.

During all of this, Winfield had to contend with Steinbrenner constantly berating him in the press. This, despite Winfield being an All-Star and, outside of the strike shortened '81 season, driving in over 100 runs in each of his first four seasons in New York. It started almost from the time he signed his contract. Winfield ran a charity that provided a host of services to the underprivileged. As part of Winfield's contract, Steinbrenner was supposed to make quarterly payments to the charity. Toward the end of 1981, The Boss stopped doing so, and eventually he questioned the methods and even the legality of how Winfield was running the charity. It would eventually end up in court.

Steinbrenner also constantly criticized Winfield's play on the field, saying he was a good player, but not as good as "Reggie."

"I wasn't sure then, and I'm still not, what his gripe is with me," Winfield wrote in his 1988 autobiography, which was scathing in its criticism of Steinbrenner. "Part of it, I think, as a frustrated athlete with marginal ability, George wants to 'own' his players, wants them up on their flippers barking for fish like trained seals. And from the beginning, I refused to bark."[57]

Now, as Winfield watched Steinbrenner try and usurp his authority as player rep, he refused, yet again, to bark. When Steinbrenner started passing out copies of the commissioner's letter, Winfield stepped in and put an end to it, in a confrontation that, as Rex Hudler later recalled, made the hair stand "up on the back of everyone's neck."[58]

"Excuse me," said Winfield. "I'll take those and distribute them. I'm the player rep on this team. It's my job. This is my team in that regard."

"Not for long. I'm the boss around here. We'll see if you're going to be around next season," responded Steinbrenner.

"Oh, yeah? Well, I'm not worried about it. Because you know and I know where I'm going to be next year, and that's right here!"

"We'll see about that!"

"Yeah, we will."

Steinbrenner then stormed out of the clubhouse. After Winfield discussed the issue with his teammates, Steinbrenner called him into Martin's office. Embarrassed about losing face in front of the players, The Boss told Winfield there could be no more confrontations like that, because they were not good for the team. Winfield let loose.

"Not good for the team!? I'll tell you what's not good for the team," and Winfield proceeded to layout all of Steinbrenner's comments during the Toronto series and how he was making things worse for the team.[59]

According to Winfield, the next day Steinbrenner called him in for another meeting where he said they would just never see eye-to-eye. He offered to trade Winfield to the team of his choice that very day. Winfield declined.

The incident was not surprising, given the history of the two. Nor was it shocking to anyone who knew Winfield well. He was a tremendous athlete, yes, but Winfield was also a smart businessman, who made sure to know detail and process.

Winfield was not going to bow down to Steinbrenner, and he was going to be certain he knew more than him as well.

Back on the field, the first home game after Baltimore kept up the malaise of the team. Niekro gave up 6 runs before the end of the third inning, and the Yankees went down 9–1. After being removed in the fifth inning, the normally even-tempered Niekro grabbed a bat and smashed the metal frame encasing the payphone outside the Yankees' clubhouse. Toronto had picked up a half game during the off day and won again that night. Their division lead was now up to seven games, with just twelve games left in the season. The loss concluded the worst, most bizarre stretch of games the Yankees had ever played.

"Oh god . . . [this] is bringing back a lot of things I tried to forget about," said Baylor over twenty-five years later when asked about that stretch of games.[60]

"The handwriting is on the wall," said Steinbrenner. "We're not eliminated, but we're very close to that perilous point."[61]

The next day, the *New York Times* ran a small two paragraph blurb on the front of its sports page. The title summed up the feeling of the city and both teams succinctly: "Subway Series Fading."

# 9

# "One Tremendous Baseball Season"

THE YANKEES HAD ELEVEN scheduled games left in the regular season, plus one possible makeup should they actually make a run for first place. To have any chance at winning the division, they were going to need to win, at a minimum, at least ten of those games. Seeing as how three of them were a season-ending series against the Blue Jays in Toronto, that meant they needed to pick up at least four games in the standings between Wednesday, September 25 and Thursday, October 3. That would put them three games out heading into Toronto, where they could control their own destiny by sweeping the series.

Following the 9–1 loss to the Tigers, the offense exploded against Jack Morris. Don Mattingly, leading the league in RBIS, doubles, extra-base hits, and game-winning hits, drilled his thirty-first home run, and Rickey Henderson set a single season team record by stealing his seventy-fifth base. Joe Niekro gave up 1 run over five innings, and the team won 10–2. Coupled with a Toronto loss, they picked up a game and were now just six back. After an off day and a rain out, they began a four-game series at home against the Orioles on Saturday, September 28. Down in the ninth, they rallied for 2 runs, with Dave Winfield winning the game on a two-out single. The next day, they swept both games of a doubleheader, picking up another half game in the standings.

The fourth game brought yet another chance for history at the Stadium. Phil Niekro tried a fourth time for win number three hundred. That Monday had been a long and emotional day for the Niekro brothers. They'd been in Wheeling, West Virginia, in the morning to visit their sick father, then driven an hour to Pittsburgh, caught a flight, and arrived at Yankee Stadium just after 5:00 p.m. Whether it was the strain of a long day, or just the motions of the baseball season, Niekro did not get his three hundredth that night. Instead, he left the game in the eighth inning with the team trailing 4–2. He would have one more chance at history, on the final day of the year in Toronto. Unable to afford a loss, the Yankees clawed back in the bottom of the ninth. Mattingly, about to be named American League Player of the Month for the second consecutive month, hit a game-tying 2-run home run and Don Baylor drove in the winning run with a single to give the team a 5–4 win. Henderson, Winfield, and Mattingly became the first trio of Yankees teammates to score 100 runs in a season since 1950. The team picked up a half game in the standings and were now five back with six to play and one possible makeup game. Any combination of Yankees losses or Blue Jays wins totaling three over those last six games, and the season was over.

"We're still knocking on the door," said Winfield. "Maybe by some freak of nature, they'll fall on their faces and we'll slip into first place and right into the history books."[1]

ON MOVED THE METS to Pittsburgh, the last series before the three games in St. Louis. That Friday night, in front of fewer than five thousand people, it looked as if the Mets' season had come to an end. Staked to a 5–2 lead in the bottom of the third inning, Tom Gorman, Wes Gardner, and Randy Niemann coughed it up. Five singles, two walks, and one big error. The Mets were now down. Trailing by 1 in the top of the ninth, Ray Knight and Keith Hernandez both singled to lead off the inning. But they never left second or first base.

The Cardinals were rained out in Montreal. The Mets were now four and a half games out, their largest deficit since watching fireworks light up the early morning sky in Atlanta. One more loss before St. Louis, and the season would be all but over. The Mets needed something, anything, to keep their hopes alive. They got it in a spark from their manager and a clutch performance by their closer.

In the second game at Pittsburgh, umpire Joe West tossed Davey Johnson in the fourth inning. With two runners on, Tony Peña hit what Johnson thought was a ground-ball double play. But West called the runner at second safe. Johnson was livid. A call like that—the way this team was going—could cost them the game and end the year. Johnson got his money's worth in the argument, eventually saying the magic words that got him tossed. It was his fourth ejection of the year, and so far, the Mets had won the other three games. It gave the team a spark of life when it needed it.

Then, in the ninth inning, up 3–1, Roger McDowell allowed a double and two walks to load the bases. From the clubhouse, Davey Johnson told Mel Stottlemyre to bring in Jesse Orosco. It was a risky move, given Orosco's recent propensity for giving up big hits. But there were few options. The tension was gut wrenching. The Mets had been through this too many times before in the last few weeks. Often, they ended up on the wrong end. Orosco had to save this game. He had to. A blown save here, even if he was not the one who loaded the bases, would be devastating beyond recovery.

Jesse, who had blown the lead or lost the game in four of his last six appearances, reared back, found what he needed, and struck out the next two hitters. He had come through bigtime. Meanwhile, the Cardinals split their doubleheader against the Expos, so the Mets picked up a half game in the standings. Four back.

One more game in Pittsburgh. One more chance for devastation from the bullpen. Up 2 in the eighth, McDowell gave up three hits, allowing Pittsburgh to tie the game. Then Orosco, less than twenty-four hours removed from his heroics, gave up a single to give the Pirates the lead.

Down a run in the ninth, and with their season yet again teetering on the brink, the Mets needed a big hit. Howard Johnson supplied it, lining a shot over the wall in right to tie the game. The Cardinals, listening to a play-by-play being supplied by phone from the Pirates' public-relations director, shuddered. They had just been defeated by the Expos, and the prospect of facing the Mets three games up instead of four was not one they relished.

Orosco kept the Pirates at bay in the ninth. Then in tenth, Gary

Carter came through, hitting a 2-run home run that gave the Mets the lead and the win. The last week had been tough, with gut-wrenching losses and miserable performances. But the Mets had pulled back to within three of first with three games coming up in St. Louis. Sure, they would have preferred to be closer, or even ahead. But they were certainly in a better position than the Yankees. And now they controlled their own destiny. Every game they won would automatically bring them a game closer to first. They essentially needed a sweep. No one was fooling themselves otherwise. Two out of three would only put them within two games of first with three games left. That probably would not be enough. They needed all three of these games.

Would that be difficult? Absolutely. The Cardinals were playing better than any team in baseball. Was it impossible? Absolutely not. This team was like any other in Mets franchise history. They were not just good, they were confident. They knew if they played their game, they were better than you. This would be their chance to show it. To show they were the team meant to play in the post-season, not the Punch and Judy Cardinals.

THE MILWAUKEE BREWERS CAME to Yankee Stadium for the team's last home series of the season. In the first game, Joe Niekro picked up the win in a 6–1 victory. A Blue Jay loss cut their lead down to four games. The next night, a cold, bitter early fall game with fewer than twelve thousand in attendance saw the Yankees lose a heart-breaker, 1–0. Despite a great performance by Bob Shirley, who went the distance, the Yankees could muster only seven baserunners against rookie Teddy Higuera, and never mounted a serious scoring threat until there were two outs in the ninth inning. The loss became more bitter when the Blue Jays fell later that night to the Tigers. Toronto's magic number dropped to two. The Yankees played their last regular-season home game the following night. Guidry turned in possibly his best performance of the year, going seven and giving up no runs. A Henderson lead-off home run put the Yankees ahead for good. The biggest cheers of the night, however, came in the eighth inning, when fans looked over at the out-of-town scoreboard and saw the Mets were losing.

The Blue Jays lost again, dropping their lead down to three games. It was almost impossible to believe, but the Yankees, behind by as much as seven games the week before, were now headed to Toronto for the final series of the year in control of their own destiny. Yes, that destiny was questionable: they had to win all three games against Toronto, win a makeup game that Monday against the Tigers, and if the Blue Jays also won their makeup game, win a one-game playoff in Toronto that Tuesday. But in this season of incredible highs and stunning lows, anything now seemed possible.

ST. LOUIS—A QUANT MIDWESTERN city on the banks of the mighty Mississippi—bore little resemblance to New York. Its skyline was not dotted with building after building that seemed to soar above the clouds, nor were its city streets teeming with life every night. Instead, you had a handful of buildings that dominated everything else in town. The Gateway Arch, a 630-foot high stainless-steel structure located just off the river, was the first thing you noticed when traveling into town. For a fee, you got to ride inside an enclosed tram right to the top. There, one could look over the city or southwestern Illinois. Or, you could try not to vomit from the thought that the only thing stopping you from plunging 630 feet to the ground was a few feet of stainless steel.

There were a few hotspots to grab a drink, maybe see a band. It certainly was not a city of prudes. After all, the Anheuser-Busch headquarters was there. So beer was never in question. But perhaps what separated St. Louis from New York, at least in the eyes of the baseball world, was the fans. Over the years, Cardinals fans had developed and embraced a notion that they were the kindest, most loving supporters of any fan base in the game. Even in the worst of times, Cardinals fans would not dream of booing one of their own. That was unthinkable. They most certainly would not do what Mets fans were doing to Foster or Doug Sisk or Knight.

Of course, opposing players did not feel that way. To them, St.

Louis could be a place where fans went a creative step further then just booing you on the field.

"In St. Louis, a lot of times, the fans call[ed] your room to try and wake you up late at night," said Staub. "Oh god, they were terrible in St. Louis with that kind of stuff. And don't even think to eat a cookie or a cake that is sent to you."[2]

But for hometown players, such hijinks were unthinkable. And luckily for St. Louis fans, there was little to boo about this team. John Tudor would have been the Cy Young Award winner in just about any other season. Willie McGee was on his way to an MVP. Vince Coleman was going to win the Rookie of the Year. Their emphasis on speed and singles over power made the game exciting. A squeeze bunt here, a double steal there. It was better—to Cardinals fans anyway—than a 3-run homer.

That kind of play worked well in Busch Stadium. Just under twenty years old, Busch followed the model of many a '60s- and '70s-style stadium: multipurpose, round, humorless. Located two blocks west of the Arch, it was one of the many cookie cutters of the era. It was not as bad, aesthetically speaking, as some of the other parks. In Philadelphia and Pittsburgh, the stands extended around the entire stadium. It was one big circle of seating where a field just happened to sit in middle. At least in St. Louis they had cut off the lower level of seating right around mid-right and left fields. After came the bullpens, two different sections of bleacher seating and then, in the middle, the batter's eye. Naturally, it was all symmetric. There were no nooks or crannies or anything remotely close to a unique aspect of the park. But at least bleacher seats were better than looking at the huge ugly black backgrounds that separated the outfield fence from the stands in Philly and Pittsburgh. It was not art. But it was something.

Perhaps the most important aspect of Busch Stadium, however, was the turf. It was like playing on concrete, but with a thin layer of carpeting over it. And in the summer, the Midwest heat bouncing off that carpeting was nearly unbearable.

The impact of the turf for a team like the Cardinals, which featured only one established power hitter but multiple people with speed, was significant. They could chop the ball down or slash it in the gap and let their speed take it from there. Routine ground balls in other parks found holes in St. Louis because the ball was not slowed down by grass. Line drives in the gap got to the wall quicker for the same reason. Every now and then, you might even see a ball hop over a fielder's body if the bounce was significant enough.

It was no coincidence that the Cardinals led the league in triples and batting average. Or that the only two teams in the National League to hit more doubles also played on turf fields. Nor was it a coincidence that despite being second to last in home runs, just barely averaging 1 every two games, St. Louis led the National League in runs scored. And stolen bases? Well, credit for that could not go to the turf, but still. A team capable of hitting more home runs was less likely to try and be stealing bases. But the Cardinals simply did not have that power. So instead, they stole and they stole a lot. By season's end, they would lead the league with 314 swipes. That total was 60 percent more than the next closest team.

"God, everyone on their team ran," said Carter. "The only one that didn't, I don't think, was Jack Clark. It was the way that their team was lined up. That field was perfect for them."[3]

This style of play—mixing team speed with the elements of their ballpark—had brought the Cardinals to this moment: a three-game lead in the division with six games left. And while the pressure should have been on the Mets, the Cardinals were perhaps feeling it too. Two wins would give them the division. But if they were swept, they would be heading into the final weekend fighting for their lives against their archrivals, the Cubs.

It all came to a head starting on Tuesday, October 1. Forty-six thousand sat in Busch Stadium to cheer on their Cardinals. The Mets, despite needing to sweep, seemed oddly relaxed. If they could take this game, they had Dwight Gooden going tomorrow, and that was just about as much a guaranteed win as you could get. And then it would all come down to the third game on Thursday. And at that point, anything could happen.

"Guys, we gotta do this," Hernandez told his teammates, whom he called together into his hotel room the night before the start of the series. "We gotta put this together against these guys right here."[4]

They spent the rest of the night watching the Cincinnati Bengals beat the Pittsburgh Steelers on *Monday Night Football*. As everyone headed out, Rusty Staub reminded them to turn their hotel room phones off, lest any Cardinals fan try to wake them up.

But to sweep the series, the Mets had to win this game first. And that would not prove easy. Ron Darling, a pebble in Davey Johnson's shoe all year despite solid numbers, was going up against Tudor, who had rendered the Mets helpless three weeks earlier at Shea.

IT WAS A COLD October night in the Midwest. Both pitchers were good but not at their sharpest. Each gave up a walk in the first but pitched out of it. Each put runners on base in the second but pitched out of it. And it continued that way. Tudor allowed a walk and then a single to Darling in the fifth, but he retired Mookie Wilson without further damage. In the seventh, HoJo was thrown out at home after Darling missed on a suicide squeeze, taking the air out of a second one-out rally. In the bottom of the inning, with two on, Darling snagged a comeback from Ozzie Smith and turned a 1-6-3 double play.

In the top of the ninth, the Mets loaded the bases with one out. Tudor got out of it. The Cardinals made no noise in the bottom of the inning. The game went into extras. Both Darling and Tudor had thrown nine shutout innings. Tudor came out and threw a scoreless tenth. Then in the bottom half of the inning, it looked like midnight might finally be approaching for the Mets. With two outs and two on, Orosco, who had replaced Darling after nine innings, faced Clark. Surely every Mets fan—and perhaps player—watching was familiar with Jesse's recent struggles. And here he was facing the one guy on St. Louis who could actually hit one out of the park.

Each wind up from Orosco brought a temporary stoppage in breathing from everyone watching. Clark had not swung a bat in over a week, hobbled by a bad back. But in this moment, few players would feel any pain. Maybe it was the week off, or maybe just a good pitch, but Clark swung late on a fastball and flied out weakly to right. In New York, thousands of bar patrons collectively exhaled in relief. The game moved on to the eleventh.

Ten innings was as far as Tudor went. Whitey Herzog brought in one of his two stoppers, lefty Ken Dayley. The lefty looked sharp, striking out Hernandez—much to the delight of his former hometown fans—and then Carter. Up came Strawberry. It seemed almost inevitable that Strawberry would strike out. Dayley was on his game, and the Mets' right fielder had trouble against left-handed pitching in the best of situations. The count was 1-1 as Dayley wound up to deliver what should have been a devastating lefty-on-lefty curve. As the ball started breaking, the clock in right field, which was part of a scoreboard that stood behind the bleachers, showed 10:44 p.m.

As the curve came in, Strawberry waited, recognized and then adjusted. His bat came through the zone with lightning speed. When he connected, the ball seemed almost to explode off his bat, like a bullet coming out a gun. There was no question the second he hit it that the ball was leaving the ballpark. Dayley did not even bother to turn around and watch it go. Right fielder Andy Van Slyke did not take a single step in pursuit of the ball. He merely gazed up at the small circular object making an orbit over his head.

We will never know how truly far the ball would have gone, because it crashed into the scoreboard clock. All that was missing was the hands and numbers exploding off, and it would have been just like the movie *The Natural*.

Estimates on just how far the ball went varied. Some said 430 feet. Some said 450 feet. Some said further. What was certain was that the Mets now had the lead, 1–0, and that Strawberry had never hit a bigger home run in his short career.

The Cardinals, stunned but not out of it, could not let the game end with a whimper. In the bottom of the eleventh, Tom Herr reached base when Wilson dropped a fly ball in center. It seemed almost like fate. The Cardinals were just meant to win this thing. Herr moved to third with two outs. The tension on the New York bench was palpable. They could not suffer another setback like this. But Ivan de Jesus lifted a lazy fly ball to center field. This time, Mookie caught it. The Mets were two games out.

"Call Cooperstown. Tell them to send down a truck. There was a baseball game here that's ready to be encased in glass and installed in the center of the Great Moments Room," wrote the *Bergen Record*'s Celizic.[5]

Davey Johnson was all smiles afterward. Johnson had been criticized by the press for starting Darling against Tudor when Gooden was available. Now, Davey looked like a genius. No doubt with a certain sense of irony, he sat in his office drinking a tall, cool Budweiser.

Meanwhile, over in the St. Louis clubhouse, Herzog sat flustered. His best pitcher had given them ten shutout innings, and they still lost. And while he said he was not conceding the next day's game to the Mets just because Gooden was pitching, there was tension in the air. When informed that Johnson had said tonight's game was more a must win for the Cardinals than the Mets, Herzog snapped back, "Who the hell's in first place?"[6]

The next day, Gooden did what he had done all season: he gave his team a chance to win. He was not overpowering, but Doc held the Cardinals down long enough in the second game to allow the Mets to build up the lead. This time, it was the bottom of the order getting it done. George Foster, HoJo, and Rafael Santana combined for eight hits and 4 runs scored. When the bottom of the ninth rolled around, the Mets were up 5–1. Gooden struck out Terry Pendleton to start, then retired Darrell Porter on a pop up. New York was one out away.

Gooden, however, lost his command. He walked Ozzie Smith. He walked pinch hitter Curt Ford. Coleman singled, making it 5–2. Then McGee hit a ground ball up the middle. It looked like the game might be over, but Santana and Wally Backman collided trying to field the ball. Everyone was safe. The tying run was now at first and the winning run was at the plate in Herr. It spoke volumes about how much faith Davey Johnson had in his twenty-year-old starter—and perhaps how little he had in his bullpen—that Gooden remained on the mound.

Herr was having an extraordinary season, if for no other reason than he had already driven in over 100 runs despite having just 8 home runs. Herr's numbers spoke not only to his talents but to the ability of the Cardinals to score through a combination of speed and hits, not power. Gooden had not fooled Herr in this game, allowing two singles and a walk to the second baseman. It was certainly within the realm of possibility that Herr could tie the game with an extra-base hit. He could even win it if Gooden grooved one.

Herr fouled off the first pitch. The crowd at Busch was on their feet. This had been a season of big moment after big moment. Many had come from Herr. They felt it in their bones. He was going to come through again.

Gooden, pitching from the full windup, went into his high leg kick, reared back, and threw a fastball as hard as he could. Herr had Gooden's timing down perfectly. He whipped the bat around and lashed the ball to right. Gooden at first was resolved to it being another base hit and, at worst, a 5–4 game. But on its way to right field, the ball found the mitt of Backman. Positioned perfectly, the Mets' second baseman snagged his counterpart's shot. Game over. The Mets were now just one game back.

The clubhouse was giddy afterward.

"It feels like they're chasing us," said HoJo.[7]

Over two games, the Mets had gotten contributions from almost everyone. Solid pitching. Timely hits. And the bullpen was rested and ready to go for the final game. Gooden, meanwhile, was 24-4. He had not been at his dominating best but still managed to become the first pitcher that year to strike out ten Cardinals in a game. And perhaps most importantly, he was now in line to pitch the one-game playoff at Shea should the two teams be tied at the season's end.

The momentum had all seemed to shift in New York's direction. They were still not in first place. And one more win by the Cardinals would just about end the season. But it was not the Mets that were in the process of blowing a division lead. It was not the Mets whose best pitcher had tossed ten shutout innings only to see his team lose the game. And it was not the Mets doing all this in front of their hometown fans.

Taking no chances, before the third game the Irish Catholic Frank Cashen went to mass just around the corner from Busch Stadium.

The priest implored his congregants to say a few prayers for the Cardinals that day. Cashen waited after the mass to have his say.

"Father, there are some Catholics that don't like the Cardinals," Cashen told him.

The priest took Cashen's arm, gently patted it and told him, in essence, tough, the Cardinals were the parish's team.[8]

It looked like St. Louis would need divine intervention. In the top of the first inning of the final game, against Danny Cox, the Mets wasted no time. Wilson led off the game with a single. He moved to second on an out, then scored on a Hernandez single, the first of his five hits in the game. Carter singled, then Strawberry. The bases were loaded with one out and the Mets already ahead 1–0. They had their cleats on Cox's neck. All they needed was someone to land the fatal blow.

That someone could have been George Foster. And what a moment it would have been for him. Foster, one of the most powerful bats in the Big Red Machine, was simply not the same player with New York. Fans had been expecting the guy who hit 52 home runs in 1977—the only player to hit over 50 in a single season between 1965 and 1990. What they got instead was a player with decent power who hit for a decent average and played decent defense. Occasionally they got flashes of the old George. But largely they saw an okay, not great player, stuck on a terrible team.

The reaction was harsh. It did not take long for Foster, one of the highest paid players in the game, to be serenaded with boos from the hometown faithful. Perhaps the situation could have been alleviated if Foster seemed more emotional, more into being a Met and playing in New York. But he never gave off that vibe. In the clubhouse he was quiet. Some would say withdrawn. Hell, even his batting stance seemed to lack effort, making one wonder how he could generate so much power with such a tired-looking swing.

Many of the '85 Mets would laugh at the mention of any of their teammates and easily be able to tell a funny anecdote about the person. At a minimum, they could talk about their intensity for the game. Such comments were lacking at the mention of Foster. Few of his teammates claimed to really know him or spend any kind of quality time with him. Some would point to his achievements with the Reds. Others would go with the more generic offering of his being a good guy. But none offered the kind of words you heard about someone like a Mookie Wilson, or a Sid Fernandez, or a Ray Knight.

Soon enough, Foster would point to race as an issue within the clubhouse and a factor in how the organization treated him. Perhaps he was right. Gooden and Strawberry certainly felt like black players were treated differently than white players. A black player in a slump had poor work ethic. A white player in a slump was just, well, in a slump. Like the Yankees, the underlying racial tension was there.

Race related or not, Foster's four seasons of misery in New York had all led up to this moment. Bases loaded, one out in the first inning of the most important game he had ever played for the Mets. A hit by Foster—a hit that could propel the Mets to their first postseason in twelve years—was just the kind of thing that could turn someone into a legend in New York.

Instead of a magic moment, Foster hit a ground ball to third. Pendleton threw home to force out Hernandez. No run scored, no big hit.

Years later, some of Foster's teammates would swear that George had hit that ground ball on a 3-0 count, and after he had gotten the take sign from the bench. They recalled being on a bench filled with players unhappy that Foster had not only swung away, but possibly killed a rally.

None of the press reports of the game that this author found say Foster swung 3-0. Attempts to find video of the at bat through the Mets, Cardinals, and Major League Baseball were futile. It was as if the moment never existed.

It seems unlikely that Foster did swing 3-0. That said, the fact that some of his teammates were absolutely certain that he had spoke volumes about his relationship with the guys he played with. Whether he swung 3-0 or not, years later, many of Foster's teammates would distinctly remember that as the crushing moment of the game, if not the season.

HoJo followed with a ground ball to Pendleton who stepped on third for the final out. The rest of the game was a frustrating mix of missed opportunities, failure to get one more out, and fan interference. In the bottom of the second, with Pendleton on third base, Porter lifted a fly ball in foul territory along the third base line. HoJo reached into the stands but was blocked from making the play by a fan. Turns out the fan was sitting in the Mets' owners box, though he did not belong there. He had sneaked down without anyone noticing. Porter ended up walking. Now, with runners on the corners, Ozzie Smith hit a ground ball to second. The Mets got one out, but could not get Smith at first. The game was tied.

In the fourth, with two out, Coleman looped a single just over short to score 2 runs. In the sixth with two out, McGee singled in another run. Meanwhile, Carter struggled to take advantage of Hernandez's performance. He followed a single in the third by hitting into a double play. When Hernandez doubled in a run with two outs in the fifth, Carter flew out to end the inning. In the seventh, Hernandez doubled, sending Dykstra to third with two out. Carter popped up to end the inning.

The ninth inning came with the Cardinals up 4–3. Busch Stadium was rocking. This was not a clinching game, but it was about as close as it could be for the hometown crowd. Reliever Ricky Horton quickly retired the first two batters. But when Hernandez singled, it gave new life to the Mets. Up came Carter. The Kid had produced one big hit after another in 1985. If he could muster one right here, it could permanently cement his status in New York for years to come.

Carter steadied himself at the plate. It would be a lie to say he was not thinking of a home run here. Maybe he would say he just wanted to hit the ball hard somewhere. But that would be code for wanting to crush the ball into the left-field stands. Instead, a perhaps overanxious Carter chopped at a letter-high fastball, sending a meek shot into right field. The third out was easily made. With that, St. Louis went nuts. A celebration ensued that would have given someone the impression the World Series just ended. An hour after the game was over, horns could still be heard honking throughout the streets around Busch Stadium.

In the clubhouse, the implications of the defeat were obvious. The Mets all said the right things.

"We are still in this."

"It ain't over till it's over."

"Long as we are not mathematically eliminated, we still have a chance."

The Cardinals played the same game.

"The Mets are a heck of a team."

"It is not done until we win the games we need to win."

"We were relaxed the whole time and knew we would pull it out."

But anyone in either clubhouse knew the truth. The Mets had been one big hit away from sweeping the series and forcing a closing weekend for the ages, with a possible one-game playoff waiting in the wings. Instead, they were now two games out with three to play. And they did not control their destiny. All St. Louis had to do was win two games against Chicago, and it was over. The Mets could sweep the Expos at Shea, and they would still need the Cubs—a team they had come to despise over the last two seasons—to take at least two of three from the Cardinals. It was not improbable. But as the Mets landed in New York at four in the morning that Friday, they knew it was unlikely. They knew that somehow, despite all they had accomplished and been through that year, the Yankees now had a better chance of making the postseason than they did.

"What a joke it would be if the Yankees should sneak into the playoffs after we've dominated Big Apple baseball all year," wrote Hernandez.[9] Surely there were countless New Yorkers who felt the same way.

IN AN ERA OF ugly ballparks, Exhibition Stadium in Toronto may have been among the worst. That was saying something. Cookie-cutter parks, like Busch Stadium, overflowing with concrete and AstroTurf were everywhere. Older parks like Yankee Stadium and Fenway were showing their age. But Exhibition was a special kind of ugly. Originally the home of a Canadian Football League team, it was used as a dual-purpose stadium when the Blue Jays entered the league in 1977. Sitting on the shores of Lake Ontario just south of downtown Toronto, the park consisted of a single-tier level of seating that wrapped around the foul lines. It stopped just short of the foul pole in left field, where a large gap of concrete divided it from a level of covered grandstand seating that ran along the left-field wall. As the wall began to bend toward center, the stands, covered by an enormous façade, kept running straight on a diagonal course along what was the sideline for football games. In right field, there was no gap in the seating. The stands ran along the right-field line and simply kept going in that direction, straight past the outfield wall. With no stands behind it, the space behind the right-field wall was empty, with only the occasional parked car visible in the vast emptiness. In night games, any ball hit over the right-field wall seemed to vanish into the abyss. The seating setup, intended more for football, meant that even with a packed house, there were vast areas of empty seats beyond the outfield walls, simply because fans there would have to turn their bodies at forty-five-degree angles to see home plate.

"It was one of the goofier baseball stadiums you are ever gonna play in," said Brian Fisher. "It was odd shaped. The turf wasn't great. Beautiful city, but just a terrible baseball field."[10]

The makeup of the stadium and its lakefront address could mean brutal weather conditions for players. Wind coming off the lake could easily sweep through a one-level stadium. And with no roof, temperatures early and late in the season could be below freezing.

Into this cold, sometimes desolate stadium, whose vast empty spaces could give it a hauntingly spooky appearance during night games, the Yankees strolled on Friday, October 4. The Yankees, after "being virtually ignored by the media in favor of the Mets and playing before private gatherings at Yankee Stadium," had now gotten everyone's attention.[11]

"We got late into Toronto [and] I have never seen a hotel lobby filled like that place was filled, with all those New York fans. It was unbelievable. It was just incredible. I had never seen support like that," said Mike Pagliarulo.[12]

The Yankees were on the verge of one of the greatest comebacks in baseball history and, considering how far back they had been, the pressure was all in the other clubhouse. The Yankees were confident they could pull this off. They just had to take it one game at a time, and that started by winning this Friday-night game. It rested, in part, on the shoulders of Whitson. If Eddie's arm had been hurt, or if he was having any lingering issues from the Baltimore brawl, it did not show. Whitson held Toronto scoreless for the first four innings. In the top of the fifth, the Yankees struck first. Bobby Meacham doubled in a run, and Henderson singled in Meacham for a 2–0 lead. But in the bottom of the inning, a two-out error by Andre Robertson gave those 2 runs back. Tied at 2, neither team could break through until the bottom of the eighth inning. With two outs and a runner on third, former Yankee Cliff Johnson singled in a run to give Toronto a 3–2 lead. The crowd of over forty-seven thousand went ballistic. They could see the division title just ahead. All they needed were three more outs from their ace reliever Tom Henke, and, for the first time ever, it was Toronto's.

NINETEEN-EIGHTY-FIVE WAS A SEASON Butch Wynegar probably wanted to forget. He'd endured injuries, the bizarre dugout phone calls from a manager that did not like him, and losing his catching job down the stretch. But there was one thing he just absolutely could not—would not—endure: making the out that ended the Yankees' season.

"I said, 'Don't be the last out.' I didn't want to run off the field while they're celebrating."[13]

These were Wynegar's thoughts as he strode to the plate with two outs in the top of the ninth inning, the Yankees down 3–2, and their chances of a miracle comeback all but evaporated. The first two hitters of the inning had been retired by Henke with ease. Now, even with rain falling down on them, forty-seven thousand Blue Jays fans were on their feet, yelling, screaming, clapping, creating a cacophony of noise that made hearing yourself think almost impossible. Mistakenly, someone had pushed a button too soon, and the scoreboard flashed "How Sweet It Is." The fans could feel it. The players in the Toronto dugout and on the field could feel it. And deep down, most of the Yankees' players could feel it too: the division race was about to end.

The count moved to 1-1. Batting left-handed, Wynegar kept his composure. He just wanted to get on base. As Henke wound up, the crowd collectively held its breath: Could this be it, could this be the pitch that gets us to the playoffs?

Henke threw a hard fastball. It was the pitch he'd gotten the first two outs on, and there was no doubt in his mind it was the best pitch to throw here. But it was across the inner part of the plate. Wynegar swung and connected so smoothly with the ball he never even felt it come off the bat. It was obvious from the second he hit it that the game was tied. Still, everyone peered through the rain and watched as the ball sailed high into the night and disappeared in the blackness behind the right-field fence. Butch Wynegar—who was 5 for his last 40, who was batting .223 overall, who had not hit a home run in nearly four months, who had not even driven in a run in the entire month of September, whose own teammates sat in the dugout wondering why Martin was not pinch-hitting for him with Ron Hassey in this critical moment[14]—had just hit the biggest home run the Yankees had seen since Bucky Dent in 1978.

The silence inside Exhibition Stadium was deafening. They had been one pitch away. One pitch everyone was certain they would get. Now, the only cheering to be heard were the euphoric screams of Wynegar's teammates as they poured out of the dugout to congratulate him. When Meacham followed with a single and Henderson walked to put runners on first and second, Blue Jays manager Bobby Cox replaced Henke with left-handed Steve Davis. Mattingly, the man most people assumed was weeks away from being named American League MVP, strode to the plate. Nervous fans chewed their fingernails and held their hands together, pleading for this last out. The home run had been bad, but if the game remained tied, all it took was 1 run in the bottom of the ninth and the division title was theirs.

They seemingly got their wish when Mattingly hit a lazy fly to Lloyd Moseby in center field. But just as Moseby was about the squeeze the ball for the last out, it popped right out of his glove and landed on the turf. Moseby, momentarily shocked, quickly picked up the ball, as if by somehow grabbing it quickly no one would notice what just happened. But it was too late. Meacham scored easily, and now the Yankees had the lead, 4–3. If Wynegar's home run had shocked the crowd, Moseby's error left them in stunned silence. Dave Righetti got three outs in the ninth, and the Yankees, miraculously, were still alive. After the game, an ecstatic Yankees clubhouse may have felt like fate was on their side.

"If Moseby played for us and did that in New York, damn, they'd probably shoot him before he got to the plate again," said Mattingly.[15]

"You walk into the clubhouse after that game and it was quiet as a church mouse," said Blue Jays first baseman Willie Upshaw. "I know myself and the guys, we pretty much left the locker room quiet and didn't spend a whole lot of time in there like we usually did."[16]

Still beaming off the euphoria of the come-from-behind win, the team set out the next afternoon to bring the race within one game. To keep their season alive, the Yankees would have to beat someone who, for many of them, had been their teammate just two years earlier. But Doyle Alexander's tenure had been rough, almost as rough as Whitson's. Alexander, a tall righty, had been traded to the Yankees in the middle of the 1976 season and helped them win the division, going 10-5. After a few years in Texas, Atlanta, and San Francisco, he returned to the Yankees via trade just before the start of the '82 season. His return was a nightmare. Alexander went 1-7 with a 6.08 ERA and had to deal with constant berating from his employer. His '83 season did not go much better and after two months, the team released him. Alexander signed with Toronto and underwent a resurgence. He won seventeen games in 1984 and, going into Saturday's game, had won sixteen more in 1985, the best back-to-back seasons of his career. Steinbrenner had already said releasing him was one of the biggest mistakes he had ever made. Now Alexander, still being paid by the Yankees, set out to end their season.

Looking to stop him was Joe Cowley, the odd duck.

"Oh boy, you are gonna get some reactions there, huh," said a laughing Pagliarulo when asked about his former teammate.[17]

Eccentric, prone to falling victim to practical jokes—he once, after consummating the relationship, thought a prostitute sent to his room was transgender because one of his teammates convinced him of such (she was not)—Cowley was tolerated in the clubhouse, but not loved. He drove teammates crazy by incessantly running counts to 3-2, always nibbling at corners and never seeming to trust his stuff to put hitters away. And his oddball behavior was, at times, just too much for some. A few thought that, like Whitson, Cowley was not equipped to handle the pressures of playing in New York.

Despite a string of no decisions and the wrath of his manager, Cowley had pitched well down the stretch, putting together a series of starts that lowered his ERA by nearly half a run. Now here he was, looking to extend the season. The wind was howling that afternoon, a stiff twenty-five-mile-an-hour breeze coming off Lake Ontario and pushing out toward right field. Cowley was going to have to keep the ball low and away to the Jays' power-hitting left-ies. That was the plan anyway. The execution fell short.

"Saturday morning, Winfield is doing dumbbell curls right by their first line," recalled Jesse Barfield. "When we saw that he was trying to intimidate us, I thought, 'You don't know what's about to hit you.'"[18]

Barfield was right. Ernie Whitt clobbered a 3-2 fastball over the wall in right-center in the bottom of the second. Then in the bottom of the third inning, Moseby, seeking redemption for the dropped fly ball the night before, sent one over the right-field wall. Moseby was still getting congratulations in the dugout when Willie Upshaw crushed a breaking ball over the wall in right too. Three lefties, 3 home runs to right field. The Yankees were down 3–0 in the third, and their string of magic had finally run out.

Where Cowley could not keep the ball away from lefties, Alex-ander did not nothing but throw them outside. Pitching the game of his life, he gave up only five hits, just two of them to lefties, and did not walk a batter. After Mattingly singled in the sixth inning, the Yankees, down 5–1, did not have another base runner. As the team came to bat in the top of the ninth inning, a Toronto fan, per-haps remembering the numerous insults to that country's national anthem in New York, jumped on top of the Yankees' dugout. He donned a Ronald Reagan mask and held an American flag in one hand and a white flag of surrender in the other. The crowd loved it. Forgetting the painful memory of the night before, they were on their feet, a euphoric noise whipping around Exhibition Stadium as the Yankees made one, then two easy outs in the ninth. Alexander, still on the mound, then watched as Hassey hit an easy fly ball to Bell in left. Bell ran in, squeezed the ball tight in his glove, and fell to his knees, his arms pumping through the air in excitement. He high-fived teammate Tony Fernandez, and the rest of the Jays came pouring out onto the field. Fans, many of them dressed in heavy winter coats, joined them and several immediately hoisted Alexander on their shoulders. They carried him off the field as if he had just returned from a historic military victory in some far away land.

"Let's just say it was sweet," said Alexander after the game.[19]

They had come close, but that was no consultation to Billy Martin.

"Second's for the birds," said Martin after the game. "I'm not taking pride in this at all. When you go after this, you go after all the marbles."[20]

His players, proud of what they accomplished, mostly felt the same way. They had come so close to one of the ultimate comebacks in baseball history. And there were countless moments along the way where they could look back and say what if: What if Billy had not left Fisher in against Cleveland? What if they'd been able to scratch 2 runs against Higuera that last Wednesday night? What if they'd just found a way to win one more game somewhere, somehow along the way? As the Blue Jays doused themselves in champagne, none of that really mattered right now.

THIRTY MINUTES AFTER THE Yankees were eliminated, the Mets saw their dream season come to an end too. They had returned home for one last series against Montreal and won the first game. But the Cardinals had beaten the Cubs, ensuring at least a tie for the division. Now, the Mets sat in their dugout in the bottom of the eighth inning gazing up at the scoreboard. At 4:43 p.m., it flashed disheartening news: Cubs—1, Cardinals—7, FINAL.

That was it. The rest of the game became meaningless. The season was now, officially, over. Carter sat starring at the final score, his hand on his chin as if trying to process the news. His teammates sat around, equally as catatonic. Then, something truly remarkable happened.

After booing the news, the crowd—initially forty-five thousand but now reduced after the Mets fell behind—stood as one and applauded. In unison, they gave their hometown heroes an ovation that lasted for over two minutes. It was an amazing sight. Just a few years removed from seeing crowds as small as five thousand at the park, the fans were giving their team an impromptu ovation for not making the playoffs.

Fans began ripping up programs and showering the field with them. In preparation for what seemed like an inevitability, the Mets had been ready with hundreds of orange and blue balloons, which they now released. On the scoreboard, a quick message from Cashen appeared thanking the fans. Few if any people actually heard it over the applause.

The next day, the season's last, many of the regulars sat. The Mets lost that game too. But once it was over, the team emerged from the dugout to thank their fans. As they did, a video showing highlights from the season played in the background. It was appropriate that in a year where the curtain call became a staple of the organization, the Mets ended the season with one big team curtain call.

Players doffed their caps. Some even threw theirs into the crowd, along with some baseballs and a few bats. It was a way to say thanks to the over 2.7 million who had come out to the ballpark to see them that year. It was not only a franchise record, but no team in New York City history had ever drawn that many.

"The most mind-boggling thing about the season was the attendance," said Cashen. "When you consider all the great Yankee teams that have been in this city, and the Dodgers and the Giants, too, it's just very gratifying to set that record."[21]

After it was over, the Mets went back to the clubhouse, appreciative of the fans showing their support, but disappointed in the final result.

"We have won more baseball games over the past two years than any team in either league [188] and have nothing to show for it but a team attendance record," wrote Hernandez.[22]

They began packing their things, thinking of what might have been, but also looking forward to what could be in 1986.

THE YANKEES STILL HAD one more game to play. It was meaningless in terms of the season. The Blue Jays were moving on, and the Yankees were not and nothing could change that. But to two men in the Yankees' clubhouse, this game had all the meaning in the world. Phil Niekro was taking his fifth shot at win number three hundred. Though most people assumed he would pitch again in the 1986, at his age, who knew? There were rumors running rampant that the Braves might want him to manage in Atlanta in 1986. Maybe he would hang 'em up before hitting that milestone. Not likely, but maybe. Perhaps the only Yankee more focused on this game than Phil was his younger brother Joe. While it seemed unlikely that Phil would retire before getting to three hundred, it was certainly a possibility that the two might not be on the same team in 1986. Even Niekro later admitted in his book that he thought about simply not pitching that day and instead waiting to sign with the Braves and win his three hundredth there. Joe wanted to be there in person to see his brother reach that milestone.

Fortunately for both, the Yankees jumped out to a 3–0 lead in the first and never looked back. They tacked on 2 more in the fifth, 2 more in the eighth, and 1 more in the ninth when Mattingly homered, his 35th of the season and his 145th RBI. Niekro, meanwhile, coasted along. He did not give up a hit until two out in the fourth. The Jays had sat most of their regulars—there was no need to take a chance on an injury with the game meaning nothing—but still, Niekro's performance was impressive. It was even more so because he was keeping their offense at bay without his best pitch. Phil, now in his twenty-second season, had always wanted to pitch one game without using the knuckleball. Now he was giving it a shot, using a combination of fastballs, breaking balls, and the occasional eephus pitch to record all his outs.

Niekro took the mound in the bottom of the ninth with his team up 8–o. As a joke, Martin had pitchers start warming up in the bullpen, though he had no intention of lifting the star of the show. After two outs, Phil gave up a double to Fernandez. Martin sent Joe out to the mound to give Niekro a chance to settle down before the next batter. When he got to the mound, Joe gave his brother some good news: their father had been taken out of intensive care earlier in the day.

Niekro had one last batter to face, his former Braves teammate Jeff Burroughs. Though he had always wanted to go a whole game without throwing one, Phil now felt he owed it to the pitch that got him here. He threw two knuckleballs to Burroughs, both for strikes. His teammates now all stood at the edge of the dugout, waiting to celebrate.

"I hope they don't try to lift Niekro up on their shoulders," Yankees television announcer Phil Rizzuto noted. "At his age, he might fall."

Niekro wound up and delivered a third straight knuckler. This one dipped and ducked away from Burroughs, who swung through it for the third out. At long last, Niekro had his three hundredth win. His teammates surrounded him, but immediately he found Joe and the two embraced. The Toronto fans gave him a warm ovation. He became the eighteenth pitcher to win three hundred games and was also the oldest pitcher to ever throw a shutout. The Yankees became the first and, as of this writing, the only team to have a three-hundred-win game pitched for and against them in the same season.

THE YANKEES FINISHED THE year 97-64, two games out of first place. It was thirteen more years before they won as many games in a season. The Mets finished the year 98-64, three games out of first place. At that time, it was the second-highest win total in franchise history, behind only the '69 championship team.

Despite their having the third- and fourth-best winning percentages in baseball, respectively, the Mets and Yankees failed to make the playoffs. In 1994 Major League Baseball expanded to three divisions and added a wildcard team in each league to the postseason.

Had such a system existed in 1985, the Yankees would have won the American League wildcard by twelve and a half games. The Mets would have won the National League East Division by thirteen and a half games over Montreal.

Instead, both teams watched as the Royals beat the Cardinals in seven games to win the World Series. No doubt, players from both teams sat back thinking they could have easily beaten either team to become world champions. Regardless of the outcome, the two teams had provided the most exciting season of baseball New York had seen in decades. At a time when winning the division still had meaning, the Mets and Yankees had fought up until the last weekend of the season, something that had never happened since the Mets joined the league in 1962—not even close.

"Who among us can say that we didn't have one tremendous baseball season around here," asked no less a curmudgeon than the *Daily News*'s Dick Young. "Shoot, we had two teams in the race almost all the way. Up and down, back and forth, down and out, and then back from the dead. Sorry, Vince Lombardi, but winning isn't everything. Trying to win is everything."[23]

For the Yankees, old stars showed why they were future Hall of Famers, and new ones emerged to be quickly embraced by their fan base. Henderson stole eighty bases, led the league with 146 runs scored, and finished third in the American League MVP voting. Winfield drove in 114 runs, his second-highest total as a Yankee, and won a Gold Glove. Guidry finished 22-6 and placed second in the American League Cy Young Award voting, losing out to the Royals' Bret Saberhagen. Mattingly led the league in doubles, RBIS, total bases, and sacrifice flies, while also winning a Gold Glove. His 145 RBIS were the most by an American League player in thirty-two years. He received twenty-three of twenty-eight first-place votes, easily winning the 1985 American League MVP.

The Mets saw years of developing their farm system come to fruition. Gooden went 24-4 with a 1.53 ERA. Doc led the league in wins, innings pitched, ERA, strikeouts, and complete games. He ran away with the National League Cy Young Award, receiving every first-place vote. Gooden even finished fourth in National League MVP voting. Strawberry set a then career high in home runs despite missing two months of the year. Darling won a then-career high sixteen games. McDowell finished with a 2.83 ERA in 127 and 1/3 innings.

The veterans came through as well. Carter hit a career high 32 home runs and became only the second Met ever to drive in more than 100 runs. After enduring the worst slump of his career, Hernandez wound up hitting .309 with 91 runs driven in. The Mets could see nothing but better days ahead.

NOW THAT THE SEASON was over, the Yankees and Mets had to look to 1986. Though they did not know it at the time, they were two teams headed in the opposite direction. Their offseason decisions that year, however, were a good indicator of how the rest of the decade would go.

The second Jeff Burroughs swung through Phil Niekro's knuckleball, the biggest question for the Yankees was who would be the manager in 1986. While many thought it would be Martin, given the performance of the team under his reign, Billy did himself no favors after the final game of the season. Noting that Earl Weaver made more money than he did but that the Orioles had gone nowhere that season, he wanted a raise. Moreover, he was upset that Steinbrenner still had not made an announcement regarding the team's investigation of the Whitson fight in Baltimore.

"I haven't said anything up to now because I didn't want to cause a disruption before the season was over," said Martin in the clubhouse after Niekro's three hundredth win. "But what kind of an organization lets a player punch and kick the manager and doesn't back the manager? I was just trying to break up a fight and he [Whitson] went after me."[24]

If Martin really wanted to come back, he was going about it horribly.

A few days later, the results of the investigation came in: Martin was not to blame for either the Whitson fight or the incident with the fan the night before. But Billy was not completely in the clear. A source close to the investigation, possibly Steinbrenner himself, told the *New York Times* that, "it looks like in both cases Billy was in places where he shouldn't be. It's always something he shouldn't be doing. Like in the fight with Whitson, it didn't say he started the fight, but he didn't walk away and instead pursued it."[25]

A week after the regular season ended, Steinbrenner announced that he was leaving the decision about manager to Clyde King and Woody Woodward, the Yankees' general manager and vice president of baseball operations, respectively. The announcement surely had to rankle Martin, who felt that he had performed more than adequately enough to be brought back. Moreover, King and Martin's relationship was on less-than-sure footing. King, a teetotaler, was no fan of Martin's hard drinking, fighting ways. The decision was just another of Steinbrenner's well-worn tactics. Not bringing back Martin would be an unpopular decision, but The Boss could just blame it on his subordinates. It would not be his fault. And if a new manager was brought in and the team flourished, Steinbrenner would proclaim himself a genius for listening to his baseball people. But no one really believed he was handing over responsibility for such a big decision to someone else.

What followed was two weeks of uncertainty about the team's future. Names of new managers were thrown out on a daily basis. King loved Yogi Berra. Would Yogi come back? No chance. He was still mad at the man in charge. Bobby Cox, manager of the Blue Jays, revealed that he rejected an offer from the Yankees, instead opting to become general manager of the Braves. King himself, who had managed the Yankees briefly in 1982, was an option. Joe Torre, the former Mets and Braves manager, now doing commentary for the Angels, was named as a possible successor and was eager for the job, should it be offered. Then Murray Chass wrote a story in the Sunday, October 27, *New York Times* that had Steinbrenner's oldest son, Hank, telling his father that if he wanted to fire Martin, blame his erratic team decisions late in the year, not the bar fights.[26] That same day, the *Daily News* reported that Martin was out and Lou Piniella was in.

As those stories were hitting newsstands, the Yankees themselves made it official. Shortly before the start of Game Seven of the World Series, Clyde King announced that Piniella would in fact be replacing Martin as the manager of the team. It was the thirteenth managerial change in twelve years of Steinbrenner ownership. Martin, away on a hunting trip, did not immediately comment, but he would stay on with the team as a consultant.

"I know it's a tough job," said Piniella in perhaps the understatement of the year. "But my god, it wasn't easy playing here. I've been here a long time and I've seen different changes in the manager's position. I'm no fool: I'm coming in with my eyes open. I know I could be replaced. I just plan on doing a good job."[27]

Perhaps the best description of the situation came from Moss Klein.

"Piniella is inheriting a good team but it's a team that has potential problems," wrote Klein a day after the announcement was made. "His job won't be easy, just as it won't be easy to replace the man who is ex-manager of the Yankees for the fourth time—for reasons that had nothing to do with his managing ability."[28]

The 1986 Yankees were a good team, but those potential problems all came to fruition. Key contributors in 1985 were shipped off. Baylor was traded in spring training. Phil Niekro was re-signed that off-season, only to be released a week before opening day. They traded for the White Sox's Carlton Fisk, who refused to agree to the deal, not wanting to play in New York. They tried for Tom Seaver, yet again, but were unable to reach a deal. Running out of White Sox players to trade for, they finally sent Cowley and Ron Hassey to Chicago for pitcher Britt Burns (two months later Hassey would actually be traded back to the Yankees). It was disastrous. Steinbrenner ignored warnings about a degenerative hip condition Burns had. Sure enough, Burns injured himself in spring training and never threw another pitch in the big leagues. The team used thirteen different starters in '86 with only Dennis Rasmussen winning more than nine games. They never captured the thrill of the '85 team on the field, and the drama off the field—which continued in spades under Piniella—just became more and more tiresome without the team actually winning.

FOR THE REST OF the 1980s, the Mets were the talk of New York. Their young, feisty, and alcohol and drug induced vibe meshed well with the times and the attitude of countless New Yorkers. While most of the '85 team returned, key additions like pitcher Bob Ojeda and rookie outfielder Kevin Mitchell were just the right pieces needed to put the Mets over the top. Davey Johnson made clear right out of spring training that he expected his team to dominate and win the whole thing. Normally such pressure could bury a team early. Instead, the Mets thrived. They swept a key four-game series in St. Louis in late April, leaving with a first-place lead in the National League East they would never relinquish.

The Mets continued to batter and pummel their opponents, literally and figuratively. They engaged in four bench-clearing brawls that year, each more entertaining than the last. Such behavior may have infuriated the opposition, but New Yorkers ate it up. An incident in Houston resulted in the arrest of four players. The team simply moved past it. Foster accused ownership of racism over who got playing time (though Foster had lost his playing time to Kevin Mitchell, who was also black). Rather than let the issue linger, the Mets simply released him. When the Mets encountered controversy, the maneuvered past it and emerged stronger. Fans loved it all.

Though Gooden wasn't pitching at his 1985 level, his numbers continued to impress. He was supplemented by Ron Darling, Sid Fernandez and Bob Ojeda, all posting impressive numbers for the year, while McDowell won fourteen games out of the bullpen. The offense, which had struggled through long stretches of the '85 season, flourished. The Mets led the league in batting average, hits, runs, walks, on-base percentage, and slugging percentage.

At the All-Star break, the Mets held a thirteen-and-a-half-game lead. On September 17, a full two and a half weeks before the season ended, the Mets clinched first place. Their postseason experience that year has been well documented. They won a hard-fought battle against the Astros, including one of the greatest baseball games ever played in Game Six, to take the National League pennant. Then, they knocked off the Red Sox in seven games to win the franchise's second-ever world championship.

Of the twenty-two Mets who took part in that World Series, only five—Kevin Elster, Lee Mazzilli, Kevin Mitchell, Tim Teufel, and Bob Ojeda—had not been a member of the team in 1985. The core nucleus that had been developed in the early '80s and solidified in

1985, had won it all. They set a new single-season team record of 2.76 million fans coming out to Flushing that year, which would be eclipsed in 1987 when they became the first New York sports team to draw over 3 million. New Yorkers loved the Mets, and would continue to love them for years.

THE REST OF DECADE was a mixture of managerial firings, off-the-field controversies, bad trades, bad free-agent signings, and bad baseball for the Yankees. They would start off competitive, only to fade as the season progressed. At the trade deadline, Steinbrenner would always make a bad move, acquiring a player he did not need in exchange for key pieces of the farm system. Young talent was never allowed to develop. By 1989, the team was in shambles. They finished 74-87, their worst record in twenty-two years. The following year, they ended up in dead last, their worst season since 1913.

The Yankees' moment to at least try and keep pace with their Flushing neighbors had come and gone. For the first time ever, the Mets—and the Mets alone—would reign as the true baseball team of New York.

The success of the Mets only further enraged Steinbrenner and made him more manic during this time period.

"George got so obsessed with the Mets that he was manipulating the attendance figures at Yankee Stadium," said Bill Madden. "When the attendance was calculated for each game before they could announce it in the press box they had to call George down in Tampa and if he didn't like the attendance figure, if he thought it was too low, he gave them a new figure. He came up with a code because at the end of the year you still have to give the proper figures. So at the end of the year, after each one of these attendance figures that George had changed, they had a seven after them. Anything that had a seven as the last number they knew had to be changed back to the real figure at the end of the year."[29]

From 1985 to 1990, the Mets took control of New York City's baseball soul through guts, grit, and getting hammered. Rather than learn from their example, Steinbrenner simply lied about how many people came to Yankee Stadium. And so it went.

# Epilogue

PERHAPS THE TWO SADDEST stories to emerge from the reju-
venated Mets era were those of Darryl Strawberry and Dwight
Gooden. Both continued to post impressive numbers throughout
the 1980s and into the '90s. But years of substance abuse took
their toll. Both players missed time, either through suspension
or for treatment because of drug and/or alcohol addiction. Strawberry left the Mets after the 1990 season for the Dodgers, but being
close to home only exacerbated his drug use. Injuries resulted in
him playing only 104 games from 1992 to 1994. Strawberry found
redemption, where else, but with the New York Yankees. He played
in the Bronx from 1995 to 1999, winning three world championships and becoming a model teammate. When he was diagnosed
with colon cancer just before the start of the 1998 playoffs, Strawberry became a rallying cry for his teammates and Yankees fans.
But in the spring of 2000, he failed yet another drug test, result-
ing in his third suspension over the previous five years. He never
played baseball again. Strawberry coped with addiction for years
afterward and eventually founded Strawberry Ministries and the
Darryl Strawberry Recovery Center with his wife, Tracy. He now
tours the country talking about his addiction in the hopes that others will seek help.

Dwight Gooden pitched relatively well during the first part of the
1990s, but he was not quite as dominating as the Dr. K of 1985. He
suffered his worst year in 1994 and followed that with a yearlong
suspension in 1995 for failing a drug test. Gooden's career might
possibly have ended there if not for, who else, the Yankees. Steinbrenner, never one to shy away from a feel-good story, signed Gooden

for the 1996 season. After being hit hard early, Doc pitched a no-hitter that May, and became one of the team's most reliable starters that summer. He was joined on the team by Strawberry. Ten years after winning it all with the Mets, Doc and Straw won it all again, but this time in pinstripes and with far less drugs and alcohol. Gooden went on to have several more productive years in the Majors before calling it quits in 2001. His post baseball career, however, was filled with instances of drug abuse and arrests. Though claiming he was clean, many friends and associates believed Gooden was still using drugs throughout the 2010s.

Gary Carter went on to hit over 300 home runs and become a Mets icon. He was named team co-captain in 1988. The Kid finished his career with one last season in Montreal—he hit a double over the head of former teammate Andre Dawson in his last at bat—before retiring after the 1992 season. He was eventually elected to the Hall of Fame. Carter succumbed to brain cancer in 2012.

Carter's co-captain was Keith Hernandez, who continued to win Gold Gloves and deliver clutch hits for the rest of the decade. He spent the last year of his career with the Indians. After retiring from the game, he gained newfound fame appearing in two 1992 episodes of *Seinfeld*, where one of the plot lines involved Hernandez allegedly spitting on two of the main characters (it turns out Roger McDowell was the real spitter). Since 2006, Hernandez has been part of one of the best color-analyst duos in baseball for the New York Mets.

The other half of that duo is Ron Darling. He drove Davey Johnson crazy for a few more solid years in Flushing. Darling spent the last part of his career in Oakland, putting in a strong 1992 season that helped the A's win the division.

Howard Johnson eventually became a full-time player with the Mets, and flourished. He posted three 30-30 seasons and led the league in home runs and RBIs in 1991. Johnson retired after the 1995 season and later became a first-base and hitting coach with the Mets and then a Minor League manager.

Rafael Santana remained the Mets' shortstop for two more seasons before a rare trade between the two teams sent him to the

Yankees. He was there for a season before injuries limited him to just thirteen more at bats in the big leagues. Santana became a coach and manager in the Minor Leagues for various organizations.

George Foster was one of the few players from the '85 team that was not a part of the '86 championship. He struggled throughout much of that year, losing his playing time to Kevin Mitchell. Foster believed the lack of playing time was racially motivated and said as much publicly. That was the last straw for the organization. He was released by the Mets in August and finished his career with the White Sox. All told, Foster hit 348 career home runs.

Mookie Wilson cemented his place in both Mets and baseball history by hitting the ground ball that went through Bill Buckner's legs in Game Six of the 1986 World Series. Wilson, one of the few members of the 1980s Mets not known for either hard partying or being an asshole, remains a fan favorite to this day. In retirement, Mookie spent many years as a Mets coach and in the front office.

Danny Heep was on the '88 Dodgers team that eliminated the Mets in the National League Championship Series. He played in the big leagues until 1991. In the late '90s, he became head coach of the University of the Incarnate Word Cardinals where he served for twenty seasons.

Ray Knight rebounded from his injury-plagued 1985 season to have one of his strongest years in 1986. He became a postseason hero by scoring the winning run in Game Six of the World Series (off Bill Buckner's error) and for hitting the go-ahead home run in Game Seven. Knight, who hit .391 in the Series, was named MVP. He moved on from the team in 1987 and retired from the game by 1989. He served a season and a half as manager of the Reds, before eventually becoming a broadcaster for the Washington Nationals.

Rusty Staub retired after the '85 season, the only man in baseball history to have five hundred hits with four different teams and one of just four to have hit a home run before their twentieth and after their fortieth birthdays. In October 2015 Staub was flying overseas from Ireland when he suffered a heart attack midflight. His heart stopped beating and attempts to revive him through CPR failed. A defibrillator gave just enough time to get him the medical attention he needed. Less than two weeks later, with the Mets at home against the Royals, Staub threw out the first pitch before Game Three of the World Series. Staub, known almost as much for his humanitarian efforts as his playing career, died in March 2018.

Ed Lynch pitched one game for the '86 Mets before being injured. Once healthy, he no longer had a spot in the rotation and was traded to the Cubs, where he finished his career. He eventually went back to school and received his law degree, then served as a scout for both the Cubs and Blue Jays.

Sid Fernandez followed up his '85 season by becoming one of the Mets' most reliable starters in the late '80s. He averaged thirteen wins a year between 1986 and 1989, making the All-Star team twice. Dukey was a key performer in relief during the '86 World Series, striking out ten batters in just over six innings. He retired from the game in 1997, only to attempt a comeback in 2001 with . . . the Yankees. Fernandez's comeback attempt did not last long, and he retired again without appearing in a big league game.

Rick Aguilera was a reliable starter for the Mets in 1986 and '87 and was the winning pitcher in the infamous Bill Buckner World Series game. The Mets traded him to the Twins in 1989 and with Minnesota, Aguilera became one of the premier closers in baseball. When he retired in 2001, he was eighth on the all-time saves list.

Roger McDowell followed up his rookie season by winning fourteen games in relief in 1986. He was the winning pitcher in the World Series–clinching game that year. McDowell further solidified his reputation as one of the game's more eccentric players through a series of hot foots, masks, and even wearing his uniform upside down. Like many of the young players from '85, he was traded away in the late '80s, going to the Phillies. After retiring, McDowell served as a pitching coach for the Braves and Orioles.

Jesse Orosco won three games for the Mets in the '86 National League Championship Series, including the clinching Game Six. He recorded the final out of the World Series that year, famously tossing his glove in the air before falling to his knees and pounding the ground. After the Mets traded him following the 1987 season, he spent the next fifteen years playing for eight different teams, including a brief stint in 2003 with the Yankees. When Orosco retired before the start of the '04 season, at the age of forty-six, no pitcher in baseball history had appeared in more games.

Doug Sisk returned in 1986 and pitched effectively over the next two seasons. After playing for the Orioles in 1988, injuries came back to plague him again. He retired after the '91 season. Though his relationship with the fans has improved somewhat, he still gets his share of snarky remarks every now and then. Appropriately, the Scum Bunch founder works for a wine importer and distributor in his home state of Washington.

It took Terry Leach another season before he became a permanent Major Leaguer. Naturally, after all that time between the Minors and the bigs, in 1987 he went 11-1 as a spot starter and reliever, including throwing yet another shutout. Leach won a World Series ring with the Twins in 1991 and eventually wrote an autobiography about his trials and tribulations in the Majors.

Tom Gorman was released by the Mets just before the start of spring training in '86. He pitched fourteen more games in the big leagues. After retirement he became active as a baseball coach in his hometown in Oregon.

Davey Johnson remained the Mets' manager for the rest of the '80s. Though the Mets never had a losing season under Johnson, he was unable to capture the magic of '86 in subsequent years. In 1990 after the team got off to a 20-22 start, he was fired. As of this writing, Johnson remains the winningest manager in the team's history. He went on to manage the Reds, Orioles, Dodgers, and Nationals, all with varying degrees of success, but never to a championship. His .562 winning percentage is among the highest all-time of any manager with over one thousand wins.

Not long after Johnson was fired, Frank Cashen stepped down from the organization. The general manager who had assembled the '80s dynamo was eventually vilified for taking it apart, piece by piece. Cashen's departure removed one of the last remaining links between the organization and their championship team. Cashen remained with the Mets in various capacities for the rest of the decade and was inducted into the team Hall of Fame (with, among others, Davey Johnson) in 2010. He died in 2014 at the age of eighty-eight.

DON MATTINGLY FOLLOWED UP his 1985 American League MVP season by setting a team single-season record for hits in 1986 and finishing second in the MVP voting. In 1987, he set a Major League record for grand slams in a single season and tied a record by homering in eight consecutive games. By the '90s, however, a back injury sapped him of his power and his offensive numbers fell. Still, he remained a fan favorite and was named team captain in 1991. Mattingly finally reached the postseason in 1995. Though the Yankees were knocked out in the first round, he hit .417 with 1 home run and 6 RBIs. He never played again, eventually coaching with the Yankees and managing the Dodgers and Miami Marlins.

Dave Winfield's feuding with Steinbrenner continued throughout the rest of the '80s, coming to a head in 1990. That May, Winfield was traded to the Angels. Two months later, Steinbrenner was banished from having any association with the Yankees after he paid a gambler thousands of dollars for information to blackmail Winfield. Still, Winfield's last years with the Yankees were productive, averaging over 100 RBIs a season. In his post-Yankees career, Winfield erased his "Mr. May" status when his extra-inning double in Game Six of the 1992 World Series drove in the Series-winning runs for the Blue Jays. Reaching three thousand hits in 1993, Winfield was elected to the Baseball Hall of Fame in 2001.

Rickey Henderson spent only three and a half more seasons with the Yankees but still established a franchise record for career stolen bases (since eclipsed). Growing increasingly disgruntled in New York, he was traded back to Oakland in 1989. Henderson went on to set all-time records in stolen bases and runs scored and even helped the Mets reach the postseason in 1999. He was elected to the Baseball Hall of Fame in 2009.

Don Baylor, whom the Yankees falsely believed had little left in the tank, was traded to the Red Sox during spring training in 1986. Baylor proceeded to have one of his best offensive seasons ever. He retired after the 1988 season, having appeared in the World Series in each of his final three seasons, for three different teams. Baylor served as the first-ever manager of the expansion Colorado Rockies, and spent three seasons managing the Chicago Cubs. He died of cancer in 2017.

Ken Griffey's wish to be traded finally came true in June 1986 when he was sent to the Braves. Griffey went on to play with his son, Ken Jr., with the Mariners. In a game in Anaheim, they homered in consecutive at bats. Junior, never forgetting the Yankees treatment of him or his father during the 1980s, went on to have a Hall of Fame career, largely at the expense of New York.

Willie Randolph manned second base in the Bronx for three more seasons, serving as team captain from 1986 to 1988. He ended his career in 1992 with the Mets. After serving as third-base coach for the Yankees for a decade, Randolph managed the Mets from 2005 to 2008, leading the team to the National League Championship Series in 2006. Randolph remains a fan favorite, both in the Bronx and in Queens, to this day.

Bobby Meacham played his last full season in the Majors in 1985. He played parts of the next three years before being traded to the Rangers, though he never ended up in a big league game with the team. Meacham went on to become a coach with the Marlins, Padres, Yankees, and Astros before managing in the Blue Jays organization.

Mike Pagliarulo erupted in 1986, hitting 28 home runs and becoming the legitimate power threat the team had hoped he would. He followed that up with 32 home runs and 87 RBIS in 1987, the best season of his career. Injuries, however, took a toll on Pags. His power numbers dropped as the decade went on. In 1991, he earned a World Series ring with the Twins, hitting a big, game-winning home run in the third game of that year's American League Championship Series. After retirement, he started his own company that helped Japanese and American teams scout players from both countries. Pags eventually reunited with Mattingly in Miami, serving as the Marlins' hitting coach.

Phil Niekro won eleven games for the Indians in 1986, showing the Yankees that he still had a little left in the tank. He spent

1987 with three different teams, the last of which was the Braves. He pitched one game for Atlanta, the last of his career, before retiring with 318 career wins. Niekro was elected to the Hall of Fame in 1997 and spent several years in postretirement managing the Colorado Silver Bullets, an all-female baseball team.

Ron Guidry lasted three more seasons in the big leagues, serving as captain—along with Randolph—during that time. Injuries limited his effectiveness as he won only sixteen more games in his career. His .651 career winning percentage—170 wins against 91 losses—is the twenty-sixth highest in Major League history. In 2003 the Yankees retired his number 49. From 2006 to 2007 he served as pitching coach for the Yankees.

Joe Cowley, traded to the White Sox after the '85 season, went on to throw what is generally regarding as one of the worst no-hitters in baseball history. Against the Angels in Anaheim on September 19, 1986, he walked seven batters and gave up a run, but did not allow a hit, winning 7–1. Cowley never won another game after that, becoming the only pitcher in history whose final big league win was a no-hitter. Somewhat true to form, Cowley seems to have disappeared. Multiple efforts to locate him through previous teams, former teammates, the players' union, and at old addresses, were unsuccessful.

Dennis Rasmussen, finally left alone to just pitch, led the Yankees with eighteen wins in 1986. His propensity to give up home runs, however, finally pushed Steinbrenner to trade him toward the end of the '87 season. Rasmussen spent parts of seven seasons with the Reds, Padres, Cubs, and Royals before retiring after the 1995 season.

Brian Fisher never enjoyed another season quite like his rookie year. In 1986 he was used more as a set-up man and middle reliever for Dave Righetti, but saw his ERA balloon. After the season ended, he was part of the one of the worst trades in team history, going to the Pirates along with Doug Drabek for Pat Clements, Cecilio Guante, and Rick Rhoden. In Pittsburgh, Fisher was converted back into a starter. Injuries finally ended his career after seven seasons.

Dave Righetti enjoyed the best season of his career in 1986, setting a then single-season record with forty-six saves. Mattingly was the only member of the '85 team to stay longer with the Yankees than Righetti, who left as a free agent after the 1990 season. At that time, Rags was the team's career leader in saves. In his final big league season, he was converted back to a starter, winning a game against the Yankees in New York. After retirement, Righetti spent eighteen seasons as pitching coach for the Giants.

Ed Whitson managed to endure an even worse 1986 with the Yankees. Despite a 5-2 record, his ERA stood at 7.54 midseason. The team could no longer afford to start him and was hesitant to use him at Yankee Stadium for fear of fan reaction. Mercifully, they traded him back to San Diego. Back in the peace of the West Coast, Whitson pitched solidly for the Padres, winning fifty-three games between 1987 and 1990. He became a local coach in retirement in Ohio, and hardly ever speaks about his time in New York and specifically will not discuss Billy Martin or even mention his name.

Billy Martin came back to manage the Yankees a fifth time in 1988. Piniella, after two tumultuous years, moved up to the general manager spot. Again, the Yankees surged under Martin's style of baseball, leading the division into June. Then, at Lace, a strip club in Texas, bouncers beat the hell out of Martin. Billy might have gotten away with the incident, had he not returned to the team's hotel in the middle of the night just as everyone was exiting because of a fire alarm. Steinbrenner stood and watched as Martin drooped out of the cab, his ear nearly detached from his head. A short time later, Billy was fired for a fifth and final time, replaced, again, by Piniella. Martin spent the next year and a half at his residence in upstate New York. Removed from the game, he seemed happy and grounded. In late 1989, he began informing people that George was going to bring him back to manage a sixth time at some point in the 1990 season. But on Christmas Day, Billy was killed in a car accident just outside of his home.

George Steinbrenner spent the rest of the 1980s fuming over the Mets' success and making life hell for his staff, managers, and players. The team crumbled as a result. By 1990 his longstanding feud with Winfield came back to haunt him when a known gambler and mob associate claimed that The Boss had offered him money for dirt on Winfield's charitable foundation. Steinbrenner said he was paying to protect Winfield from public exposure. No one believed him. Late that summer, he was given a lifetime ban from having any association with the Yankees. When fans at Yankee Stadium heard the news, they stood and applauded. In his absence, the team, led by Gene Michael, rebuilt their Minor League system, allowed young prospects to flourish, and made shrewd trades and free-agent signings. In 1993 Steinbrenner's ban was lifted and he returned to the day-to-day operations. Publicly, he seemed a bit more mellow, though there were certainly flashes of the old Boss. But the Yankees were on the cusp of a dynasty, and winning kept him and his players happy. Moreover, when Steinbrenner—voiced by Larry David—became a reoccurring character on the hit television show *Seinfeld*, it humanized him in a way few thought possible. By the end of the century, fans were actually glad The Boss was back and loved it when he would question an umpire, an opposing team, or even one of his own players. When he died in 2010 at the age of eighty, George Steinbrenner—who for years had been vilified by fans and players alike—was eulogized as a tough but caring owner who did whatever it took for his team to win. To this day, Yankees fans will occasionally be heard grumbling, "If only George was still around." Such sentiment would have been unthinkable in 1985.

In one of the most bizarre twists around that entire 1985 season, four years later Billy Martin ended up moving to the hometown of none other than Albert Millus, the Yankees fan whose encounter with Ed Whitson started their legendary brawl. Millus, who worked for the town, ended up meeting Martin in Billy's home while he was doing some renovations. Millus never heard from or saw Whitson after that night in Baltimore.

# NOTES

## 1. A Seismic Shift

1. Gary Carter phone interview, April 26, 2010.
2. Pearlman, *Bad Guys Won*, 39.
3. Carter interview.
4. Golenbock, *Amazin'*, 416.
5. Carter interview.
6. Carter interview.
7. Carter interview.
8. Frank Cashen phone interview, February 8, 2011.
9. Cashen interview.
10. Carter interview.
11. Carter interview.
12. Al Harazin phone interview, February 10, 2011.
13. Bud Harrelson phone interview, June 11, 2010.
14. Mike Riordan in person interview, February 4, 2018.
15. Mookie Wilson phone interview, January 13, 2011.
16. Golenbock, *Amazin'*, 362.
17. Katz, *Split Season*, 63.
18. Wally Backman interview, February 26, 2011.
19. Terry Leach phone interview, December 2, 2010.
20. Rusty Staub phone interview, January 18, 2011.
21. Golenbock, *Amazin'*, 374.
22. Dan Castellano, "Ryan Two-Hits Mets, 4–0," *Star Ledger*, September 1, 1982.
23. Walt Terrell phone interview, January 17, 2011.
24. Tom Gorman phone interview, March 29, 2011.
25. Pearlman, *Bad Guys Won*, 22.
26. Cashen interview.
27. Harazin interview.
28. Cashen interview.
29. Cashen interview.
30. Golenbock, *Amazin'*, 368.
31. Harazin interview.
32. Cashen interview.
33. Staub interview.

34. Dick Young, "Odds to Win the Pennant: Mets 4–1, Yankees 100–," *Record*, July 9, 1984.

35. Joseph Durso, "Mets in Fight for First as Yanks Fight for Respect," *New York Times*, July 12, 1984.

36. Joseph Durso, "Mets Are Swept, Four Ejected," *New York Times*, August 9, 1984.

37. Jack O'Connell, "Chicago Not Kind to Mets," *Bergen Record*, August 9, 1984.

38. Dan Castellano, "Mets Lose, 5–4; Take Aim at '85," *Star Ledger*, October 1, 1984.

39. Castellano, "Mets Lose, 5–4; Take Aim at '85."

### 2. "Never Played the Game"

1. Moss Klein, "Henderson Proves a 'Steal,'" *Star Ledger*, June 23, 1985.

2. Murray Chass, "Yanks and A's Complete Deal for Henderson," *New York Times*, December 6, 1984.

3. Rich Bordi phone interview, August 12, 2010.

4. Bus Saidt, "Rickey Henderson," *Trenton Times*, December 19, 1984.

5. Rex Hudler phone interview, February 3, 2011.

6. Dale Berra phone interview, October 14, 2010.

7. Moss Klein, "Henderson a Yank, If He Signs," *Star Ledger*, December 6, 1984.

8. Madden, *Steinbrenner*, 22.

9. Golenbock, *George*, 88.

10. Golenbock, *George*, 113.

11. Madden, *Steinbrenner*, 184–85.

12. Madden and Klein, *Damned Yankees*, 56.

13. Golenbock, *George*, 207.

14. Madden, *Steinbrenner*, 210.

15. Moss Klein, "Yanks Won't Be the Same without Reg," *Star Ledger*, January 23, 1982.

16. Don Markus, "Reggie Heads West," *Bergen Record*, January 24, 1982.

17. Madden, *Steinbrenner*, 220.

18. Madden and Klein, *Damned Yankees*, 212.

19. Associated Press, "Steinbrenner Is Disputed," *New York Times*, September 1, 1982.

20. Joseph Durso, "Padres Sign Gossage to Five-Year Contract," *New York Times*, January 7, 1984.

21. Moss Klein, "Yanks Trade Nettles to San Diego," *Star Ledger*, March 31, 1984.

22. Klein, "Yanks Trade Nettles to San Diego."

23. Bill Madden phone interview, November 15, 2010.

24. Moss Klein, "Weaver's Availability Puts Yogi in Jeopardy," *Star-Ledger*, October 1, 1984.

25. George Vecsey, "The Boss Is Back," *New York Times*, October 1, 1984.

26. Winfield and Parker, *Winfield*, 220.

27. Madden, *Steinbrenner*, 179.

28. Moss Klein phone interview, May 10, 2010.

### 3. Attendance Envy

1. Bill Francis, "Davey Johnson's Managerial Skills Lead Him to Cooperstown's Doorstep," National Baseball Hall of Fame, https://baseballhall.org/discover-more/news/johnson-davey.

2. Golenbock, *Amazin'*, 392.

3. Fernandez interview.

4. Roger McDowell phone interview, January 25, 2011.

5. Wilson interview.

6. Madden and Klein, *Damned Yankees*, 281.

7. Moss Klein, "Howser 'Managed' to Help Dent," *Star-Ledger*, March 3, 1985.

8. Dave Anderson, "Steinbrenner's Peace Plan," *New York Times*, March 3, 1985.

9. Moss Klein, "Mattingly, Righetti Share That 'Neglected Feeling,'" *Star-Ledger*, March 11, 1985.

10. Tom Verducci, "Boss Lays Bomb on Mattingly," *Newsday* through the *Bergen Record*, March 11, 1985.

11. Klein, "Mattingly, Righetti Share."

12. Anderson, "Steinbrenner's Peace Plan."

13. Pearlman, *Bad Guys Won*, 142.

14. Dan Castellano, "Foster to NL Rivals: Mets in Driver's Seat," *Star-Ledger*, March 2, 1985.

15. Jack O'Connell, "Strawberry Signs Away His Worries," *Bergen Record*, March 13, 1985.

16. Jack O'Connell, "Johnson's Stamp on This Camp," *Bergen Record*, March 8, 1985.

17. Jack O'Connell, "Newfound Fame Doesn't Appeal," *Bergen Record*, March 11, 1985.

18. O'Connell, "Newfound Fame Doesn't Appeal."

19. Dan Castellano, "Mets Enjoy Following Their Leader . . . Keith Hernandez," *Star-Ledger*, March 31, 1985.

20. George Vecsey, "Torn between Shadow and Sunshine," *New York Times*, March 9, 1986.

21. Golenback, *Amazin'*, 385.

22. Hernandez and Bryan, *If at First*, 9.

23. Craig Wolff, "Hernandez: Consummate Pro with the Intensity of an Artist," *New York Times*, June 9, 1985.

24. Wolff, "Hernandez: Consummate Pro."

25. "Met Tickets a Hot Item," *Star-Ledger*, March 2, 1985.

26. Jack O'Connell, "Mets' Bandwagon Is Quickly Filling Up," *Bergen Record*, March 10, 85.

27. "$36M Deal Struck to Upgrade Shea," *Bergen Record*, March 13, 1985.

28. Jack O'Connell, "Mets' Past, Future Meet in One Game," *Bergen Record*, March 14, 1985.

29. Claire Smith, "Yanks Will Wait a Little More before Panicking," *Bergen Record*, March 13, 1985.

30. Moss Klein, "Andre Hits HR; Yanks Fall Again," *Star-Ledger*, March 13, 1985.

31. Tom Verducci, "Rooftop with the Boss: Some Yanks in for a Jolt," *Newsday* through the *Bergen Record*, March 14, 1985.

32. Jack O'Connell, "Mets Batter Bruised Yanks," *Bergen Record*, March 19, 1985.

33. Dan Castellano, "Mets Drub Yankee Subs," *Star-Ledger*, March 20, 1985.

34. Mike Pagliarulo phone interview, December 12, 2010.

35. Bobby Meachem phone interview, December 16, 2010.

36. Madden and Klein, *Damned Yankees*, 130.

37. Gooden and Klapisch, *Heat*, 177.

38. Moss Klein, "George: Mets' Numbers Just Don't Seem to Add Up," *Star-Ledger*, March 21, 1985.

39. Claire Smith, "Yankees Hold Off Mets; Take Turn to Gloat," *Bergen Record*, March 25, 1985.

40. Smith, "Yankees Hold Off Mets."

41. Moss Klein, "George: Mattingly Injury Mishandled," *Star-Ledger*, March 31, 1985.

42. Moss Klein, "Ailing Yanks Won't Get Well Enough to Win," *Star-Ledger*, April 7, 1985.

43. Klein, "Ailing Yanks."

44. Moss Klein, "Rickey, Count Hobble onto DL," *Star-Ledger*, April 4, 1984.

45. Dan Castellano, "Don't Tell Mets They Can't Overtake Cubs," *Star-Ledger*, April 7, 1985.

## 4. Fun to Be a Met

1. Bordi interview.

2. Phil Niekro phone interview, June 7, 2010.

3. Niekro interview.

4. Niekro interview.

5. Niekro and Bird, *Knuckleballs*, 24.

6. Niekro interview.

7. Niekro interview.

8. Niekro and Bird, *Knuckleballs*, 25.

9. Gooden and Klapisch, *Heat*, 10.

10. Gooden and Klapisch, *Heat*, 17.

11. Joseph Durso, "Gooden Debut Was Painful," *New York Times*, July 4, 1985.

12. Mel Stottlemyre phone interview, March 29, 2011.

13. Dave Anderson, "The Prodigy and the Prof," *New York Times*, July 25, 1985.

14. Anderson, "The Prodigy."

15. Marty Noble, "Gooden's Pitch Proves Popular with Sponsors," *Bergen Record*, July 10, 1985.

16. Lann Robbins, "Some New Stars Excite Old Fans," *Bergen Record*, April 10, 1985.

17. Golenbock, *Amazin'*, 427.

18. Dan Castellano, "Boo Birds Still Bothering Sisk," *Star-Ledger*, April 18, 1985.

19. Doug Sisk phone interview, March 22, 2017.

20. Dan Castellano, "Gary: Fantasyland Finish," *Star-Ledger*, April 10, 1985.

21. Rich Chere, "Three-Hitter Keeps Mets Perfect, 1–0," *Star-Ledger*, April 13, 1985.

22. Golenbock, *Amazin'*, 424.

23. Roger Jongewaard phone interview, January 8, 2011.

24. Golenbock, *Amazin'*, 381.

25. Jack O'Connell, "Another Day, Another Hero," *Bergen Record*, April 14, 1985.

26. Rich Chere, "Strawberry HR in 9th Edges Reds, 2–1," *Star-Ledger*, April 14, 1985.

27. Dave D'Alessandro, "Unbeaten Mets Find Status Quo Is Good Enough," *Bergen Record*, April 15, 1985.

28. D'Alessandro, "Unbeaten Mets."

29. Joseph Durso, "Mets Take Fifth in a Row," *New York Times*, April 15, 1985.

30. Murray Chass, "Mets' Shadow Covers Yanks," *New York Times*, April 16, 1985.

31. Chass, "Mets' Shadow."

32. Michael Martinez, "Wynegar Gets Things Going," *New York Times*, April 17, 1985.

33. Niekro and Bird, *Knuckleballs*, 27.

34. Don Baylor phone interview, February 18, 2011.

35. Baylor interview.

36. Baylor interview.

37. Terrell interview.

38. Dave Anderson, "Sad Switch for Yanks," *New York Times*, April 29, 1985.

39. Hernandez and Bryan, *If at First*, 26.

40. Niekro and Bird, *Knuckleballs*, 38.

41. Niekro and Bird, *Knuckleballs*, 40.

42. Golenbock, *Wild, High and Tight*, 395.

43. Madden and Klein, *Damned Yankees*, 70.

44. Murray Chass, "Fourth Time Around, Martin Will Stress Discipline," *New York Times*, April 29, 1985.

45. Madden and Klein, *Damned Yankees*, 70.

46. Pepe, *The Ballad of Billy and George*, 185.

47. Berra interview.

48. Madden interview.

49. Jack O'Connell, "Met and Bucs Stage Stinker," *Bergen Record*, April 18, 1985.

50. Joseph Durso, "Mets Hold Off Cardinals," *New York Times*, April 23, 1985.

51. Michael Katz, "Darling Stars as Mets Win," *New York Times*, April 27, 1985.

52. Michael Katz, "Mets Outlast Pirates in 18th on Error, 5–4," *New York Times*, April 29, 1985.

53. Dan Castellano, "Gooden 4-hits Astros, 4–1," *Star-Ledger*, May 1, 1985.

### 5. Billy and George

1. Leavy, *Last Boy*, 180.

2. Golenbock, *Wild, High and Tight*, 12.

3. Golenbock, *Wild, High and Tight*, 18.

4. Golenbock, *Wild, High and Tight*, 138.

5. Pepe, *The Ballad of Billy and George*, 31.

6. Golenbock, *Wild, High and Tight*, 332.

7. Madden and Klein, *Damned Yankees*, 71.

8. Pepe, *The Ballad of Billy and George*, 187.

9. Chass, "Fourth Time Around."

10. Murray Chass, "Yankee Scenario Is All Too Familiar," *New York Times*, April 29, 1985.

11. John Schulian, "George Revives a Bad Marriage," *Bergen Record*, May 1, 1985.

12. Moss Klein, "Tension, Excitement Routine for George and Billy," *Star-Ledger*, April 30, 1985.

13. "Billy Watch Begins Anew," *Bergen Record*, May 1, 1985.

14. Bill Pennington, "A Stormy Start for Billy and Yankees," *Bergen Record*, April 30, 1985.

15. Moss Klein, "George Blames Players for Firing," *Star-Ledger*, April 30, 1985.

16. Michael Martinez, "Martin Institutes Changes, but He Loses in Debut," *New York Times*, April 30, 1985.

17. Niekro and Bird, *Knuckleballs*, 45.

18. Dan Castellano, "Heep 5 RBI, Dykstra HR Power Mets over Reds," *Star-Ledger*, May 4, 1985.

19. Castellano, "Heep 5 RBI."

20. Dan Castellano, "Carter Slam in 8th Zaps Braves, 5–3," *Star-Ledger*, May 8, 1985.

21. Von Hayes phone interview, June 22, 2010.

22. Rich Chere, "Gooden's 13 Ks Win, 5–0," *Star-Ledger*, May 11, 1985.

23. Carter interview.

24. Dave Anderson, "Mets' Values Old-Fashioned," *New York Times*, May 7, 1985.

25. Dan Castellano, "Strawberry Injury Takes Bat from Carter, Foster," *Star-Ledger*, May 16, 1985.

26. Ray Knight phone interview, December 11, 2010.

27. Knight interview.

28. John Harper, "Ray Knight Wishes '86 Mets Were Remembered More for Grit and Passion Than Hard-Partying Ways," *New York Daily News*, May 28, 2016.

29. Dan Castellano, "Johnson Sparks Mets, 3–2," *Star-Ledger*, May 20, 1985.

30. William C. Rhoden, "Mets Win, 3–2; Yanks Beaten," *New York Times*, May 20, 1985.

31. Dan Castellano, "Fernandez Hurt, Aguilera Called," *Star-Ledger*, May 21, 1985.

32. Joseph Durso, "Depleted Mets Lose No-Hitter to Farm," *New York Times*, May 24, 1985.

33. Jack O'Connell, "Mets Welcome Day Off to Regroup," *Bergen Record*, May 22, 1985.

34. Craig Wolff, "Knight's Confidence Boosted," *New York Times*, May 29, 1985.

35. Joseph Durso, "McDowell's Success a Tribute to Faith," *New York Times*, June 2, 1985.

36. Ronn Reynolds phone interview, March 29, 2011.

37. Durso, "McDowell's Success."

38. Jack O'Connell, "Surgery Gave Mets a Sinking Sensation," *Bergen Record*, July 7, 1985.

39. Craig Wolff, "Mets Win as McDowell Ends Dodgers' Threat," *New York Times*, May 27, 1985.

40. Mike Celizic, "Martin Revival Opens to Yawns," *Bergen Record*, May 5, 1985.

41. Michael Martinez, "Yankees Win in Martin's 3d Return," *New York Times*, May 4, 1985.

42. Dave Anderson, "Even Billy Bore Didn't Need Tickets," *New York Times*, May 5, 1985.

43. Jack O'Connell, "Billy Ball Is Working," *Bergen Record*, May 5, 1985.

44. Michael Martinez, "Martin Getting Results," *New York Times*, May 7, 1985.

45. "Yankees to Seek Trade for Griffey," *New York Times*, May 7, 1985.

46. Moss Klein, "Cowley Unhappy over Pen Exile," *Star-Ledger*, May 10, 1985.

47. Moss Klein, "Randolph Upset Batting 6th but He Won't Gripe," *Star-Ledger*, May 7, 1985.

48. "Sounding Off: It's No Fun Being a Yankee Fan," *New York Times*, May 5, 1985.

49. Berra interview.

50. Michael Martinez, "Yanks Top Angels for Sixth Straight," *New York Times*, May 19, 1985.

51. Moss Klein, "Yankees Win 6th Straight," *Star-Ledger*, May 19, 1985.

52. Moss Klein, "Yanks Rout A's on 19 Hits, 13–1," *Star-Ledger*, May 27, 1985.

53. Rich Chere, "George Praising Billy? It Must Be Fantasyland," *Star-Ledger*, June 4, 1985.

### 6. The Russians Attack Atlanta

1. Dan Castellano, "Gooden's 14 Ks Silence Giants, 2–1," *Star-Ledger*, May 31, 1985.

2. Dan Castellano, "Sisk's Save of Schiraldi Takes Met Spotlight, 7–3," *Star-Ledger*, June 3, 1985.

3. Marty Noble, "Gooden Dodges a Bullet," *Bergen Record*, June 5, 1985.

4. Rich Chere, "Cards Score Six in 13th to Top Sisk, Mets, 7–2," *Star-Ledger*, June 8, 1985.

5. Hayes interview.

6. Jack O'Connell, "Deflated Mets Ring Up Record Deficit," *Bergen Record*, June 12, 1985.

7. Dan Castellano, "Mets Smothered by Phils, 26–7," *Star-Ledger*, June 12, 1985.

8. Niekro and Bird, *Knuckleballs*, 79.

9. Special to the *New York Times*, "Johnson Reminds Mets, 'Do Not Forget,'" *New York Times*, June 13, 1985.

10. Murray Chass, "Expos Are Happier with Carter Gone," *New York Times*, March 29, 1985.

11. Jack O'Connell, "Carter Girds for Reception in Montreal," *Bergen Record*, June 14, 1985.

12. Jack O'Connell, "Mets Plunge into 4th Place," *Bergen Record*, June 16, 1985.

13. Jack O'Connell, "Bullpen Woes Vex Johnson," *Bergen Record*, June 16, 1985.

14. Joseph Durso, "Tumbling Mets Fall to Expos in 9th," *New York Times*, June 16, 1985.

15. Durso, "Tumbling Mets."

16. Joseph Durso, "Mets Tighten Race in East," *New York Times*, June 18, 1985.

17. Jack O'Connell, "Mets Answer Gibes by Cubs' Sutcliffe," *Bergen Record*, June 18, 1985.

18. Hernandez and Bryan, *If at First*, 151.

19. Dave Anderson, "The Year of the Gag: A Study in Contrasts," *New York Times*, June 23, 1985.

20. Anderson, "The Year of the Gag."

21. Michael Martinez, "Martin Says Yanks Lack Basic Training," *New York Times*, June 14, 1985.

22. Rich Chere, "Billy Upset with King; George Rips Mattingly," *Star-Ledger*, June 14, 1985.

23. Martinez, "Martin Says Yanks."

24. Rich Chere, "Tigers HRS Sink Yanks, 4–0," *Star-Ledger*, June 15, 1985.

25. Bill Pennington, "Sweep," *Bergen Record*, June 20, 1985.

26. Klein, "Henderson Proves a 'Steal.'"

27. Ron Guidry phone interview, August 19, 2010.

28. Guidry interview.

29. Guidry interview.

30. Guidry interview.

31. Marty Bystrom phone interview, October 26, 2011.

32. Rich Chere, "Pasqua's 2 Rip Rangers," *Star-Ledger*, July 12, 1985.

33. Bill Pennington, "Niekro Dwells on Present," *Bergen Record*, July 14, 1985.

34. Moss Klein, "Yanks on a Streak, Don't Want a Strike," *Star-Ledger*, July 16, 1985.

35. Murray Chass, "Mattingly Leads Yanks into 2d," *New York Times*, July 13, 1985.

36. Michael Martinez, "More Than a Token Chance for a Subway Series," *New York Times*, July 18, 1985.

37. Jack O'Connell, "Tempers Flare as Cubs Halt Skid," *Bergen Record*, June 27, 1985.

38. Jack O'Connell, "Talk Leaves Mets Shaken, but Not Stirred in 2–1 Loss," *Bergen Record*, July 1, 1985.

39. Dan Castellano, "Mets Drop 6th Straight; Mookie on 21-day DL," *Star-Ledger*, July 2, 1985.

40. Castellano, "Mets Drop 6th."

41. Rich Chere, "Local Fans Make Pitch: Strike 2 Could Be Final Out," *Star-Ledger*, July 2, 1985.

42. Gorman interview.

43. Wilson interview.

44. Dan Castellano, "Strawberry a Reluctant 'Star,'" *Star-Ledger*, July 7, 1985.

45. Sam Gardber, "Thirty Years Ago in Atlanta, a Baseball Marathon Led to Fireworks Going Off at 4 a.m.," Fox Sports, https://www.foxsports.com/mlb/story/thirty-years-ago-in-atlanta-a-baseball-marathon-led-to-fireworks-going-off-at-4-a-m-070215.

46. Gorman interview.

47. David Simpson, "Unbelievable, Unforgettable," Associated Press through the *Bergen Record*, July 6, 1985.

48. Simpson, "Unbelievable, Unforgettable."

49. Backman interview.

50. Fernandez interview.

51. Michael Martinez, "Mets Win 7th with 4 Homers," *New York Times*, July 9, 1985.

52. "Mets' Winning Streak Reaches 9," *New York Times*, July 11, 1985.

53. Jack O'Connell, "'G' Whiz: New York Showing a Pair of Aces," *Bergen Record*, July 14, 1985.

### 7. Hospital Management

1. Dan Castellano, "Schedule May Favor Mets," *Star-Ledger*, July 18, 1985.

2. Rich Chere, "Mets Rip Braves, 15–10, Set Club Mark," *Star-Ledger*, July 22, 1985.

3. Dave D'Alessandro, "Mets Seeing Red Again," *Bergen Record*, July 24, 1985.

4. Joseph Durso, "Met Hitting Fails Again," *New York Times*, July 24, 1985.

5. Orosco interview.

6. Orosco interview.

7. Stottlemyre interview.

8. Joseph Durso, "Aguilera Impressive in Victory," *New York Times*, July 30, 1985.

9. Jack O'Connell, "Doctor Tries Surgery," *Bergen Record*, July 31, 1985.

10. Peter Alfano, "Mets Win, 5–2, for Sweep," *New York Times*, August 1, 1985.

11. Jack O'Connell, "Billy Sparks New Feud," *Bergen Record*, July 18, 1985.

12. Moss Klein, "Hrbek Slams Yanks; Billy Erupts," *Star-Ledger*, July 19, 1985.

13. Jack O'Connell, "Martin Bemoans Yanks' Metrodome Doom," *Bergen Record*, July 19, 1985.

14. Bordi interview.

15. Marty Noble, "A Case of Royal Blues," *Bergen Record*, July 23, 1985.

16. Dennis Rasmussen phone interview, May 28, 2010.

17. Niekro and Bird, *Knuckleballs*, 121.

18. Moss Klein, "Royals Complete Sweep of Yanks, 5–3," *Star-Ledger*, July 25, 1985.

19. "Yanks Lose Again to Royals," *New York Times*, July 24, 1985.

20. Butch Wynegar phone interview, May 20, 2010.

21. Moss Klein, "Yanks Rout Blyleven, 8–2," *Star-Ledger*, July 30, 1985.

22. Moss Klein, "Wrong Number Can't Billy," *Star-Ledger*, July 30, 1985.

23. "Yanks Have to Settle for Split," *Bergen Record*, July 31, 1985.

24. Wynegar interview.

25. "Waddell Start Stops Guidry Streak," *Bergen Record*, August 1, 1985.

26. Piniella and Madden, *Lou*, 121.

27. Rich Chere, "Chisox Edge Bumbling Yanks, 6–5, in 11," *Star-Ledger*, August 3, 1985.

28. Meachem interview.

29. Michael Martinez, "Yankees Run into a Defeat," *New York Times*, August 3, 1985.

30. Berra interview.

31. Michael Martinez, "Seaver Arrives Smoothly at Milestone," *New York Times*, August 5, 1985.

32. Bill Pennington, "Seaver Comes 'Home' for Milestone," *Bergen Record*, August 5, 1985.

33. Martinez, "Seaver Arrives."

34. Moss Klein, "Seaver Reaches Historic 300th," *Star-Ledger*, August 5, 1985.

35. Brian Fisher phone interview, November 9, 2010.

36. Niekro, and Bird, *Knuckleballs*, 136.

37. Golenbock, *Amazin'*, 426.

38. Dan Castellano, "Mets Nip Cubs on Johnson HR," *Star-Ledger*, August 4, 1985.

39. Joseph Durso, "11 Straight for Gooden," *New York Times*, August 5, 1985.

40. Joseph Durso, "Mets Reluctantly Head Home," *New York Times*, August 7, 1985.

41. Jack O'Connell, "Mets Strike Out on Their Own," *Bergen Record*, August 7, 1985.

42. Durso, "Mets Reluctantly."

43. Murray Chass, "'There's a Strike,' Players Are Told by Union Head," *New York Times*, August 6, 1985.

44. Jack O'Connell, "Mets Make U-turn," *Bergen Record*, August 8, 1985.

45. Dan Castellano, "Carter, Foster, Strawberry Homer in 14–7 Romp," *Star-Ledger*, August 9, 1985.

46. Jack O'Connell, "Orosco Freezes Phillies," *Bergen Record*, August 14, 1985.

47. Hernandez and Bryan, *If at First*, 245.

48. George Vecsey, "Gooden: Death and Taxes," *New York Times*, August 11, 1985.

49. Joseph Durso, "At Last, Strawberry Arrives," *New York Times*, August 11, 1985.

50. Durso, "At Last, Strawberry."

51. Jack O'Connell, "It's True: Year Can Make Big Difference," *Bergen Record*, September 1, 1985.

52. Jack O'Connell, "Bullpen Saves One for Sid," *Bergen Record*, August 13, 1985.

53. Joseph Durso, "Gooden Fans 16, Wins 13th in Row," *New York Times*, August 21, 1985.

54. Durso, "Gooden Fans 16."

55. Ike Kuhns, "Dwight K's 16 for 13th in Row, 3–0," *Star-Ledger*, August 21, 1985.

56. Sam Goldaper, "Praise for Gooden from Pitching Elite," *New York Times*, August 26, 1985.

57. Jack O'Connell, "Mets Are Good Enough to Give Gooden No. 20," *Bergen Record*, August 26, 1985.

58. Craig Wolff, "Mets Stopped by Valenzuela," *New York Times*, August 27, 1985.

59. Dan Castellano, "Mets Bow to Reuss, 2–1, Head West Trailing by 3," *Star-Ledger*, August 28, 1985.

60. Malcolm Moran, "No Joy for Yanks' Armstrong," *New York Times*, August 8, 1985.

61. Rich Chere, "Absent Henderson Faces Heavy Fine," *Star-Ledger*, August 9, 1985.

62. Moss Klein, "Yanks Blast Bosox, 10–6," *Star-Ledger*, August 10, 1985.

63. Pagliarulo interview.

64. Moss Klein, "Yanks Win; Billy Defies George on Drill," *Star-Ledger*, August 15, 1985.

65. Pat Calabria, "Steinbrenner Pointedly Defers to Billy," *Bergen Record*, August 16, 1985.

66. "Yankees Within Five of the Top," *Bergen Record*, August 18, 1985.

67. Moss Klein, "Yankees Trail Jays by 5 after Trimming Bosox, 3–1," *Star-Ledger*, August 18, 1985.

68. Billy Sample phone interview, December 7, 2010.

69. Craig Wolff, "Best Catch of Career Stuns All," *New York Times*, August 20, 1985.

70. Mike Celizic, "Mattingly Assays the Work of Hitting," *Bergen Record*, September 4, 1985.

71. Moss Klein, "Mattingly, Brett Have Best MVP Credentials," *Star-Ledger*, September 9, 1985.

72. Sample interview.

73. Ron Drogo, "Yanks Trim Mariners, 4–3," *Star-Ledger*, September 5, 1985.

74. Niekro and Bird, *Knuckleballs*, 148.

75. Michael Martinez, "Yanks' Niekro Wins No. 296," *New York Times*, August 24, 1985.

76. Moss Klein, "Randolph 1st 2-HR Game Tops A's, 7–3," *Star-Ledger*, September 6, 1985.

77. Moss Klein, "George Called 'Out' (of Line) for Replay," *Star-Ledger*, September 6, 1985.

78. "Hernandez Tells Jury of His Cocaine Use," *New York Times*, September 7, 1985.

79. Hernandez and Bryan, *If at First*, 284.

80. Dan Castellano, "Mets Fall to Dodgers, 7–6," *Star-Ledger*, September 8, 1985.

81. Golenbock, *Amazin'*, 437.

82. Jack O'Connell, "Mets Take Round 1," *Bergen Record*, September 11, 1985.

83. Joseph Durso, "Mets Edge Cards, 5–4, as Johnson Hits Grand Slam," *New York Times*, September 11, 1985.

84. Rich Chere, "Foster Proved 'Hit' with Mets," *Star-Ledger*, September 11, 1985.

85. Durso, "Mets Edge Cards."

86. Malcolm Moran, "For Sisk, Darkness Is Beginning to Lift," *New York Times*, September 12, 1985.

### 8. "I'm Going to Kill You"

1. "New York–New York: A Battle for the Fans," *Bergen Record*, September 12, 1985.

2. William Geist, "Fever Rises: Mets First, Yanks Gaining," *New York Times*, September 13, 1985.

3. Moss Klein, "Hassey's 3-Run H R Narrows Gap to 1 1/2," *Star-Ledger*, September 13, 1985.

4. Murray Chass, "Hassey Sparks 6-Run Rally in 7th as Yankees Win," *New York Times*, September 13, 1985.

5. Bill Pennington, "Hassey Hassles Jays," *Bergen Record*, September 13, 1985.

6. Bill Pennington, "Niekro to Try for No. 300," *Bergen Record*, September 13, 1985.

7. Douglas Martin, "Blue Jays Fans Upset with New York's 'Yankee Hospitality,'" *New York Times*, September 18, 1985.

8. Moss Klein, "Yanks Fall 3 1/2, 7–4," *Star-Ledger*, September 15, 1985.

9. Michael Martinez, "Mets Keep Pace as Yankees Slip," *New York Times*, September 16, 1985.

10. Martinez, "Mets Keep Pace."

11. Jerry Izenberg, "Things That Go, Bump!!," *Star-Ledger*, September 16, 1985.

12. Mike Celizic, "The Boss Shows Up, and Yanks Disappear," *Bergen Record*, September 16, 1985.

13. Martinez, "Mets Keep Pace."

14. Celizic, "The Boss Shows Up."

15. Dan Castellano, "Mets Divide with Expos, Lead Cut to 1/2," *Star-Ledger*, September 14, 1985.

16. Castellano, "Mets Divide with Expos."

17. Joseph Durso, "Johnson Cool in Command," *New York Times*, September 15, 1985.

18. Golenbock, *Amazin'*, 438.

19. Dan Castellano, "Mets Rebound, Beat Expos, 6–2," *Star-Ledger*, September 16, 1985.

20. Joseph Durso, "Gooden Masterful Again, Fanning 11 in Two-Hitter," *New York Times*, September 17, 1985.

21. Dave Anderson, "The 'Natural Resource,'" *New York Times*, September 17, 1985.

22. Dan Castellano, "Mets 5-Hit by Phils, 5–1, Fall 2 Back as Lynch Fails," *Star-Ledger*, September 18, 1985.

23. Joseph Durso, "Mets Gain on Cardinals with Pitching and Power," *New York Times*, September 20, 1985.

24. Vinny DiTrani, "Gooden Takes Pirates Deep," *Bergen Record*, September 22, 1985.

25. Dan Castellano, "Gooden H R, 4 R B I Sink Pirates," *Star-Ledger*, September 22, 1985.

26. Dan Castellano, "Mets Stumble, Fall 3 Back," *Star-Ledger*, September 23, 1985.

27. Joseph Durso, "Carter Homer Powers Mets," *New York Times*, September 24, 1985.

28. Joseph Durso, "Mets Collapse in Ninth Inning," *New York Times*, September 26, 1985.

29. Anderson, "The 'Natural Resource.'"

30. Fisher interview.

31. Fisher interview.

32. Ron Drogo, "Indian 6-Run 9th Jars Fisher, 9–5," *Star-Ledger*, September 17, 1985.

33. Fisher interview.

34. Golenbock, *Wild, High and Tight*, 399.

35. Moss Klein, "Tigers 5 HRS Rock Guidry," *Star-Ledger*, September 18, 1985.

36. Pagliarulo interview.

37. Bill Pennington, "Yanks' Woes Mount with Loss," *Bergen Record*, September 19, 1985.

38. Baylor interview.

39. Moss Klein, "George's Criticism Unwarranted . . . Again," *Star-Ledger*, September 19, 1985.

40. Murray Chass, "Martin Jokes after Brawl," *New York Times*, September 23, 1985.

41. Bill Pennington, "Week Turns Yankee Dream to Nightmare," *Bergen Record*, September 22, 1985.

42. Bill Pennington, "Winning Is a Lost Art for Yankees," *Bergen Record*, September 20, 1985.

43. Klein, "Tigers 5 HRS."

44. Murray Chass, "Sinking Yankees 6 1/2 Back," *New York Times*, September 12, 1985.

45. Klein interview

46. Ian O'Connor, "Whit's Wisdom to Javy: 'I've Been There,'" ESPN, http://www.espn.com/new-york/mlb/columns/story?columnist=oconnor_ian&id=5149683, May 1, 2010.

47. Madden and Klein, *Damned Yankees*, 98.

48. Murray Chass, "Yankees Trounce Angels," *New York Times*, September 1, 1985.

49. Chass, "Sinking Yankees 6 1/2 Back."

50. Madden and Klein, *Damned Yankees*, 100.

51. Albert Millus phone interview, January 17, 2011.

52. Piniella and Madden, *Lou*, 122.

53. Steve Jacobson, "Yankees a Hotbed for Hotheads," *Newsday* through the *Bergen Record*, September 29, 1985.

54. Mike Celizic, "Martin Dragged Down by His Drug," *Bergen Record*, September 25, 1985.

55. Moss Klein, "Billy Broke Arm in Whitson Fray; Job in Jeopardy," *Star-Ledger*, September 23, 1985.

56. Celizic, "Martin Dragged Down."

57. Winfield and Parker, *Winfield*, 186.

58. Hudler interview.

59. Winfield and Parker, *Winfield*, 238–39.

60. Baylor interview.

61. "Niekro Mirrors Yanks' Broken Season," *New York Times*, September 26, 1985.

## 9. "One Tremendous Baseball Season"

1. Moss Klein, "Phil Fails but Yanks Win in 9th, 5–4," *Star-Ledger*, October 1, 1985.

2. Staub interview.

3. Carter interview.

4. Golenbock, *Amazin'*, 440.

5. Mike Celizic, "Baseball Gods Smile on Mets in Masterpiece," *Bergen Record*, October 2, 1985.

6. Jack O'Connell, "One Down, Two to Go," *Bergen Record*, October 2, 1985.

7. Jack O'Connell, "Momentum Shifts to Mets," *Bergen Record*, October 3, 1985.

8. Cashen interview.

9. Hernandez and Bryan, *If at First*, 326.

10. Fisher interview.

11. Moss Klein, "The Dream Is Over for Yanks, Mets," *Star-Ledger*, October 6, 1985.

12. Pagliarulo interview.

13. Murray Chass, "Yankees and Mets Triumph and Stay Alive," *New York Times*, October 5, 1985.

14. Meachem interview.

15. Moss Klein, "Yanks, Down to Last Out, Stun Jays," *Star-Ledger*, October 5, 1985.

16. Willie Upshaw phone interview, January 8, 2011.

17. Pagliarulo interview.

18. Jesse Barfield phone interview, October 26, 2011.

19. Klein, "The Dream Is Over."

20. Murray Chass, "Mets and Yankees Are Eliminated as Cards and Blue Jays Win Titles," *New York Times*, October 6, 1985.

21. Dan Castellano, "Mets Fall; 98-64 Mark 2d Best in Club History," *Star-Ledger*, October 7, 1985.

22. Hernandez and Bryan, *If at First*, 327.

23. Dick Young, "A Vintage Baseball Season for Fans of New York Teams," *Bergen Record*, October 7, 1985.

24. Moss Klein, "Billy Seeking Big '86 Raise or He'll Walk," *Star-Ledger*, October 7, 1985.

25. "Martin Investigation Finished," *New York Times*, October 11, 1985.

26. Murray Chass, "Now, a Young Steinbrenner Is Sounding Off for Yankees," *New York Times*, October 27, 1985.

27. Murray Chass, "Piniella Accepts Yanks' Offer," *New York Times*, October 28, 1985.

28. Moss Klein, "Martin Firing: Script Is Familiar," *Star-Ledger*, October 29, 1985.

29. Madden interview.

# BIBLIOGRAPHY

THE FOLLOWING PEOPLE WERE interviewed exclusively for this book, and their cooperation and stories are much appreciated: Wally Backman, Jesse Barfield, Don Baylor, Dale Berra, Rich Bordi, Marty Bystrom, Gary Carter, Frank Cashen, Ken Dayley, Sid Fernandez, Brian Fisher, Tom Gorman, Ron Guidry, Al Harazin, Bud Harrelson, Von Hayes, Rex Hudler, Roger Jongewaard, Moss Klein, Ray Knight, Terry Leach, Bill Madden, Roger McDowell, Bobby Meacham, Albert Millus, Rance Mulliniks, Phil Niekro, Jesse Orosco, Mike Pagliarulo, Dan Pasqua, Dennis Rasmussen, Shane Rawley, Ronn Reynolds, Mike Riordan, Billy Sample, Doug Sisk, Rusty Staub, Mel Stottlemyre, Walt Terrell, Willie Upshaw, Mookie Wilson, and Butch Wynegar.

## Published Sources

Carter, Gary, and Phil Pepe. *Still a Kid at Heart: My Life in Baseball and Beyond.* Chicago: Triumph Books, 2008.

Golenbock, Peter. *Amazin': The Miraculous History of New York's Most Beloved Baseball Team.* New York: St. Martin's Griffin, 2002.

―――. *George: The Poor Little Rich Boy Who Built the Yankee Empire.* Hoboken: John Wiley & Sons, 2009.

―――. *Wild, High and Tight: The Life and Death of Billy Martin.* New York: St. Martin's Press, 1994.

Gooden, Dwight, and Bob Klapisch. *Heat: My Life On and Off the Diamond.* New York: William Morrow, 1999.

Hernandez, Keith, and Mike Bryan. *If at First . . . : A Season with the Mets.* New York: McGraw-Hill Book Company, 1986.

Katz, Jeff. *Split Season, 1981: Fernandomania, the Bronx Zoo, and the Strike That Saved Baseball.* New York: Thomas Dunne Books, 2015.

Leavy, Jane. *The Last Boy.* New York: Harper Perennial, 2011.

Madden, Bill. *Steinbrenner: The Last Lion of Baseball*. New York: HarperCollins, 2010.

Madden, Bill, and Moss Klein. *Damned Yankees*. New York: Warner Books, 1990.

Niekro, Phil, and Tom Bird. *Knuckleballs: An Astonishing Inside Look at 300-Game Winner Phil Niekro Including the Two Most Interesting Owners in Baseball—Turner and Steinbrenner*. New York: Freundlich Books, 1986.

Pearlman, Jeff. *The Bad Guys Won!* New York: HarperCollins, 2004.

Pepe, Phil. *The Ballad of Billy and George: The Tempestuous Baseball Marriage of Billy Martin and George Steinbrenner*. Guilford CT: Lyons Press, 2008.

Piniella, Lou, and Bill Madden. *Lou: Fifty Years of Kicking Dirt, Playing Hard, and Winning Big in the Sweet Spot of Baseball*. New York: HarperCollins, 2017.

Sample, Billy. *A Year in Pinstripes . . . and Then Some*. Billy Sample, 2016.

Strawberry, Darryl, and John Strausbaugh. *Straw: Finding My Way*. New York: HarperCollins, 2009.

Winfield, Dave, and Tom Parker. *Winfield: A Player's Life*. New York: W. W. Norton & Company, 1988.

# INDEX

Aguilera, Rick, 127, 147, 148–49, 158, 268, 280, 282

Alexander, Doyle, 25, 203, 253, 255

Allen, Neil, 8, 12, 42, 66–67, 68, 157

American League Championship Series, 21, 89, 94

American Ship Building Company, 19

Anderson, Dave, 104, 130

Anderson, Sparky, 107, 160

Andujar, Joaquin, 63, 67, 122, 193, 201

Arlington Memorial Hospital, 163

Armstrong, Mike, 184, 229

Aspromonte, Bob, 105

Atlanta Braves, 4, 5, 57, 102, 142–45, 147–49, 153–55, 218, 257–58, 261, 268, 271, 272

Atlanta Fulton County Stadium, 142

Backman, Wally, 8, 41, 50, 52, 83, 107, 124, 148, 149, 153, 155, 173, 199, 202, 211, 215, 244–45

Baines, Harold, 79

Baltimore Orioles, 10, 26, 34, 40, 75, 79, 89, 132–33, 222–24, 260, 268, 269

Bamberger, George, 9, 10, 34, 71, 157

Barfield, Jesse, 203, 254

Barrett, Marty, 188–89

Bauer, Hank, 88

Bavasi, Peter, 165

Baylor, Don, 50, 75–78, 81, 100, 112, 116, 117, 151, 170, 190, 207, 221, 234, 236, 270–71

Beane, Billy, 70

Bell, George, 203, 255

*Bergen Record*, 40, 46, 111, 180, 189, 204, 208, 230, 244

Berra, Dale, 17, 81, 115, 132, 167–68, 186

Berra, Yogi, 23, 27–29, 36–37, 46–47, 49, 74, 79, 80–82, 96, 131, 138, 139, 164, 185, 261

Berton, Joe, 53

Blocker, Terry, 123

Boggs, Wade, 55, 58, 188

Bordi, Rich, 17, 51, 55, 161, 189, 222, 226

Boston Red Sox, 21, 26, 32, 52, 55, 58–59, 73–75, 78–79, 88, 111, 154, 185, 186, 187–89, 199, 225, 263, 270

Boswell, Dave, 90

Boswell, Tom, 219

Boyd, Dennis "Oil Can," 59

Bremigan, Nick, 162

Brenly, Bob, 182

Brewer, Jim, 88

Brock, Greg, 120

Brock, Lou, 16

Bronfman, Charles, 3

Brooks, Hubie, 5, 8, 13, 105, 127, 209

Brown, Bobby, 115

Brown, Chris, 70, 181

Browning, Tom, 68, 155

Bry, Richie, 16

Buckner, Bill, 55, 187, 267, 268

Buhner, Jay, 191–92

Burke, Michael, 20

Burns, Britt, 262

Burroughs, Jeff, 258, 260

Busch Stadium, 240–41, 245, 248–49

Bush, George H. W., 60

Butler, Brett, 218–19

Bystrom, Marty, 136, 220–21

California Angels, 24–25, 75, 116–17, 135, 161, 189–90, 226, 261, 270, 272
Camp, Rick, 145–48
Candelaria, John, 230
Candlestick Park, 119
Carlton, Steve, 83, 102
Carter, Gary, 1–6, 13–14, 33, 50, 63–64, 67–68, 72–73, 78, 84, 98, 102, 103, 107, 110, 119, 122, 125–29, 141, 146–47, 150–51, 155–56, 158–59, 177–79, 181, 192–93, 197, 199, 202, 210–13, 215, 216, 219, 238, 241, 243, 246, 248, 256, 260, 266
Carter, Jimmy, 111
Cashen, Frank, 1, 5–6, 10, 11–12, 19, 31, 34–35, 43, 62, 70, 104, 108, 124, 127, 157, 212, 245–46, 256, 269
Castellano, Dan, 13, 65, 141
Caudill, Bill, 203
CBS, 20, 46
Cedeno, Cesar, 199
Celizic, Mike, 111, 189, 208, 230, 244
Cerone, Rick, 24, 37, 90, 218
Chapman, Kelvin, 140, 155
Charles, Ed, 105
Chass, Murray, 73, 92–93, 97, 206, 229, 261
Chere, Rich, 68, 102, 168
Chicago White Sox, 35, 46, 77–79, 167, 169–70, 172, 187, 191, 262, 267, 272
Christensen, John, 53
Chrysler, 4
Cincinnati Bengals, 242
Cincinnati Reds, 6, 11, 21, 68, 72, 83, 88, 91, 101, 105, 112, 150, 155, 247, 267, 269, 272
Clark, Jack, 66, 122, 241–42
Clements, Pat, 272
Cleveland Indians, 20, 77, 163, 165–66, 184, 217–19, 255, 266, 271
Cleveland Pipers, 19
Cobb, Ty, 72
Coleman, Vince, 122, 202, 240, 244, 248
Collins, Dave, 25
Colorado Rockies, 271
Colorado Silver Bullets, 272
Columbus Clippers, 74–75, 162, 184, 218
Comiskey Park, 79
Connor, Mark, 46, 112, 167, 226

Cook, Murray, 27
Cooper, Joseph, 93–94
Copacabana, 88–89, 231
Cosell, Howard, 162
Cotto, Henry, 117
Country Club Plaza, 115
Cowens, Al, 161
Cowley, Joe, 29, 50, 80–81, 113, 116, 136, 162, 165, 169, 171, 217, 224, 253–54, 262, 272
Cox, Bobby, 252, 261
Cox, Danny, 122, 197–98, 246
Creighton University, 161
Cross Keys Inn, 223–24, 227, 230

Dangerfield, Rodney, 67
Darling, Ron, 12, 49, 68, 82–83, 100, 128, 147, 151, 154–55, 177, 181, 217, 242, 244, 260, 263, 266
Davis, Alvin, 62
Davis, Chili, 192
Davis, Jody, 128
Davis, Ron, 116
Davis, Sammy, Jr., 88
Davis, Steve, 252
Dawson, Andre, 2, 126, 127, 266
Dayley, Ken, 243
Della Femina, Jerry, 31
Della Femina, Travisano and Partners, 8
Dernier, Bob, 13
Detroit Tigers, 28, 30, 60, 90, 107, 112, 122, 130, 132–33, 137, 173, 219–22, 229, 235, 238–39
Dillard, Harrison, 25
DiMaggio, Joe, 137, 187
Doubleday, Nelson, 10–11, 19, 36
Downey, Jack, 85
Drabek, Doug, 272
Duncan, Dave, 170
Duncan, Mariano, 195
Durso, Joseph, 122
Dykstra, Len, 53, 101–2, 143, 145–46, 149, 195, 248

Elster, Kevin, 263
Evans, Darrell, 229
Evans, Dwight, 55
Exhibition Stadium, 249, 252, 255

Falcone, Pete, 8
Feller, Bob, 62
Felske, John, 212
Fenway Park, 52, 55, 74, 88, 185, 249
Fernandez, Sid, 12, 36, 49, 102–4, 108, 123,
    127, 148, 176, 180, 182, 210, 263, 268
Fernandez, Tony, 255, 258
Ferraro, Mike, 22
Finch, Sidd, 53
Fisher, Brian, 169, 171, 204, 218–19, 221,
    250, 255, 272
Fisk, Carlton, 167, 262
Fitzgerald, Mike, 5
Flynn, Doug, 8
Foli, Tom, 37, 51
Ford, Curt, 244
Ford, Whitey, 20, 88
Forster, Terry, 143
Fort Lauderdale, 36, 78
Foster, George, 11–12, 39–40, 49–50, 68,
    101, 102, 110, 119, 122, 129, 141, 142,
    150, 154, 156, 177, 183, 195, 197–98, 210,
    213–16, 239, 244, 246–47, 263, 267
Fowler, Art, 95
Franco, John, 68, 71
Franco, Julio, 219
Frey, Jim, 71, 104, 172–73

Gamble, Oscar, 37
Garber, Gene, 147
Gardenhire, Ron, 101, 102
Gardner, Wes, 236
Garrett, Wayne, 105
Gehrig, Lou, 187
Geist, Bill, 201
Gibson, Bob, 151
Gooden, Dwight "Doc," 12, 36, 38, 40, 46,
    48–49, 60–64, 66, 72, 83–84, 98, 102–
    3, 105, 108, 110, 119–21, 123, 126, 129,
    139–40, 142–43, 150–51, 154–55, 158–59,
    174–83, 192, 194, 199, 211–12, 214–15,
    217, 241, 244–45, 247, 259, 263, 265–66
Gorman, Lou, 11
Gorman, Tom, 10, 50, 65, 124, 144–48,
    236, 269
Gossage, Rich "Goose," 7, 26–28, 276
Griffey, Ken, 25, 37, 50, 58, 62, 75–76, 81,

108, 111–14, 116–17, 136, 188–89, 191,
    207–8, 230, 271
Griffey, Ken, Jr., 113, 271
Griffin, Mike, 48
Grimes, Burleigh, 182
Guante, Cecilio, 272
Guerrero, Pedro, 195
Guidry, Ron, 25, 28, 50–51, 74–76, 81, 99,
    133–37, 139, 151, 163, 178, 182, 203–4,
    220, 231, 238, 259, 272
Guillen, Ozzie, 167
Gullickson, Bill, 158

Harazin, Al, 1, 5–16, 11–12
Harper, Terry, 144
Harrah, Toby, 37, 132
Harrelson, Bud, 6, 105
Hassey, Ron, 100, 191, 204, 206, 222,
    228–30, 252, 255
Hayes, Von, 102, 123–24
Heep, Danny, 47, 68, 101–2, 104–5, 122–
    24, 146, 150, 154, 202, 211, 267
Henderson, Rickey, 15–17, 47, 49, 50–51,
    74, 78, 79, 81, 97, 111–12, 114, 132, 133,
    137–39, 151, 160, 167, 178, 184–85, 190,
    206, 235, 238, 251, 259, 270
Henke, Tom, 203, 251–52
Hernandez, John, 29–30
Hernandez, Keith, 12–13, 40–45, 49–50,
    63, 66, 68, 78, 82–84, 109–10, 119, 120,
    121, 126, 129, 140, 143–48, 150–51, 156–
    57, 159, 172–75, 177–79, 183, 192–95,
    197, 202–3, 209, 213–15, 217, 222, 236,
    241, 243, 246, 247–49, 257, 266
Herr, Tommy, 215, 243–45
Herzog, Whitey, 42, 67, 243–44
Higuera, Teddy, 238, 255
Hoffberger, Jerry, 10–11
Horner, Bob, 142
Horowitz, Jay, 53
Horton, Ricky, 248
Horton, Willie, 90, 112, 229
Houk, Ralph, 20–21
Houston Astros, 9, 86, 101, 105, 106, 150,
    155–57, 160, 263, 271
Howard, Frank, 10, 34–35
Howser, Dick, 21–22

Hoyt, LaMarr, 118
Hudler, Rex, 17, 206, 233
Hudson, Charles, 124
Hunter, Jim "Catfish," 135
Hurdle, Clint, 123–24, 154
Hussey, Richard, 178

Jackson, Reggie, 24–25, 31, 79, 92, 187, 206
Jacobson, Steve, 230
John, Tommy, 135
John Birch Society, 76
Johnson, Cliff, 251
Johnson, Davey, 12–13, 33–36, 39–40, 47–
    48, 52, 62, 71, 83, 89, 108, 110, 119–21,
    125–28, 140–41, 142–43, 145, 155, 158–
    59, 173, 175–82, 209–12, 217, 237, 242,
    244, 263, 269–70
Johnson, Howard, 33, 50, 105–7, 122, 150,
    156, 180, 198, 202, 237, 266
Jones, Ruppert, 226
Jongewaard, Roger, 70

Kaline, Al, 60
Kansas City Athletics, 89
Kansas City Royals, 21, 111–15, 136, 149,
    162, 187, 259, 268, 272
Kemp, Steve, 26–27, 37
Key, Jimmy, 203
King, Clyde, 23, 80, 113, 131, 201, 261
Kingdome, 172
Kingman, Dave, 12
Kipper, Bob, 215
Kirby, Andrea, 40
Klapsich, Bob, 146
Klein, Moss, 31, 37, 51, 98, 166, 188, 221,
    222, 224, 226, 262
Knight, Ray, 39, 46, 50, 52, 101, 105–9,
    112, 144, 146, 149, 156, 177, 183, 195,
    211–13, 236, 239, 247, 267
Koch, Ed, 46, 60
Koosman, Jerry, 180

Lacy, Lee, 223–24
LaGuardia Airport, 59, 175, 177
Lamp, Dennis, 203, 204
Lasorda, Tommy, 13
Latham, Bill, 50, 214
Leach, Terry, 8, 154–55, 177, 182, 192,
    215, 269

Leary, Tim, 62
Lemon, Bob, 21, 23, 25, 37, 93, 111
Lemon, Chet, 62
Lollar, Tim, 77
Lopes, Davey, 217
Los Angeles Dodgers, 3–4, 8, 13, 21, 23–
    24, 108, 183, 192, 194–95, 256, 265,
    267, 269, 270
Lynch, Ed, 49, 68, 102, 128, 142, 147, 155,
    195, 202, 212

MacPhail, Lee, 26, 176
Madden, Bill, 19, 82, 229, 264
Mahler, Mickey, 220–21
Major League Baseball Players Associa-
    tion, 118, 151, 175–77
Mantilla, Felix, 105
Mantle, Mickey, 16, 20, 85, 88, 187
Martin, Alfred "Billy," 15, 16, 21, 23, 30,
    79–82, 85, 87–100, 111–17, 130–31, 135–
    36, 139–40, 151, 153, 160–68, 171–73,
    184, 186–87, 190, 196, 201, 204, 206,
    208–9, 217–31, 233, 252, 255, 258, 260–
    61, 273–74
Martin, Juvan "Jenny," 85
Martinez, Michael, 139
Matthews, Gary, 139–40
Mattingly, Don, 28, 30–31, 38–39, 47, 49–
    50, 81, 98, 111–12, 115–16, 130–31, 137–
    38, 151, 164, 178, 184–85, 187–89, 191,
    206, 207–8, 232, 235–36, 252–54, 257,
    259, 270, 271, 273
Mayberry, John, 25–26
Mazzilli, Lee, 31, 263
McClendon, John, 20
McClure, Bob, 186
McDonald, Joe, 12
McDowell, Roger, 12, 36, 50, 64–65, 68,
    103, 107, 109–10, 119–20, 126, 139, 142,
    157, 173, 177, 182, 198, 213, 217, 237, 260,
    263, 266, 268
McGee, Willie, 122, 202, 240, 244, 248
McHale, John, 2–5
McIllvane, Joe, 11
McMurtry, Craig, 5
McPhail, Marlin, 61
Meacham, Bobby, 29, 48, 50, 99, 167–68,
    251, 252–53, 271

Memorial Stadium, 132, 230
Merrill, Stump, 112
Metrodome, 114–15, 160
Miami Marlins, 270, 271
Michael, Gene, 22–23, 43, 112, 167–68, 274
Miller, Saul, 36
Millus, Albert, 227, 274
Milwaukee Brewers, 24, 130, 133, 135–36, 191–92, 199, 238
Minnesota Twins, 89–90, 102, 114, 136, 156–57, 164, 268, 269, 271
Mitchell, Kevin, 263, 267
Monbouquette, Bill, 167
Montefusco, John, 51, 99, 226
Montreal Expos, 1–6, 125–28, 130, 139–41, 153, 157, 158, 159, 175, 177, 181, 192, 208–11, 214–15, 236–37, 249, 255, 259, 266
Morales, Jerry, 7
Moreno, Omar, 37
Morgan, Joe, 105
Morris, Jack, 235
Moseby, Lloyd, 203, 252–54
Mullen, John, 56
Municipal Stadium, 164
Munson, Thurman, 21, 93
Murcer, Bobby, 77, 138
Murphy, Dale, 142, 143
Murray, Dale, 46–47, 51, 81
Murray, Eddie, 223

National Basketball Association, 19
Neal, Charlie, 105
Nettles, Graig, 27–28, 162
Newark Airport, 82, 166
Newark Star-Ledger, 13, 31, 37, 52, 54, 65, 68, 98, 102, 141, 168, 188
New Haven Journal-Courier, 98
New York Daily News, 75, 82, 229, 259
New York Mets, 1, 4–14, 18–19, 29, 31–34, 36, 38, 40–43, 45–54, 59–61, 63–68, 70, 72–73, 78, 82–84, 97–98, 100–105, 107–11, 114, 116, 119–30, 136, 139–51, 153–59, 168–84, 190, 192–200, 201–3, 205, 208–17, 231, 236–50, 255–56, 258–71, 273
New York Times, 43, 47, 73, 92, 104, 114, 122, 130, 139, 201, 206, 229, 234, 260, 261

New York Yankees, 7, 12, 14, 15–32, 33, 37–40, 46–52, 54, 55, 57–58, 73–76, 78–82, 84, 85–100, 104, 111–17, 129–39, 151, 160–72, 174, 178, 182, 184–92, 196, 199–200, 201, 203–8, 217–34, 235–36, 238–39, 247, 249, 250–55, 257–62, 264–65, 267, 268–74
Nichols, Kid, 56
Niekro, Joe, 84, 222, 235, 238, 257–58
Niekro, Phil, 28, 50, 55–58, 60, 74, 79–81, 99–100, 112, 125, 137, 162, 172, 182, 189–91, 205–6, 220–21, 231, 234, 235, 236, 257–58, 260, 262, 271–72
Niemann, Randy, 236
Nixon, Richard, 92, 129, 136, 170
Nunez, Ed, 189

Oakland Athletics, 6, 15–17, 81, 87, 94, 95, 117, 130, 184, 185, 190–91, 266, 270
Oakland Coliseum, 94, 117
Oakland Oaks, 87
O'Connell, Jack, 40, 180
O'Dowd, Mary, 206
O'Hare Airport, 79, 81–82
Ojeda, Bob, 262–63
Orosco, Jesse, 50, 64–66, 82, 110, 125–26, 143, 156–57, 173, 176, 195, 199, 202, 217, 237, 242, 268–69
Ownbey, Rick, 42

Pacella, John, 7
Pacific Coast League, 86–87
Pagliarulo, Mike, 29, 47–48, 50, 132, 186–87, 191, 220–22, 250, 253, 271
Parker, Dave, 194
Parks, Dallas, 26
Parrish, Lance, 62, 99
Pasqua, Dan, 191
Pavlick, Greg, 109
Pendleton, Terry, 122, 244, 247, 248
Perry, Gaylord, 172
Phelps, Ken, 51, 100
Philadelphia Phillies, 2, 3, 44, 83, 102, 106, 123–25, 154, 175, 180, 211–16, 240, 268
Piersall, Jim, 88
Piniella, Lou, 96, 115, 138, 163–67, 186, 220, 229, 261–62, 273

Pittsburgh Pirates, 2, 26, 44, 57, 82–83, 101, 141–42, 148, 181, 199, 211–12, 214–16, 230, 236–37, 272
Pittsburgh Steelers, 242
players' strike: 1981, 2, 8, 15, 18, 22, 118, 232; 1985, 152, 172, 175–77, 184–85, 209
Plimpton, George, 53
Pocoroba, Biff, 17
Pompton Lakes High School, 7
Porter, Darrell, 197, 244, 248

Raines, Tim, 2, 126, 193–94
Ramirez, Rafael, 5
Randle, Lenny, 117
Randolph, Willie, 22, 47, 50, 51, 73, 75, 76, 99, 113–16, 137, 190, 271, 272
Rasmussen, Dennis, 29, 112, 161–62, 262, 272
Rawley, Shane, 212
Reagan, Nancy, 45
Reynolds, Ronn, 53, 109, 147
Rhoden, Rick, 272
Rice, Jim, 55, 58
Righetti, Dave, 28, 39, 48, 51, 75, 100, 163, 190, 206, 218–19, 253, 272–73
Riordan, Mike, 7
Ripken, Cal, Jr., 235
Robertson, Andre, 75, 251
Robinson, Bill, 13
Robinson, Brooks, 76
Robinson, Frank, 76
Robinson, Jackie, 87
Rose, Pete, 42, 72, 101–2
Royal, Darrell, 63
Rucker, Dave, 124
Ruth, George "Babe," 15, 79, 187
Ryan, Nolan, 9, 150, 160

Saidt, Bus, 17
Sambito, Joe, 65
Sample, Billy, 48, 76, 112, 113, 188, 189
Sandberg, Ryne, 139
San Diego Padres, 27–28, 50, 75, 108, 120, 161, 182, 192, 225, 226, 231–32, 271, 272, 273
Santana, Rafael, 50, 108, 244, 266–67
Sapir, Eddie, 81, 96–97, 222
Schiraldi, Calvin, 49, 124, 126

Scioscia, Mike, 120
Scum Bunch, 64–65, 269
Seaver, Tom, 6–7, 35, 46, 168–72, 174, 191–92, 204, 262
7-Up, 4
Shea Stadium, 7–10, 31, 45, 59, 63, 65, 67, 68, 83, 104, 108, 114, 120, 122, 129–30, 141, 151, 153–54, 156, 171, 177–79, 182, 196–99, 201–3, 205, 213–15, 242, 245, 249
Sheehy, Pete, 175
Shields, Steve, 143
Shirley, Bob, 80, 116–17, 133, 188, 206, 238
Sisk, Doug, 41, 60, 64–66, 68, 101, 108, 120, 122–24, 126, 130, 141, 143–44, 147, 183, 213–14, 239, 269
60 Minutes, 46
Skinner, Morris F., 161
Smalley, Roy, 37
Smith, Lee, 173
Smith, Lonnie, 67, 193
Smith, Ozzie, 51, 202, 242, 244, 248
Smoltz, John, 56
Soto, Mario, 68, 101
Spahn, Warren, 56
Speier, Chris, 172–73
Sports Illustrated, 53, 58
Staub, Rusty, 8–9, 12, 35–36, 43–44, 215, 240, 242, 267–68
Stearns, John, 7
Steinbrenner, George, 16, 19–32, 36–49, 51–52, 57, 60, 73–75, 78–82, 85, 90–99, 113–17, 129–32, 138–39, 162–63, 165–69, 171–72, 174, 185–87, 189–91, 196, 201, 206–8, 217, 219–22, 224–25, 229–34, 253, 260–62, 264, 265, 270, 272–74
Stengel, Casey, 87, 89
Sterling, John, 145–46
Stieb, Dave, 203–4
St. Louis Cardinals, 8, 12, 41–42, 44–45, 51, 57, 63–64, 66–68, 83, 121–23, 125, 127, 129, 140–42, 151, 153–55, 157–59, 175, 180–83, 193, 195–202, 209–14, 216–17, 236–49, 255, 258–59
Stone, Jeff, 124
Stottlemyre, Mel, 53, 61, 157, 194, 237
St. Petersburg, 33, 39

Strawberry, Darryl, 12, 38, 40, 50, 68–72, 83–84, 94–95, 110, 122, 140, 145, 149, 151, 153–56, 175, 177–79, 195, 197–99, 202, 211, 213–14, 243, 246–47, 260, 265–66
Strong, Curtis, 44–45, 193–94
Sutcliffe, Rick, 128, 140

Taveras, Frank, 8
Terrell, Walt, 9–10, 13, 76
Teufel, Tim, 263
Texas Rangers, 46, 90–91, 105, 116, 136, 163, 271
Thomas, Andres, 5
Tidewater, 62, 70, 101, 103, 108
Toronto Blue Jays, 25, 125, 130, 136–37, 151, 184–85, 187, 188, 190–92, 200, 203–6, 217, 219, 221, 224, 230–32, 234, 235–36, 238–39, 250–55, 257, 261, 268, 270, 271
Torre, Joe, 8–9, 34, 261
*Trenton Times*, 17
Trevino, Alex, 120
Tudor, John, 68, 122–23, 199, 201, 212, 240, 242–44
Turner, Ted, 44

Ueberroth, Peter, 176, 231
University of Miami, 61, 221
University of Southwestern Louisiana, 134
University of Texas, 75
Upshaw, Willie, 253–54

Valenzuela, Fernando, 8, 108, 120, 194–95
Van Slyke, Andy, 122, 243
Veterans Stadium, 123, 154, 216
Virdon, Bill, 21, 91

Wagner, Honus, 125
Warner Lambert, 4
Washington, Claudell, 142, 175
Weaver, Earl, 34, 79, 94, 260
West Palm Beach, 1, 6
Whitfield, Terry, 120
Whitson, Ed, 50, 73–74, 77, 79, 100, 115, 117, 136, 139, 165, 168, 191, 207, 224–31, 251, 253, 254, 260–61, 273, 274
Whitt, Ernie, 204, 254
Wiggins, Alan, 223
Williams, Dick, 94
Willingham, Herb, 5
Wilson, Glenn, 125
Wilson, Mookie, 7, 13, 36, 45, 50, 82, 101, 141, 144, 149, 195–97, 202–3, 213, 242, 243, 246, 247, 267
Winfield, Dave, 12, 30, 38, 47, 49–50, 51, 75–76, 100, 111, 116, 117, 136–37, 139, 151, 160, 165, 171, 184, 187, 204, 206–8, 226, 227, 231–34, 235–36, 259, 270, 273–74
Woodward, Woody, 38, 261
Wrigley Field, 13, 51, 72, 79, 159, 172, 179–80
Wynegar, Butch, 50, 73, 75, 164–66, 204, 222–23, 251–53

Yankee Stadium, 20, 25, 31, 77, 92, 100, 104, 111, 136, 138, 167–72, 186–88, 191, 204, 205, 225, 230, 235–36, 238, 249, 250, 264, 273–74
Youmans, Floyd, 5
Young, Dick, 259

Zachary, Pat, 8
Zimmer, Don, 22